COLORADO

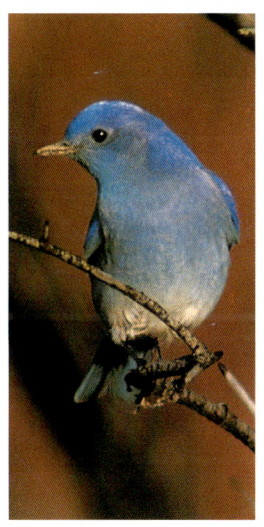

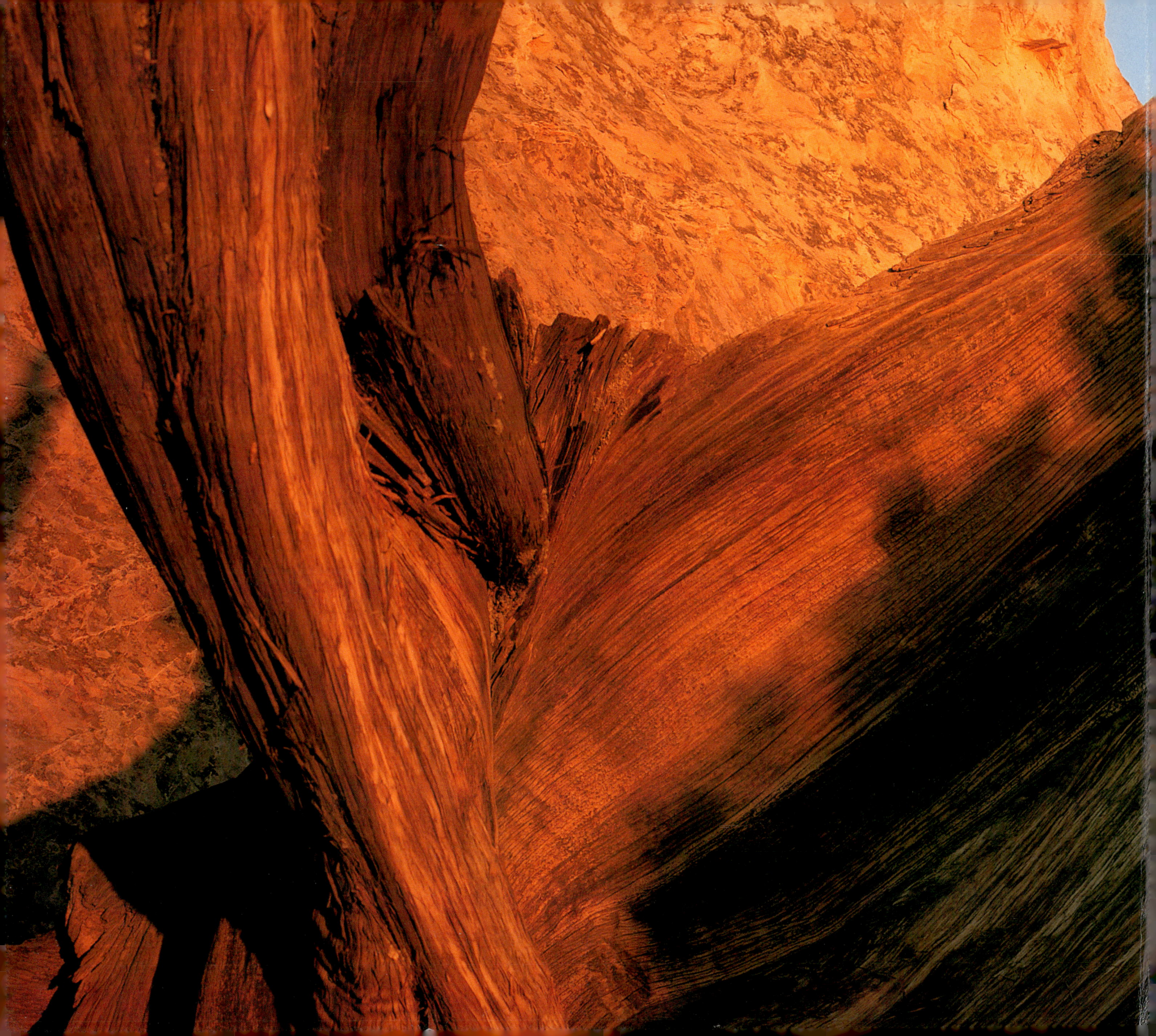

COLORADO

ART WOLFE

WITH GAVRIEL JECAN

SASQUATCH BOOKS
SEATTLE

TEXT BY CRAIG CHILDS

COLORADO

- Dinosaur National Monument
- Continental Divide
- Rocky Mountains
- Park Range
- Medicine Bow Mountains
- Cache la Poudre River
- Pawnee National Grassland
- South Platte River
- Rocky Mountain National Park
- White River Plateau
- Colorado River
- Denver
- Maroon Bells-Snowmass Wilderness
- South Platte River
- Colorado National Monument
- Grand Junction
- Gunnison River
- Sawatch Range
- Garden of the Gods
- Colorado Springs
- Uncompahgre Plateau
- Black Canyon of the Gunnison National Park
- Dallas Divide
- Continental Divide
- Sangre de Cristo Range
- Pueblo
- Arkansas River
- Great Sand Dunes National Monument
- San Juan Mountains
- Rio Grande River
- Mesa Verde National Park
- Durango

CONTENTS

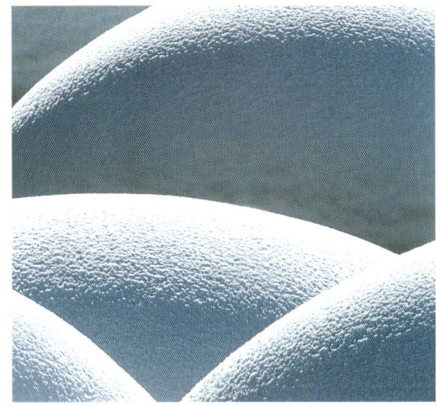

MOUNTAIN 10

RIVER & LAKE 40

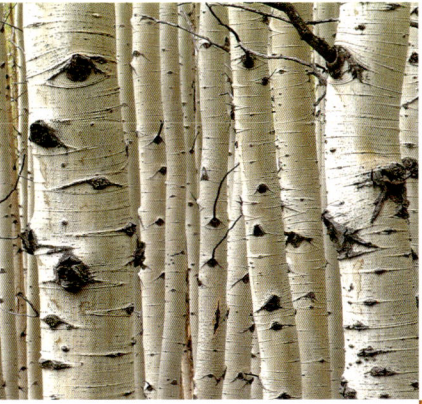

CANYON & MESA 72

FOREST 102

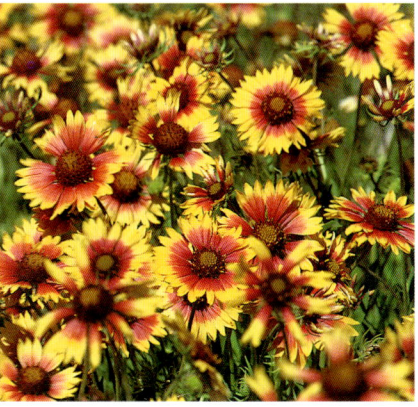

VALLEY, PRAIRIE & PLAIN 136

DEDICATION & ACKNOWLEDGMENTS

To one of my very favorite Coloradans: Nancy Jenkins. Her strength of purpose, her enduring spirit, and her incredible grace in the face of seemingly endless challenges have been an inspiration to so many people inside and outside of Colorado, including her former colleagues at the Denver Museum of Natural History, the many members of the North American Nature Photography Association, and especially me.

Some books may well be the inspiration of only one or two people, but no book becomes a reality without a true team effort. The team that made this book a reality includes some very talented people. I owe them all a debt of great gratitude: Gary Luke, Karen Schober, Linda Stark, Kim Foster, Sarah Smith, Aley Mills, Laura Gronewold (Sasquatch Books); Gary M. Stolz, Ph.D. (U.S. Fish and Wildlife Service); Mary Jean and Scott Pope; Scott Dressel-Martin; and, of course, all of those in my office—Colin Brynn, Mel Calvan, Christine Eckhoff, Erin Johnson, Gilbert Neri, Ray Pfortner, Craig Scheak, Deirdre Skillman, and Lisa Woods, plus our interns Christina Maner and Bryan Thuis, who continue to help me attain ever greater heights.

— A.W.

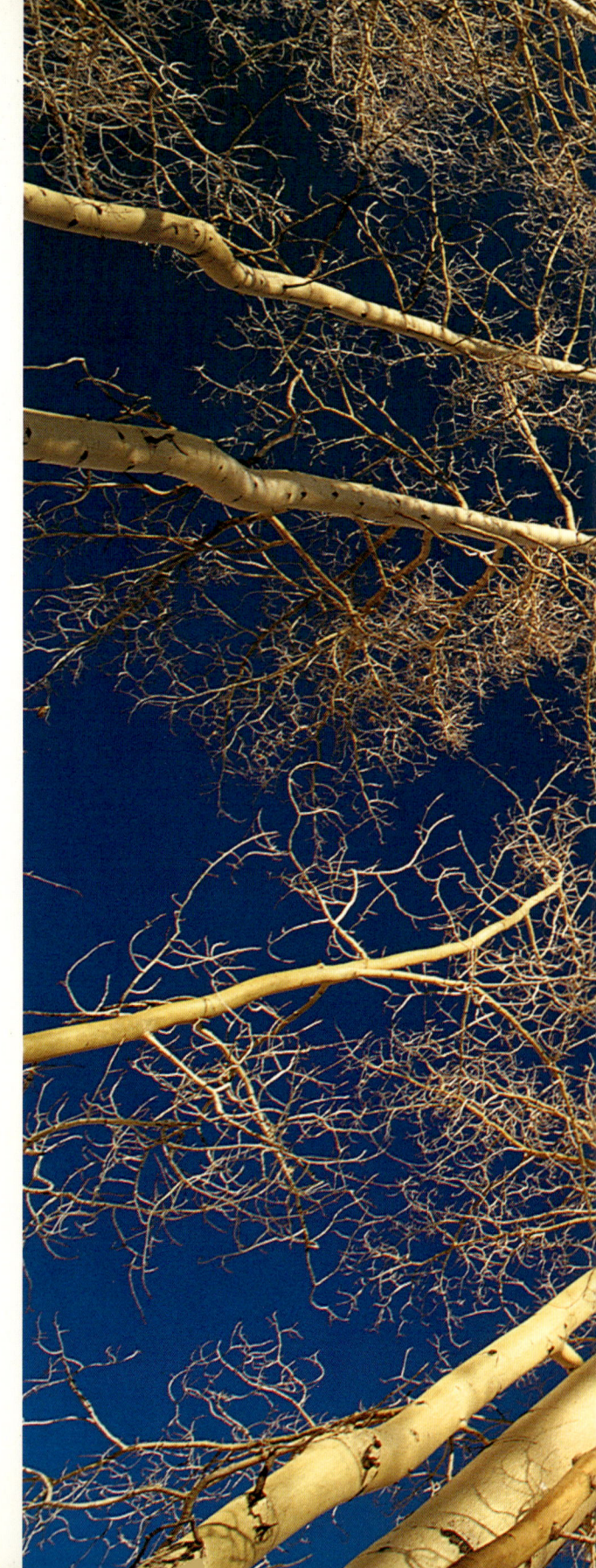

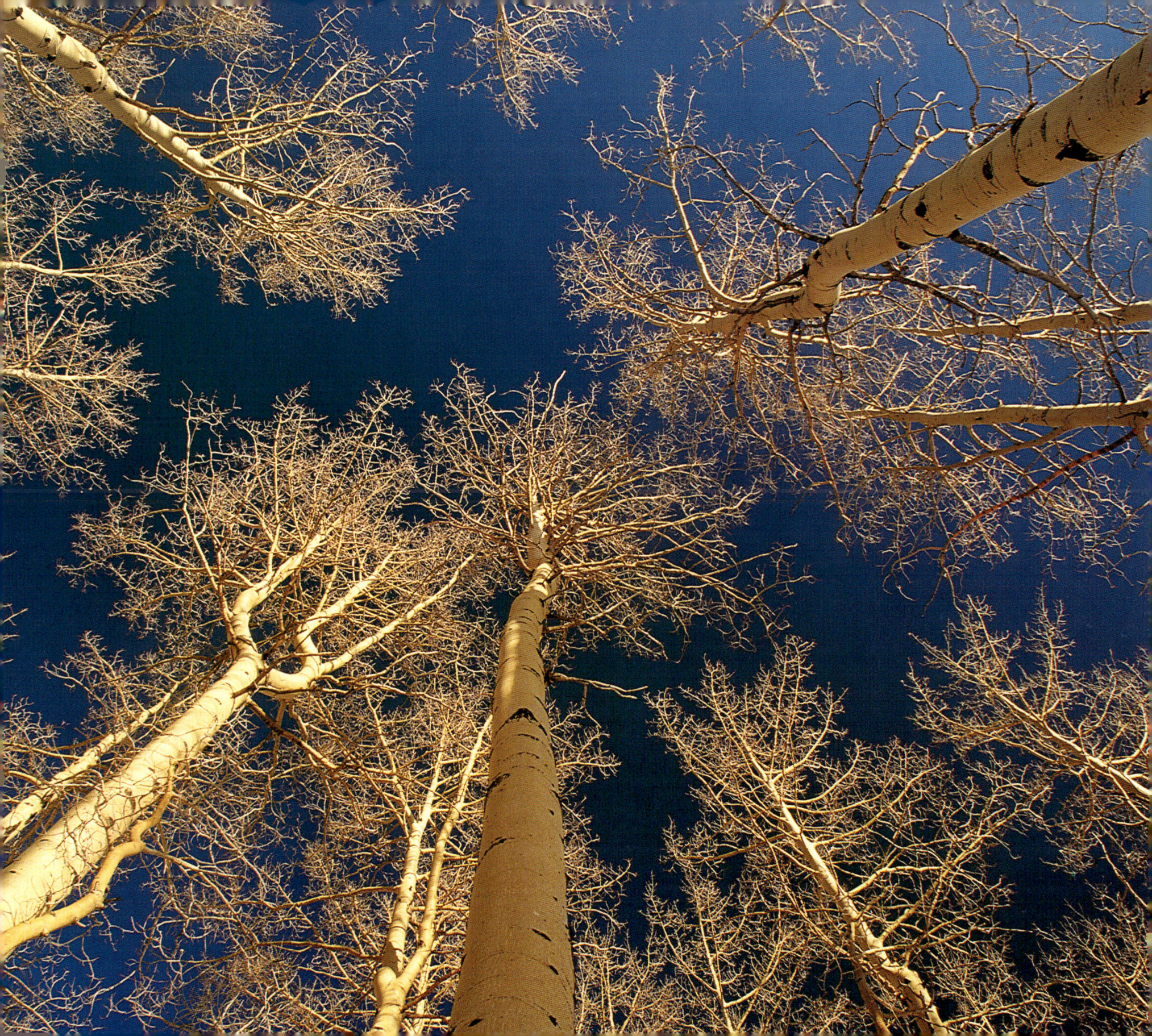

INTRODUCTION

Colorado is a state of contrasts and contradictions. It is a place of far-stretching plains, rolling foothills, and precipitous peaks. When most people think of Colorado, it is the mountains that come to mind. It is an understandable reaction, for the mountains here are truly expansive.

The San Juan Mountains—one of more than fifty ranges that constitute the Rockies—cover 10,000 square miles (6.4 million acres), about 10 percent of the entire state. Over one thousand Coloradan peaks reach above 10,000 feet, and more than fifty exceed 14,000 feet. Colorado is the "high point" of the Rocky Mountains. While Americans may dream of visiting the Andes, the Himalayas, or the Alps for a "big mountain" experience, the American Rockies hold towering monuments that are every bit as inspiring. Colorado's Mount Elbert, in the Sawatch Range, is only 259 feet shorter than Switzerland's Matterhorn.

Still, Colorado is more than its towering peaks. It is also a semi-arid desert and a temperate piedmont. This "ruddy" state, named *colorado* by the Spanish, is red rocks, deep canyons, reflective snow, and tumbling waters. It is a state of such picturesque beauty that a photographer can feel overwhelmed at the possibilities and at the range of emotions brought forth by the land.

If the observer is open to the prospect, then all emotions and senses are assailed by Colorado. There is the simple thrill of climbing a peak or hiking into a canyon, the joy at seeing a bighorn sheep with energetic young, the pulse of adrenaline at running a river, and the night-time dreams of unending wilderness interrupted by the howls of a coyote. For me, Colorado transcends the physical, and each image I capture is as much a rendition of scent, sound, taste, and touch, as it is of sight. In fact, at times I believe that there is another sense—a sixth sense—that is brought out by the wilderness. It is the sense of integration, of belonging to the wild. It combines each of the other five senses into something so much larger and all-encompassing. When I stand in the shade of a forest, among the blowing grasses of the prairie, or at the base of a tumultuous waterfall, it is a sixth sense that helps create my most memorable pictures.

Emotions have a physical impact on people. The heart races, the skin prickles, pupils dilate, breathing quickens. We are galvanized into action by the emotions we feel, be they love or fear. There is another emotion that I feel when I stand in the heart of Colorado—melancholy. Although elk, bighorn sheep, mountain lion, and others still make their home in the state, three creatures are noticeable in their absence: the brown bear, gray wolf, and American bison. That they are missing from the parks and preserves is a sad reminder that Colorado has been changed by people—some say irrevocably. But I am optimistic at heart, and one day, I hope, all three will reclaim their former homes. It is only when the land is alive with the beating hearts of the wild that it becomes truly a living, breathing country capable of stirring souls.

My optimism is founded in history, for Colorado has long valued its natural treasures, enshrining many of them as parks and monuments. The 265,727-acre Rocky Mountain National Park was established in

1915 through the pioneering dedication of Enos Mills, who saw in the Rockies something that should be preserved for all time and for all people; his is a story that shows just how much impact a single voice can have. When explorers uncovered evidence of life long vanished (such as the bones of *Stegosaurus*, now the state dinosaur), other monuments were established to protect what remains, and so were born Dinosaur National Monument, Florissant Fossil Beds National Monument, and Colorado National Monument. Fossils abound in these places, poking through the surface and baked by the sun, silent testament to a past when Colorado was inhabited by "terrible lizards" and verdant swamps.

Colorado, then, is home to the stunning grandeur of mountains, the mysteries of ancient dinosaurs, and even to an incongruous natural oddity—a sea of sand far from the lapping waters of an ocean. Born of sediments eroded from the San Juan and Sangre de Cristo Mountains and ultimately picked up by the wind, the Great Sand Dunes National Monument covers 37 square miles (23,680 acres) with undulating, rippling dunes—a tiny slice of desert in the Rocky Mountain state.

Colorado is also home to the newest U.S. national park—another reason for my optimism. From 1933 until the turn of the millennium, the Black Canyon of the Gunnison was a national monument. In 1999 it became the nation's fifty-fifth national park, the latest addition to an incredible legacy. This 30,300-acre park encompasses 14 miles of the 53-mile-long Black Canyon gorge, carved by the Gunnison River. With its deepest point at 2,660 feet, it is Colorado's Grand Canyon.

I particularly love the seasonal transitions in Colorado. As winter turns to spring, flowers push their way up through a late season snowstorm; as spring transforms into summer, meadows are lush and everything is growing; as summer blends to fall, all the energy of growth is gradually redirected to prepare for the cold to come; and, as fall turns to winter, life becomes stoic and rugged in the face of adversity.

Colorado is a land of still-rising mountains, 100 million years in the making, of river-carved canyons, wind-blown dunes, of mesas and plateaus, desertlike vistas, and endless prairies. The landscapes of Colorado complement one another. There is no single Colorado, there is only the whole thing. To know Colorado you must immerse yourself in it, allow the *colorado* to color your skin and get into your blood.

There are two emotions that I hope you will feel while viewing and reading this book: enthrallment and inspiration. The former allows you to appreciate the world around you, the latter will move you to act to secure its protection. I take photographs not simply to document the present, but to ensure that there is a future for such places. Those who come to Colorado to run its rivers, climb its mountains, hike its valleys, or ski its slopes are witnesses to a land that, in the grand scheme of things, is still fresh and new, still forming, still changing.

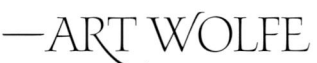

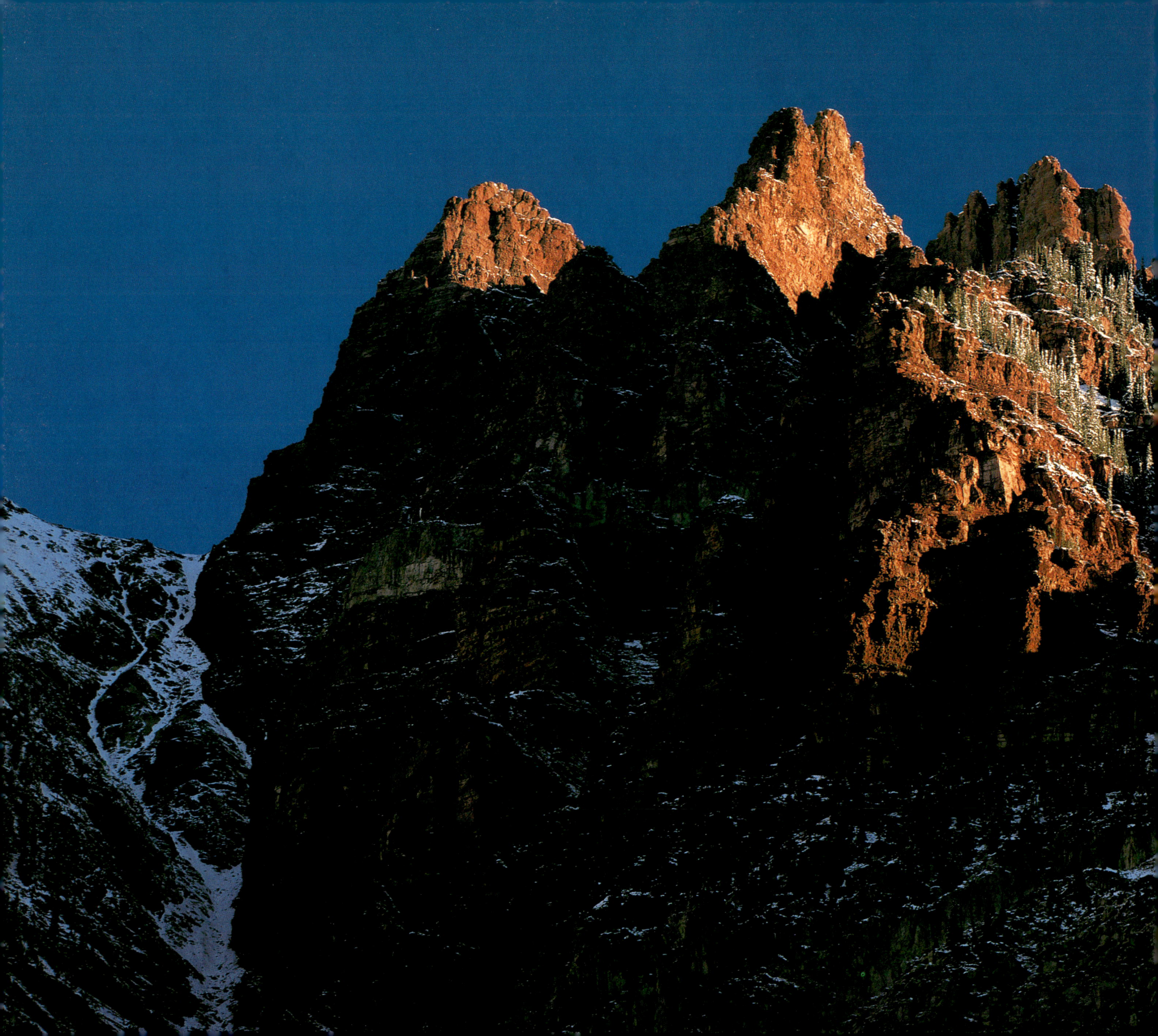

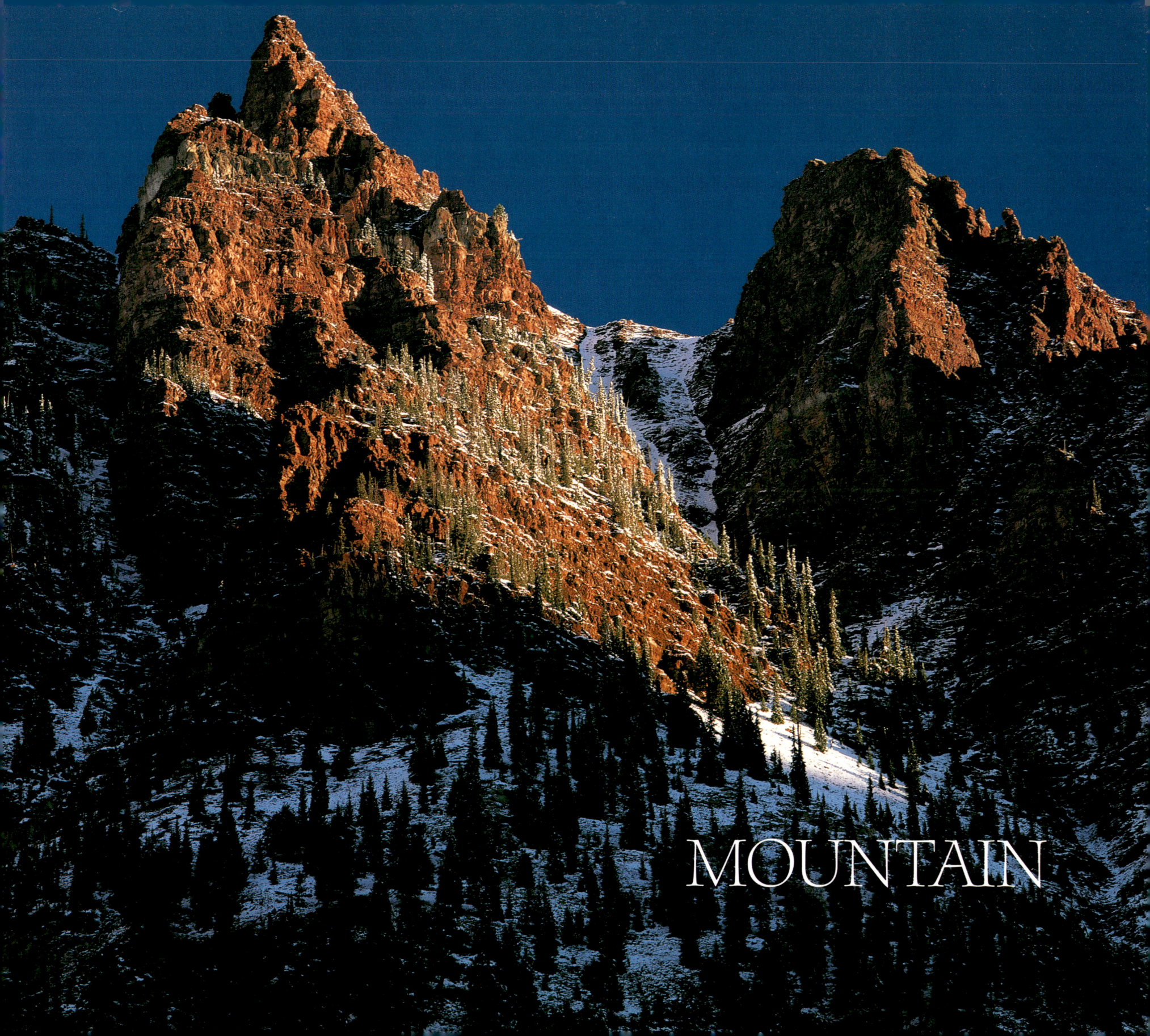

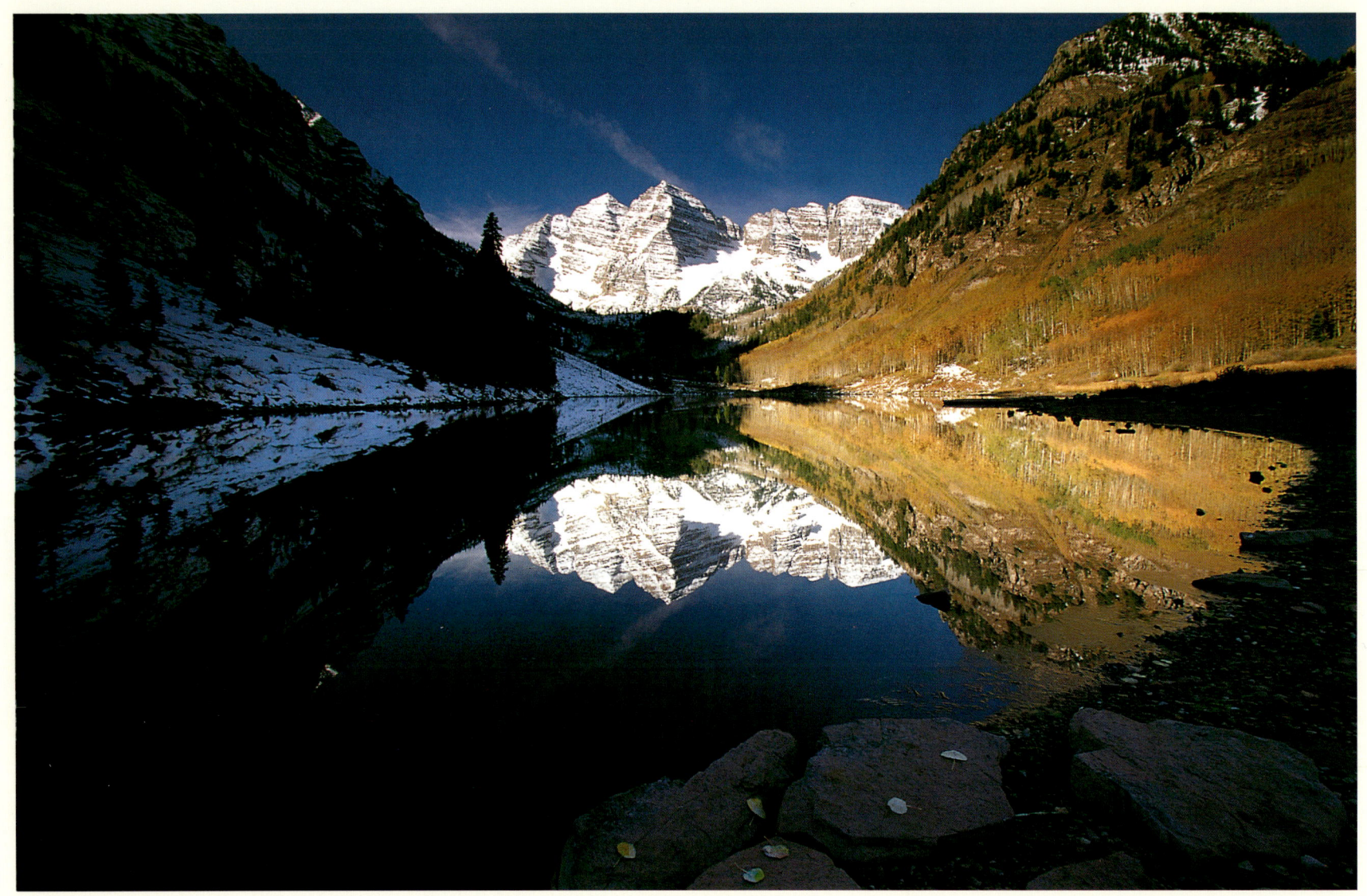

O n a summer day I walked into a spur of the Rocky Mountains that stretches from southwest Colorado almost to New Mexico. I walked through the shouldering towers above a place called Bear Creek with ten days of supplies hanging like a Sherpa's load

Overleaf: Sievers Mountain, Maroon Bells-Snowmass Wilderness

Left: Maroon Bells, Maroon Bells-Snowmass Wilderness

Right: White-tailed ptarmigan (*Lagopus leucurus*), Rocky Mountain National Park

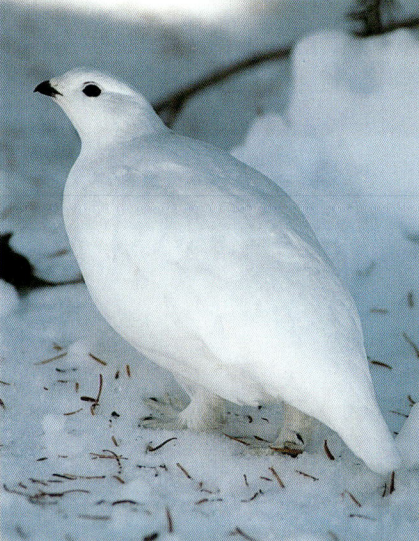

from my back. This was the place where rocks came loose at my heels and cracked all the way down, whistling and bursting to dust before reaching the creek. Vaulted walls came up, spinning out of sight in the mist of waterfalls.

When I reached 12,000 feet I laid my back against the treeless tundra where mountains came around me like knitting needles through an afghan. Gardens of plant species, those obdurate and intricate enough to thrive on a three-month growing season, grabbed at the rocks like knuckled fingers. Between the short, stiff grasses were flowers the size of sand grains, flowers that had taken ten or twenty years to show their first blooms in this harsh climate. Nothing tall grew up here. The largest trees had been wrestled to the ground by wind, stunted and twisted to knee-height.

In the evening I found shelter in the lee of a ridge, spread my gear, and fell asleep with my head against the curt alpine sedges. I curled with my knees up, the way a coyote will sleep on the ground.

Storms came through in my sleep, but did nothing to wet the ground. Gusts pushed against ragged timberline pines already imbued with the memory of wind, bent and gnarled toward the east. As clouds uncoupled and rolled west, I woke and saw through their gaps to the stars.

Running your hand across a relief globe, you will feel the smoothness of the Great Plains suddenly interrupted by a wad of wrinkled mountains in Colorado. From an airplane the mountains appear like a big tangle, islands of interconnected peaks surrounded by smooth, vacuous parks; long ranges of summits crossing each other at odd angles—the likes of the West Elks, the Sangre de Cristos, the Sneffels, the La Garitas, and the Mosquitos. From on the ground, traveling on foot, the mountains swallow everything. From inside the Gore Range or in the backside of the Maroon Bells Mountains, it looks like there is no way out, nothing but mountains everywhere.

In the morning dark clouds moved among the peaks. I walked alongside the clouds. They spiraled between mountains, broke against them, and fell into the abandoned glacial valleys and cirques. They feathered down avalanche couloirs and over the ground, snagging on the outcrops.

For years I lived in these mountains, around the town of Ouray, where I watched weather such as this stagger through. These mountains breathed down my neck like a waiting animal when I was in town. Every day they leaned over me as I walked to work, as I stopped in the post office and the bakery. I memorized the unusually sharp outlines of peaks, how they made monster faces against the sky, and I itched to walk through their eyes and teeth and cheekbones. They are the northwestern extent of the San Juan Range, heaving a crown out of the last extensive high country before the deserts of Western Colorado.

I sat on the ground in the remnants of ancient volcanoes, my pack behind me as a backrest. A short-tailed weasel appeared at the point of a rock. It was elastic and quick. It moved like a magician, leaping from the rock before I could think.

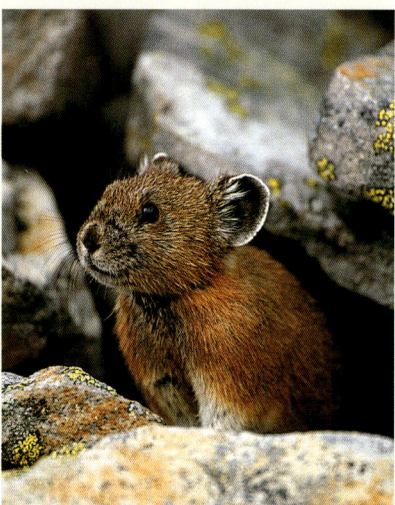

It was hunting ground squirrels and mice, nosing into burrows with an electrified metabolism. Five hundred heartbeats each minute within a tubular rib cage. Like the plants taking decades to put out their first blooms, this creature has also made peculiar adaptations to the high mountains. It must eat and eat and eat, feeding the tiny furnace of its body, its spine articulated so that it can turn back on itself inside of a rodent burrow and pop out to daylight. There is no time for anything but the impatient seeking of prey. The weasel sprang from behind a rock five feet from the tips of my boots. It leveled its gaze, sniffed the air, and was gone in the same instant. It hopped like popcorn as it took tangential paths to the east, out of my view.

For many more days I walked south and east with my gear, embedding myself into the mountains. On the fifth night I camped at the base of a peak called Wetterhorn, a 14,000-foot heap of cliffs and boulders. Rings of surrounding ledges and ridges led to summits and basins and boulder fields, riding into the oblivion of the alpine horizon. I left camp in the morning and dropped eight hundred feet into one of the valleys, coming fifteen hundred feet up the opposite side.

I walked the crater rims where snow hugged the slopes to either side. These were the apexes where raptors had left marmot skulls like shrines. A skull was at each high point, half buried in the gnarled, tiny flowers of rockjasmine and alpine pussytoes. Wetterhorn and its council of peaks looked like a tattered bird spreading its wings above all of this. Travel around its base was torturous with sudden plummets and steep ascents. Looking at this mountain, just looking at it, is like putting a knife through your hand. It is that kind of mountain. It rises from a steep bed of spilled boulders forming a single tombstone slab.

These mountains shift and buckle with high- and low-angle faults, broad upwarps, anticlines, and folds. Water freezes to ice, pressing about one thousand pounds per square inch into whatever crack it has gotten into. While the mountain range rises over millions of years, it is chipped to pieces by ice; the rock slabs collapse into talus cones, where more ice breaks them down even further. Mountain ranges come and go. These mountains were preceded by the Ancestral Rockies, preceded by another and another. Material is diced and crushed as the mountains dissolve. Rock debris runs down arterial creeks until it turns into mud in the desert rivers below.

As I returned to my camp from a day of poking around Wetterhorn, the surrounding mountains turned black against the sky so that each notch was crisp. So much moisture was in the air from the passing clouds that water beaded in my nostrils. The smell was an ocean-full of water. I stood over the hum of creeks and waterfalls, cradled by the endless and the absolute. Mountains went on forever.

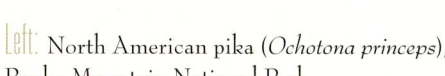

Left: North American pika (*Ochotona princeps*), Rocky Mountain National Park

Right: Least chipmunk (*Eutamias minimus*), Rocky Mountain National Park

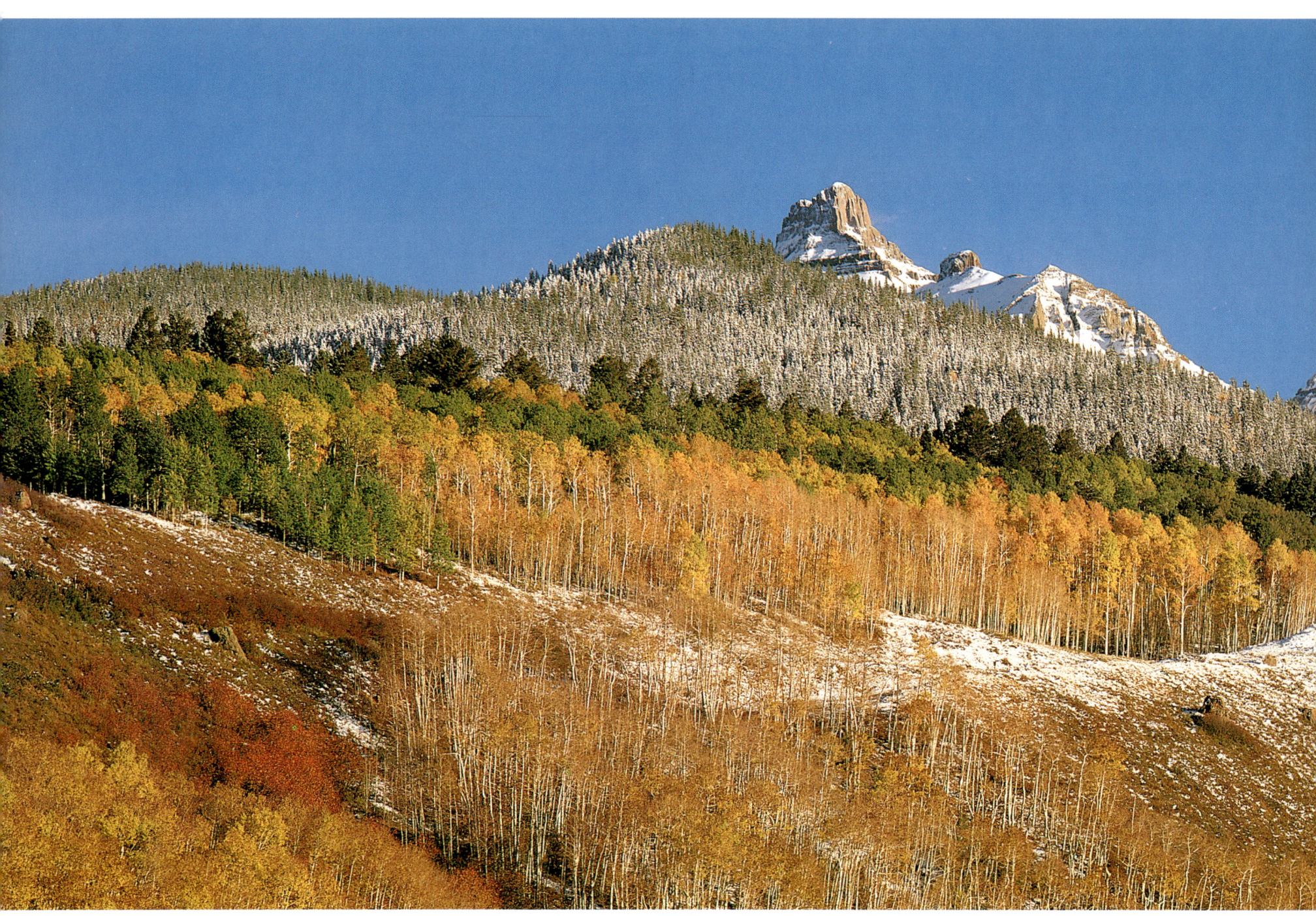

Mount Sneffels region

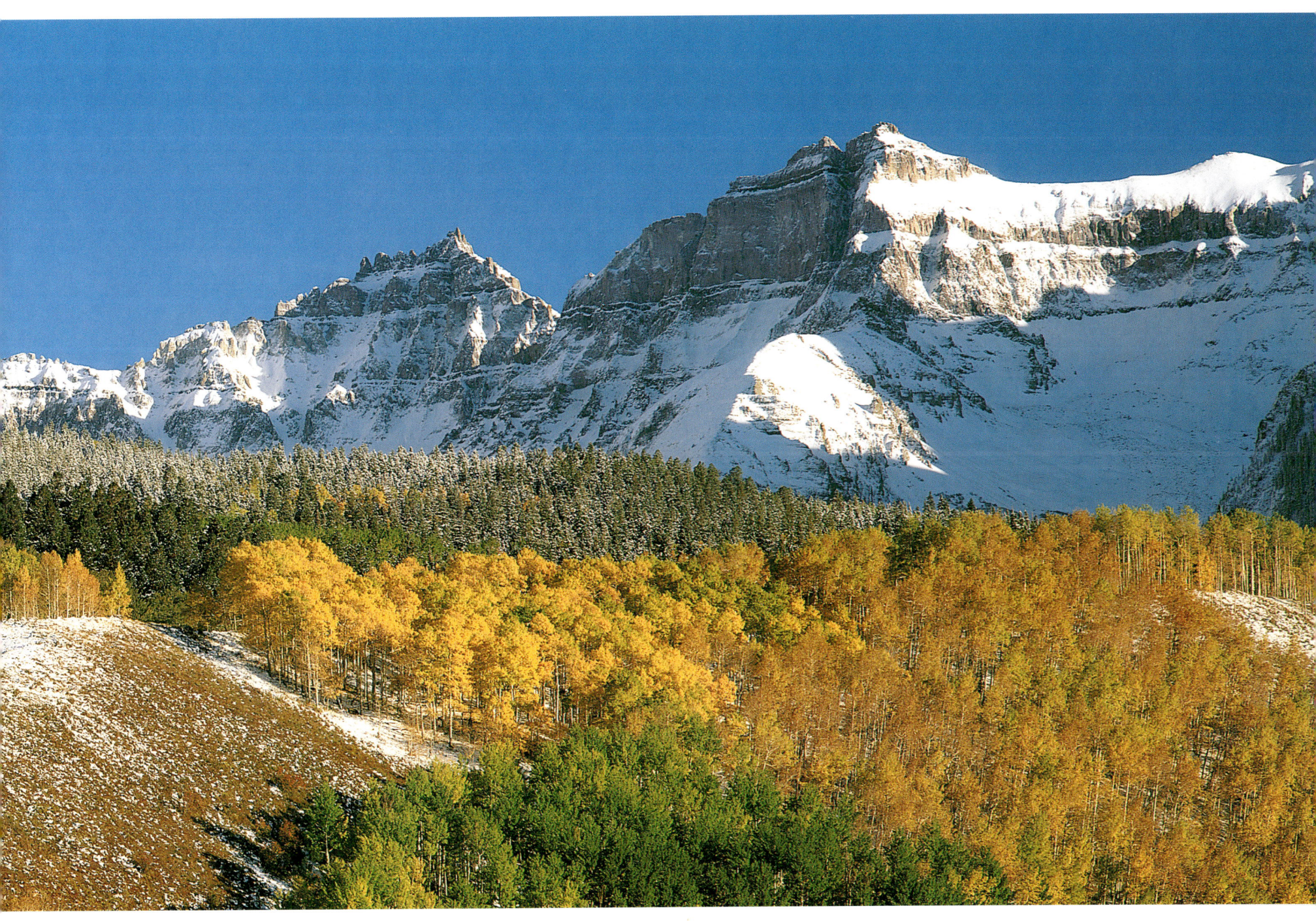

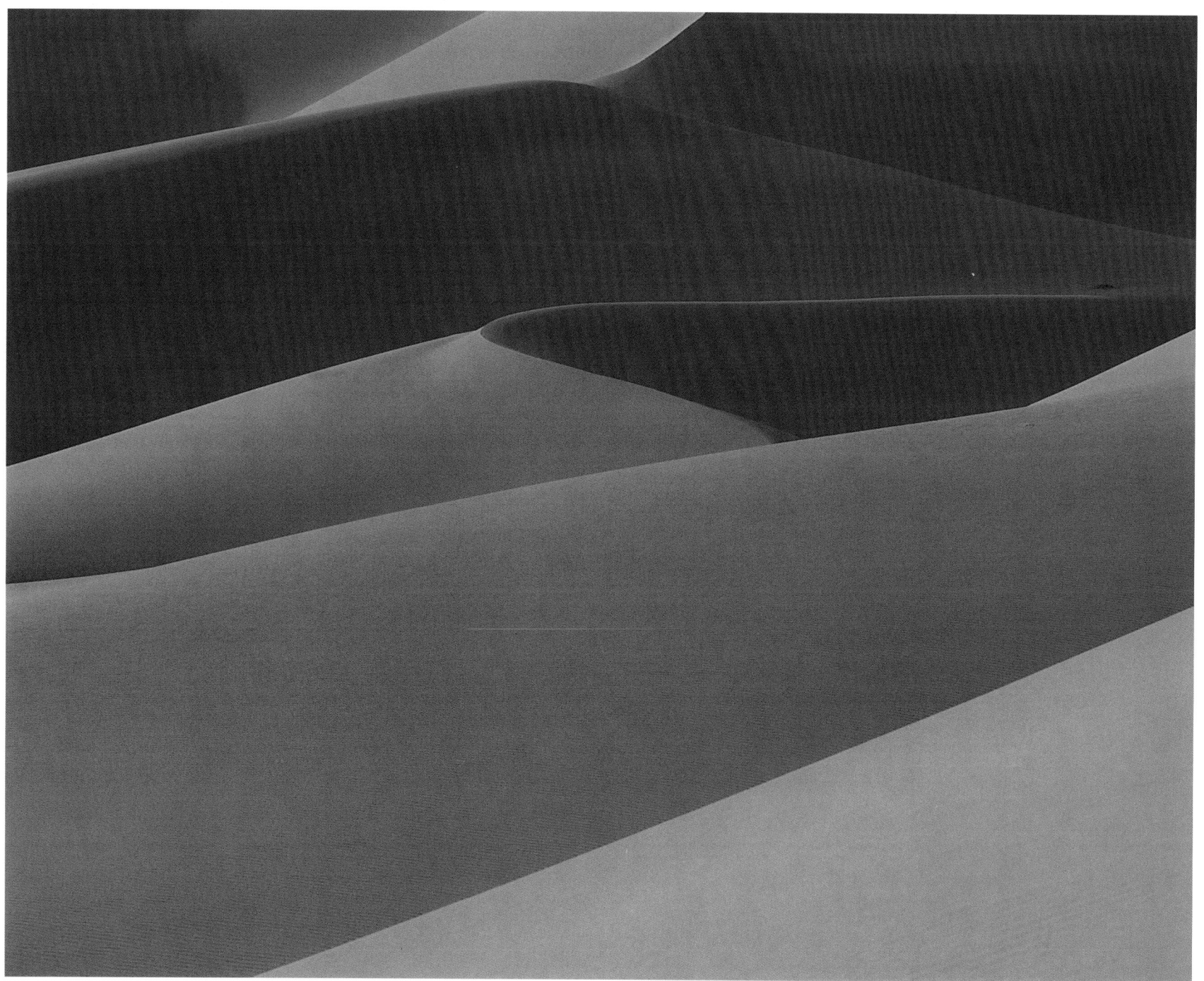

Great Sand Dunes National Monument

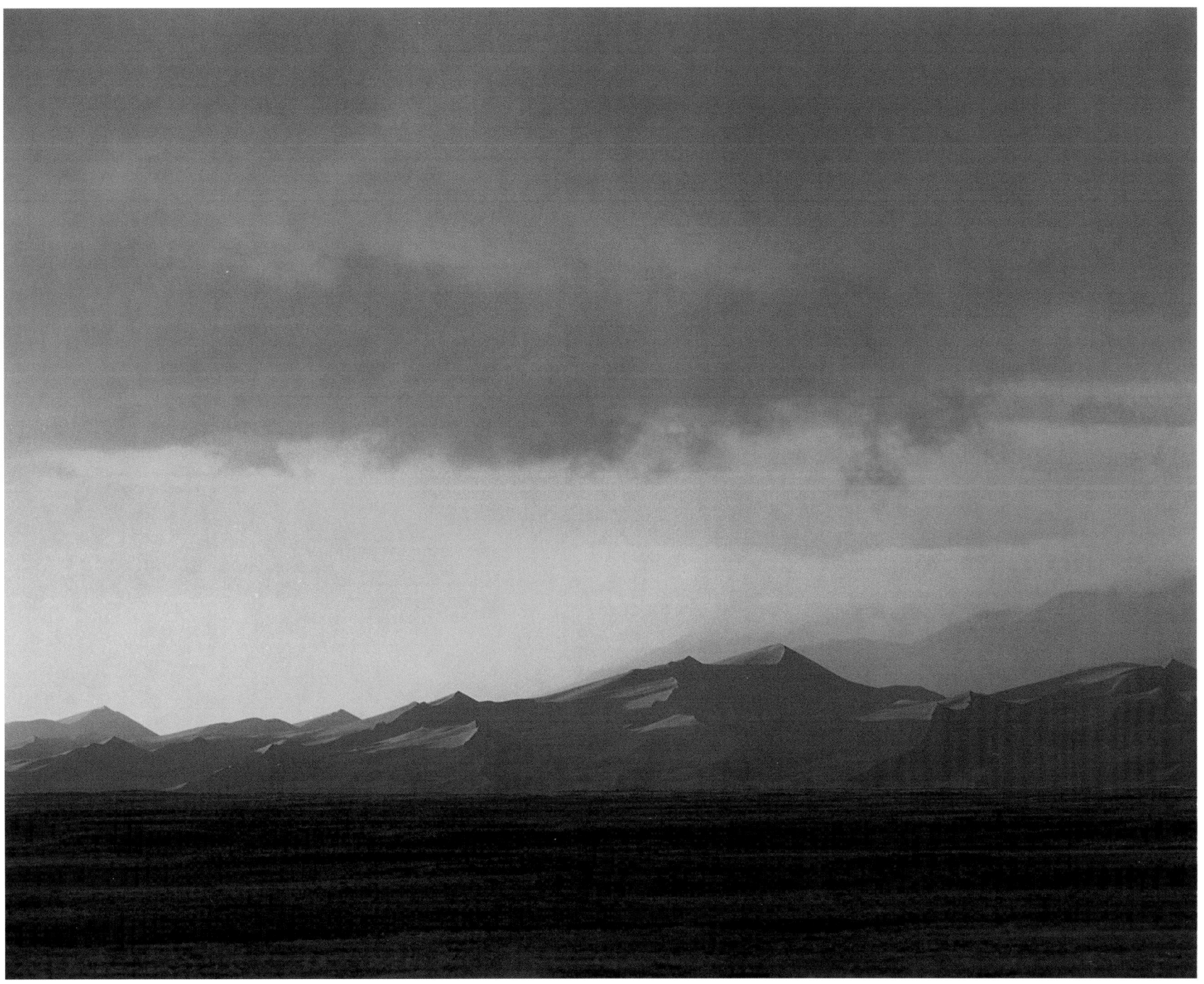

Great Sand Dunes National Monument

Below: Alpine forget-me-not (*Eritrichium elongatum*), moss campion (*Acaulis silene*), alpine buttercup (*Rununculus adoneus*), and lichen, Medicine Bow Mountains

Right: Lichen, Rocky Mountain National Park

Far right: Alpine buttercup (*Rununculus adoneus*), alpine forget-me-not (*Eritrichium elongatum*), and lichen, Rocky Mountain National Park

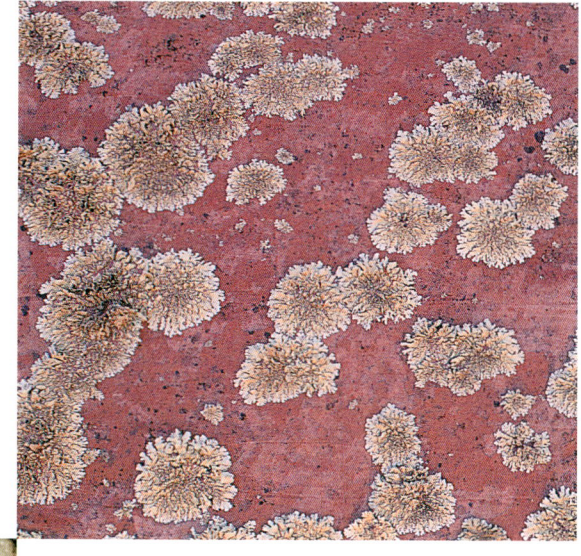

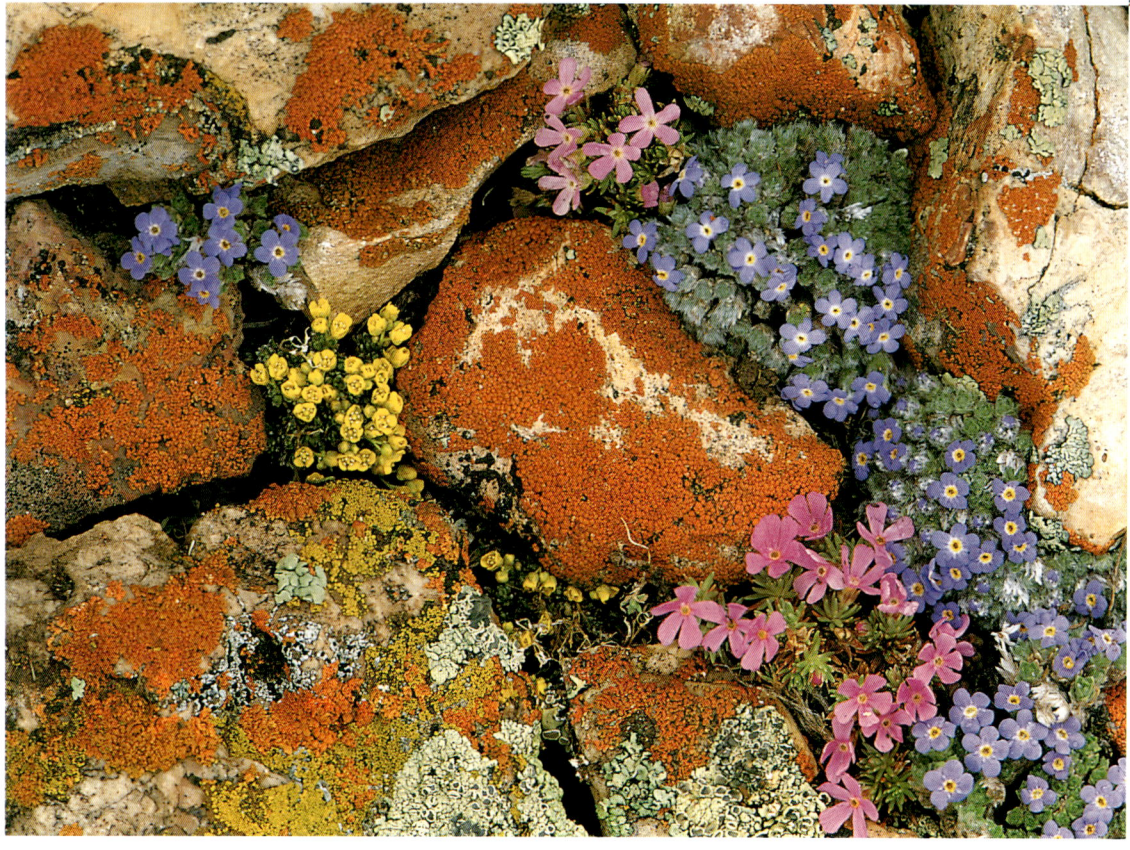

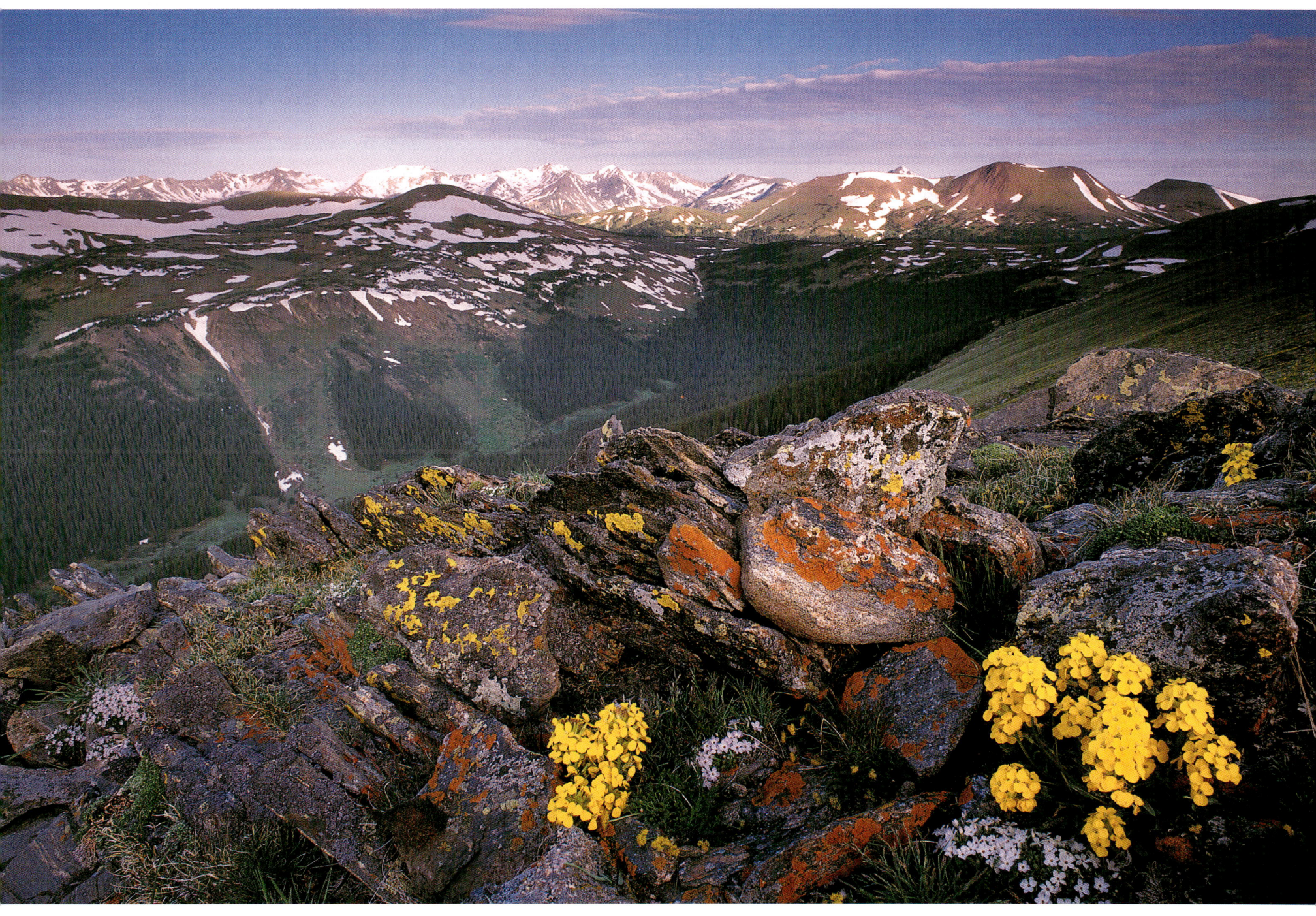

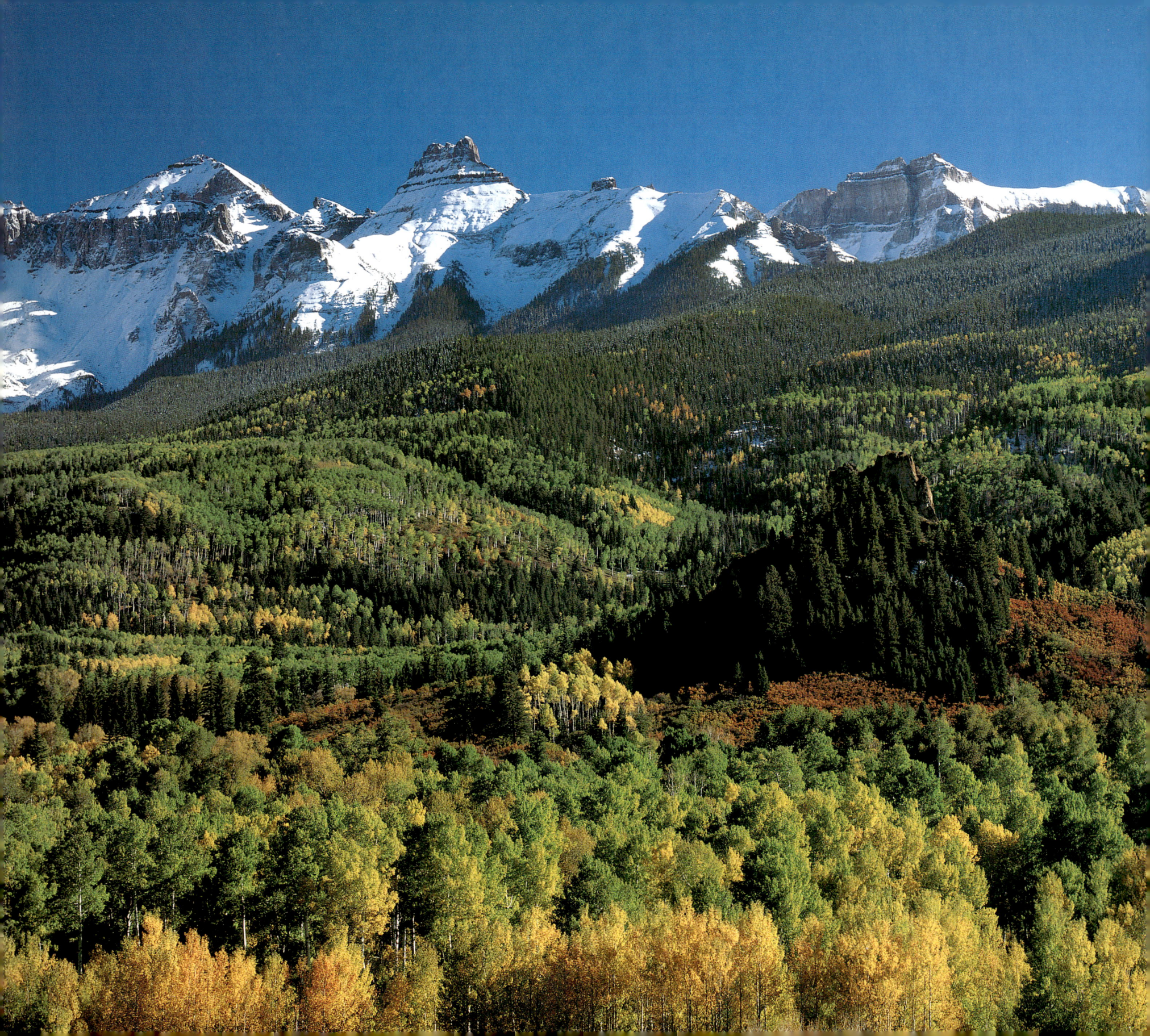

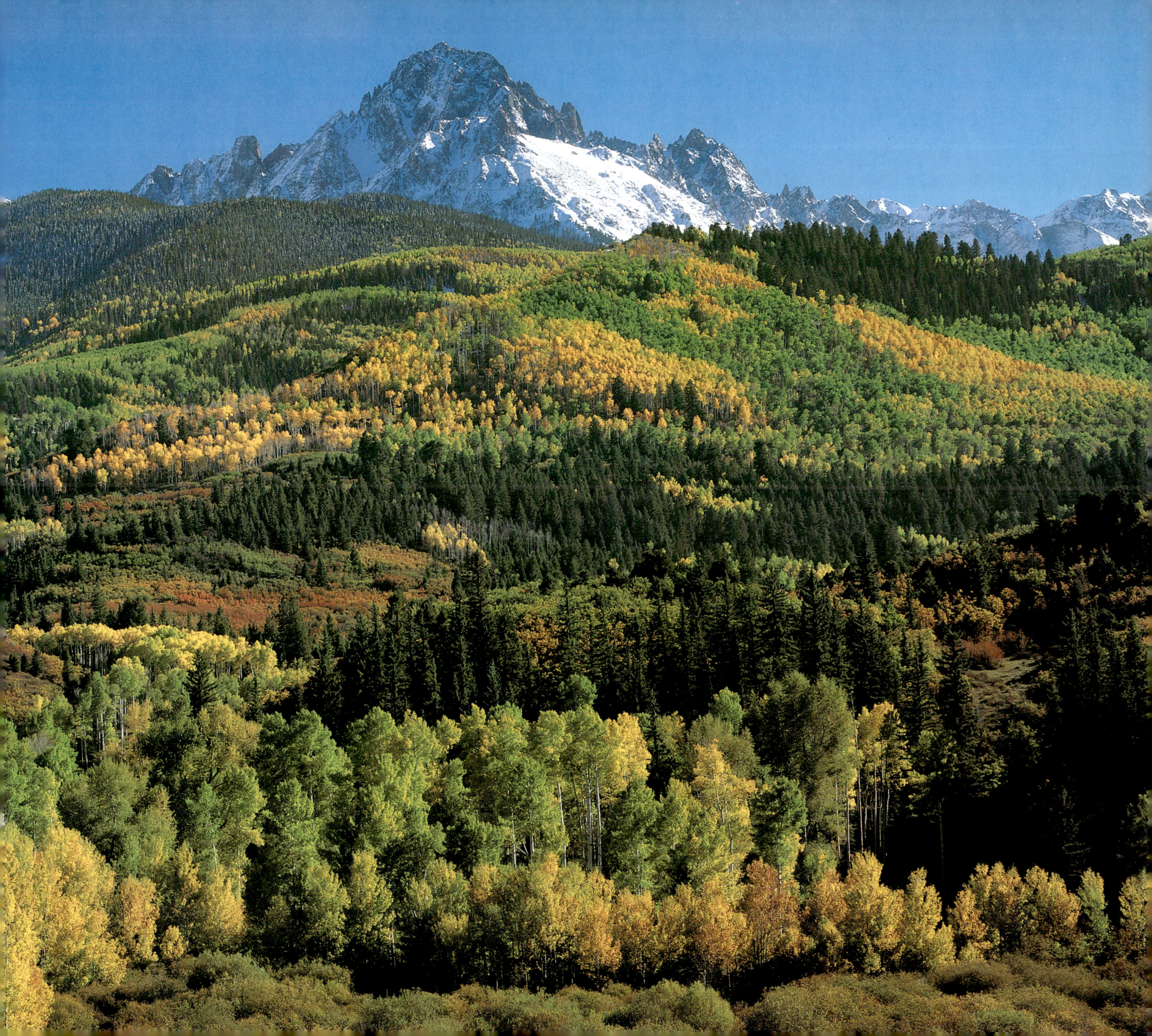

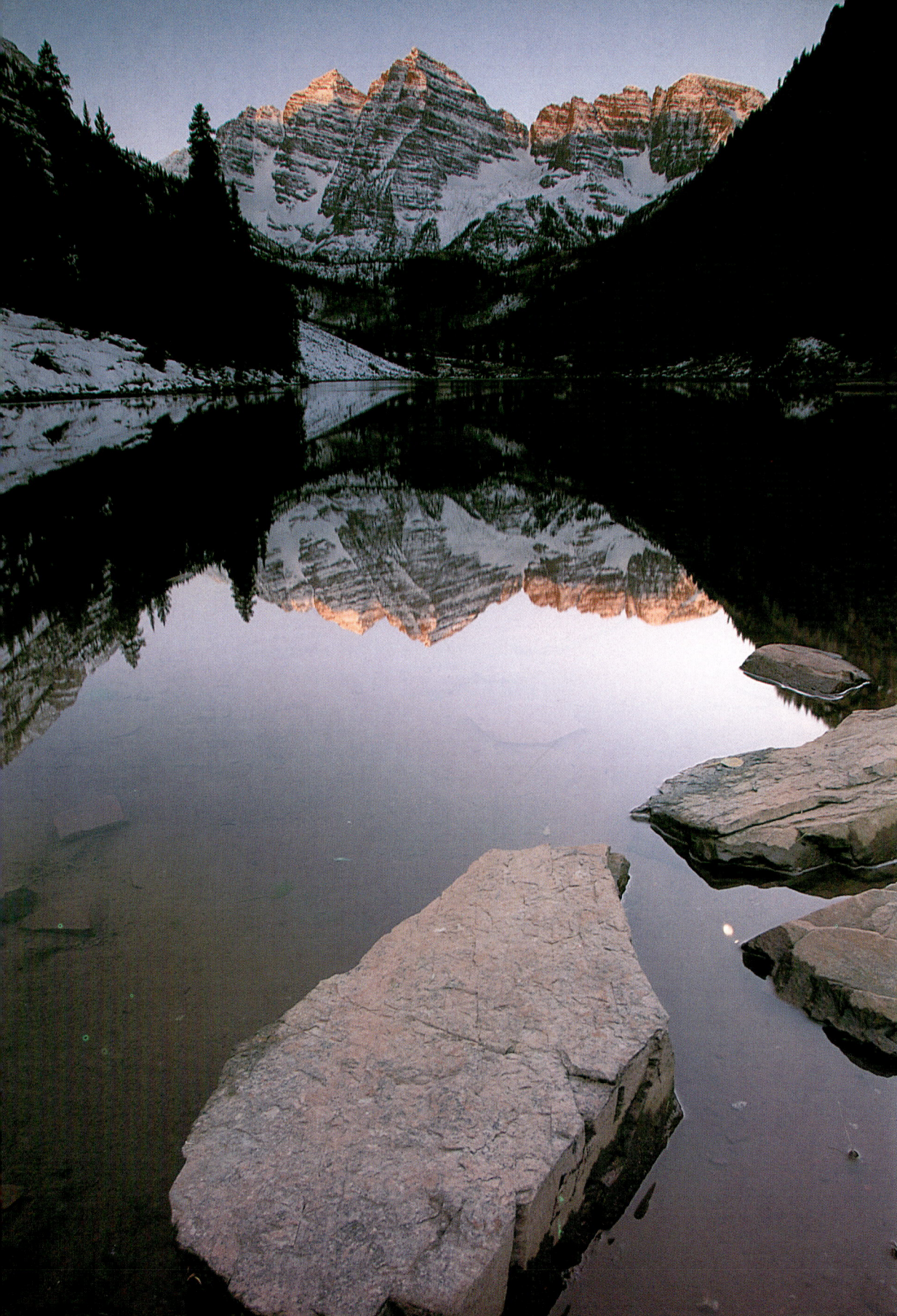

Overleaf: San Juan Mountains

Left: Maroon Bells, Maroon Bells–Snowmass Wilderness

Right: Dallas Divide, Uncompahgre National Forest

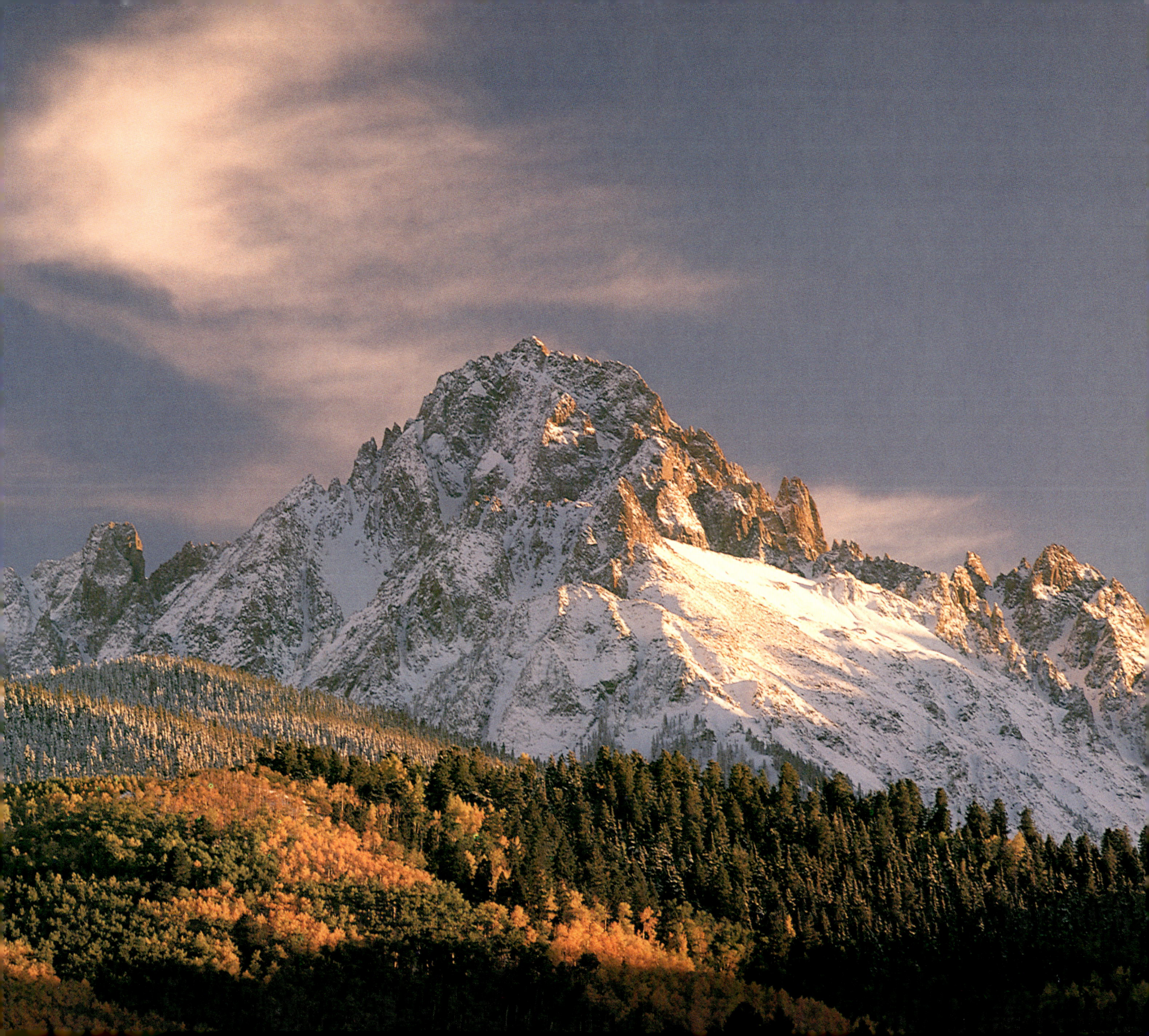

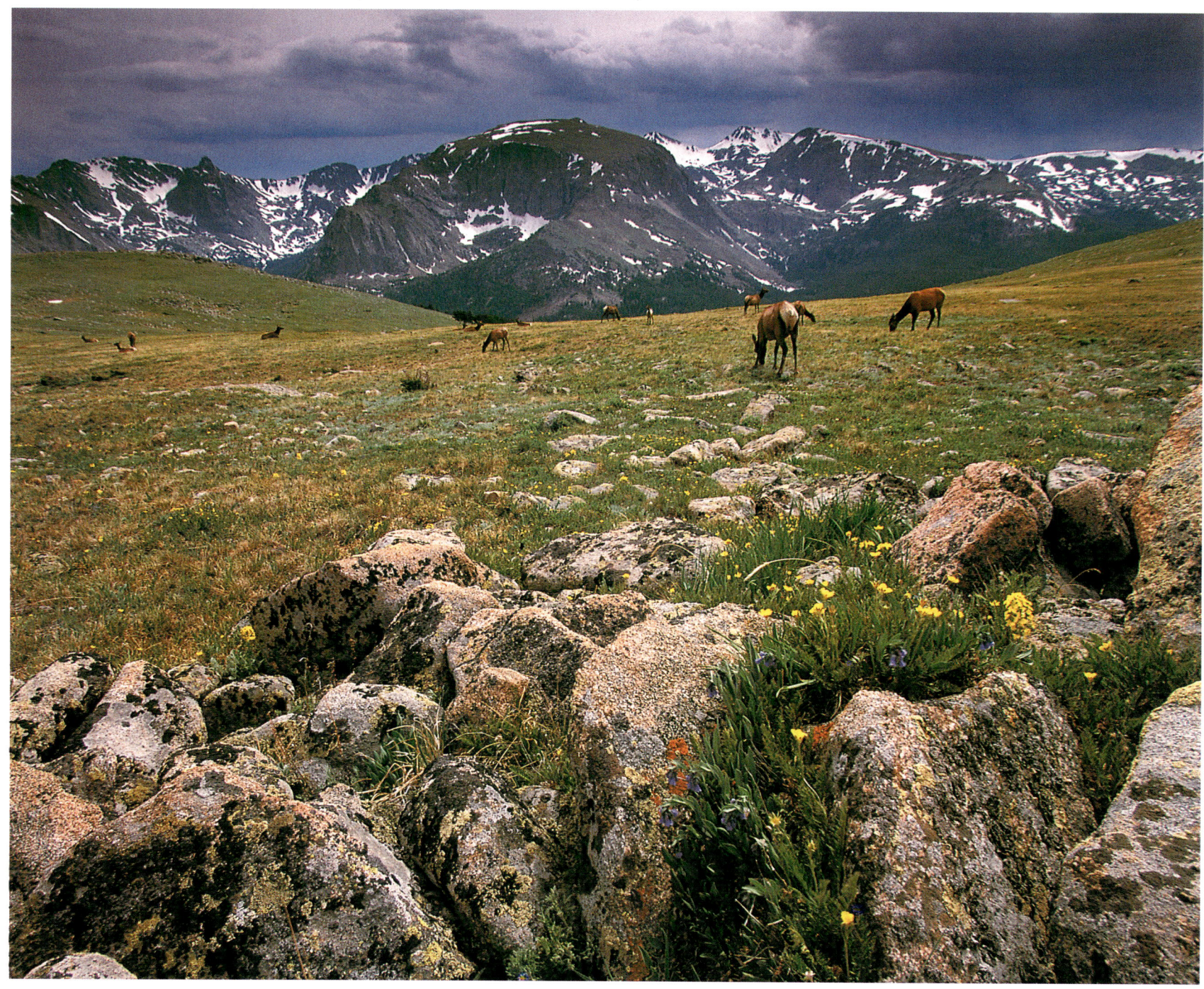

Left: Elk (*Cervus elaphus*), Rocky Mountain National Park

Right: Mount Sneffels region

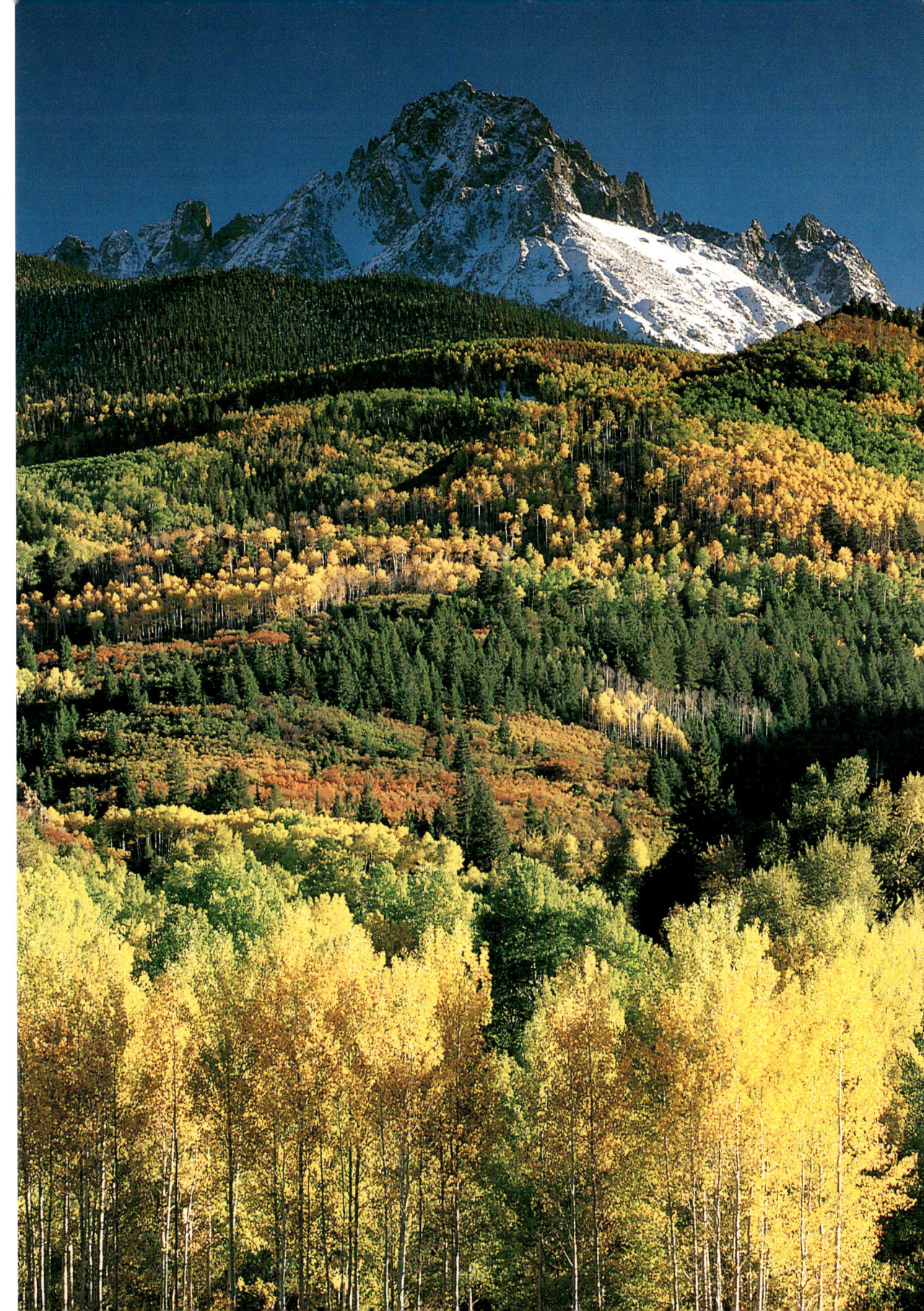

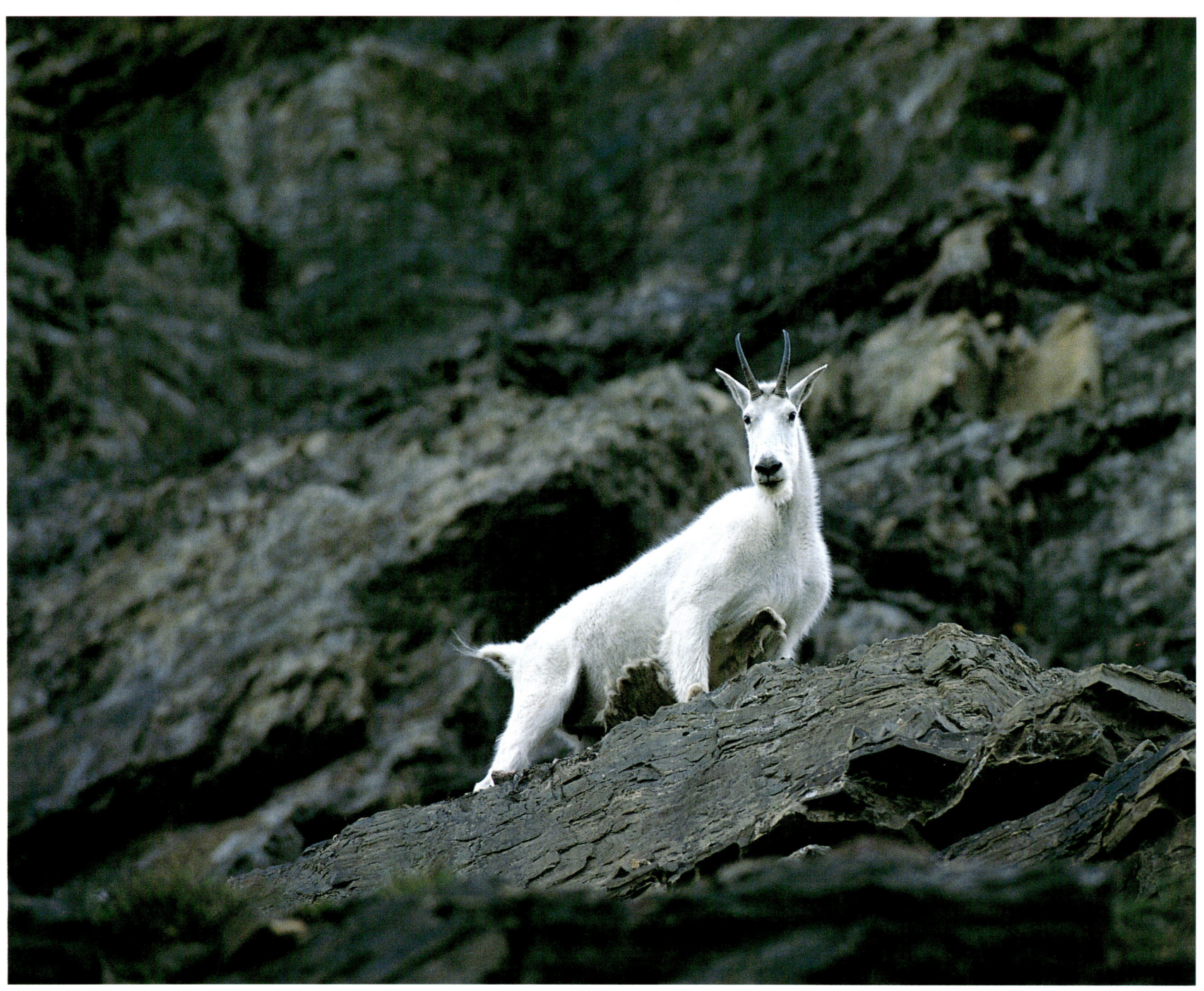

Mountain goat (*Oreamnos americanus*), Mount Evans, Arapaho National Forest

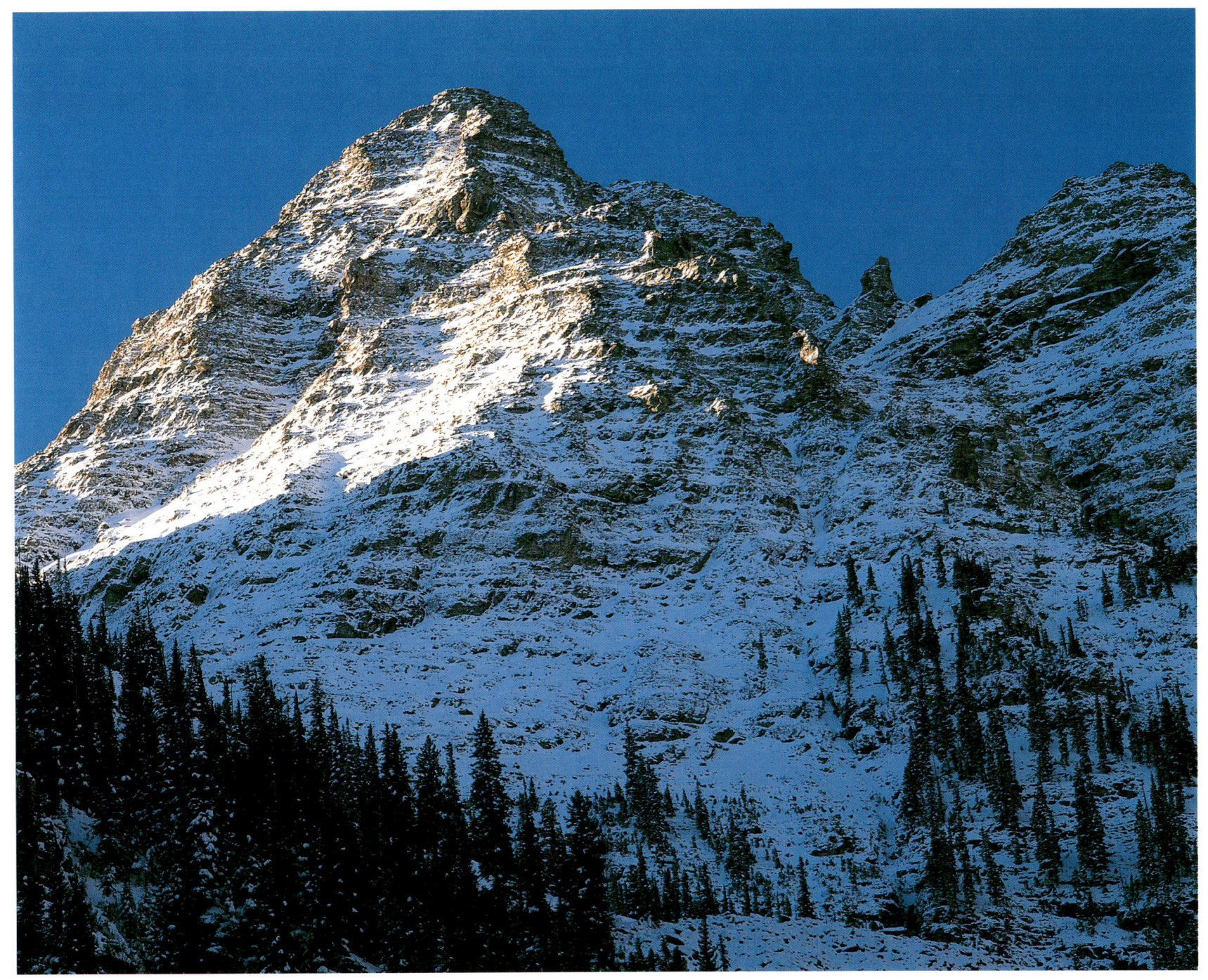

Pyramid Peak, Elk Mountains

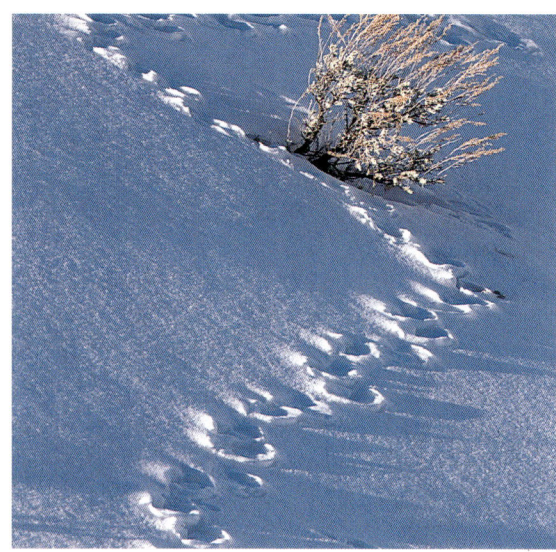

Left: Tracks in the snow, Sangre de Cristo Range

Below: Mule deer (*Odocoileus hemionus*), San Juan Mountains

Right: Elk (*Cervus elaphus*), Rocky Mountain National Park

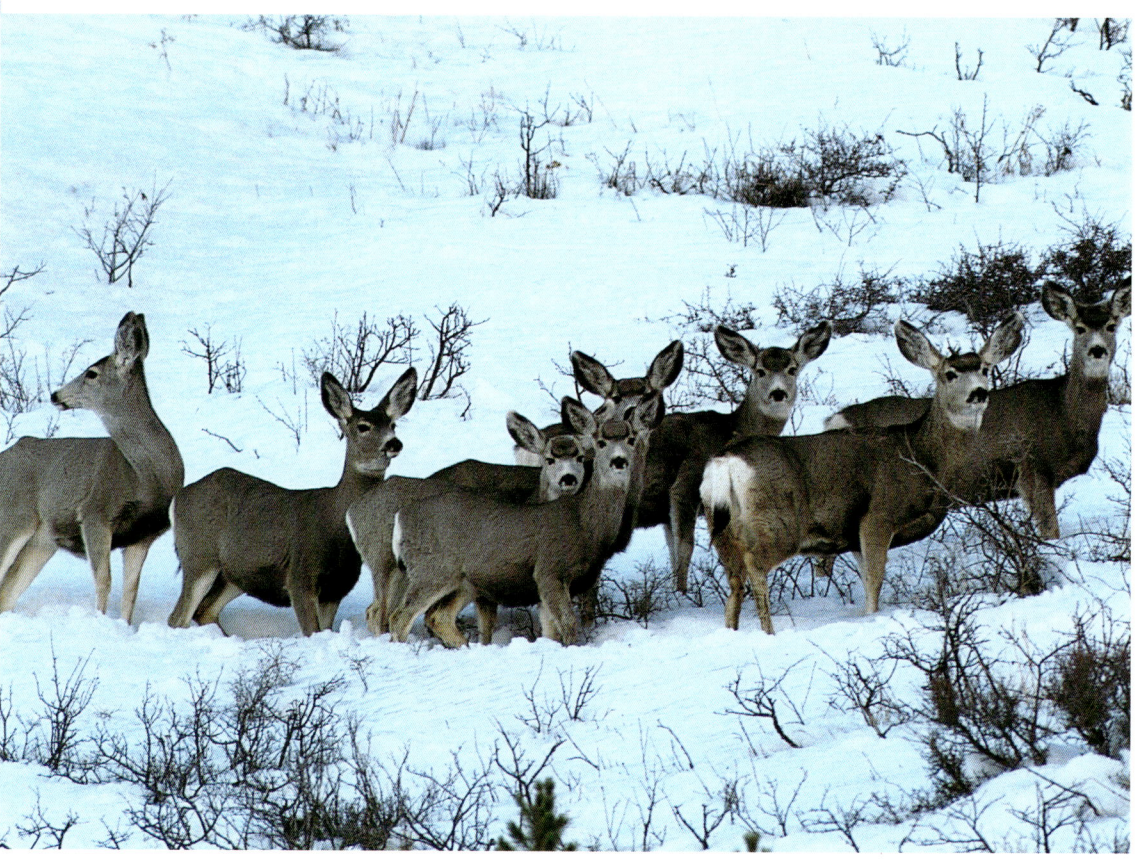

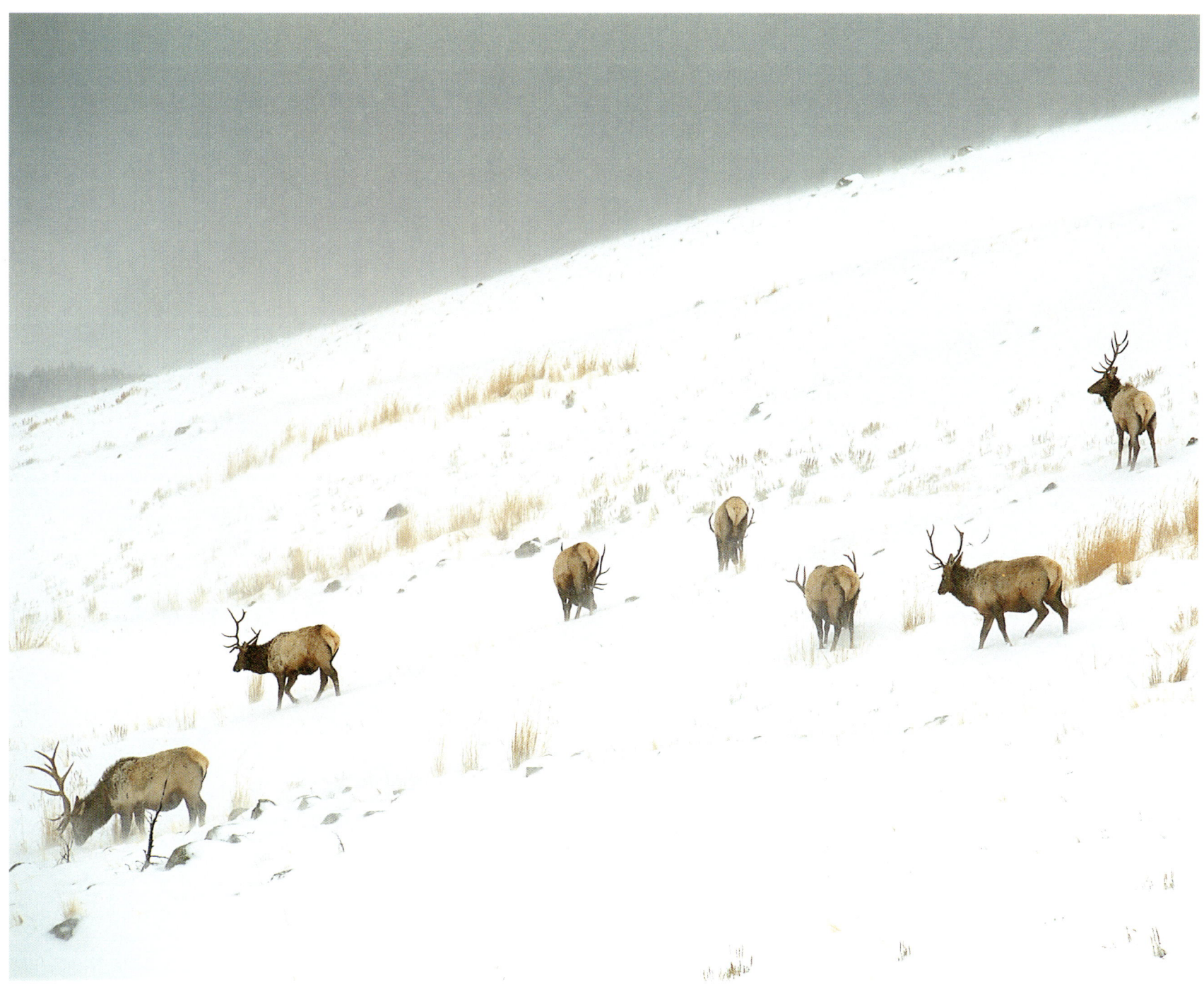

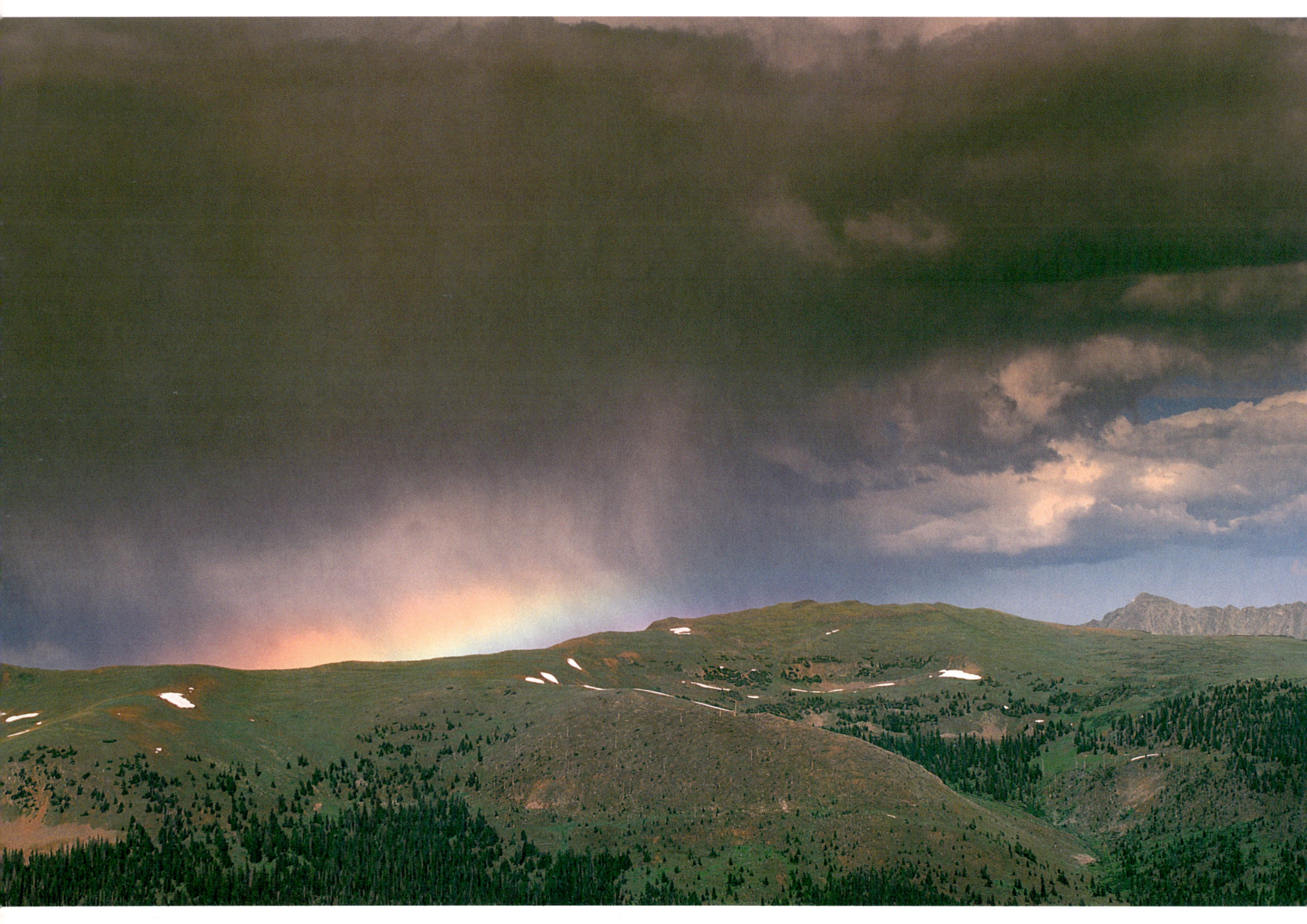

Left: Rocky Mountain National Park

Right: Subalpine buttercup (*Ranunculus eschscholtzii*) and lichen, Rocky Mountain National Park

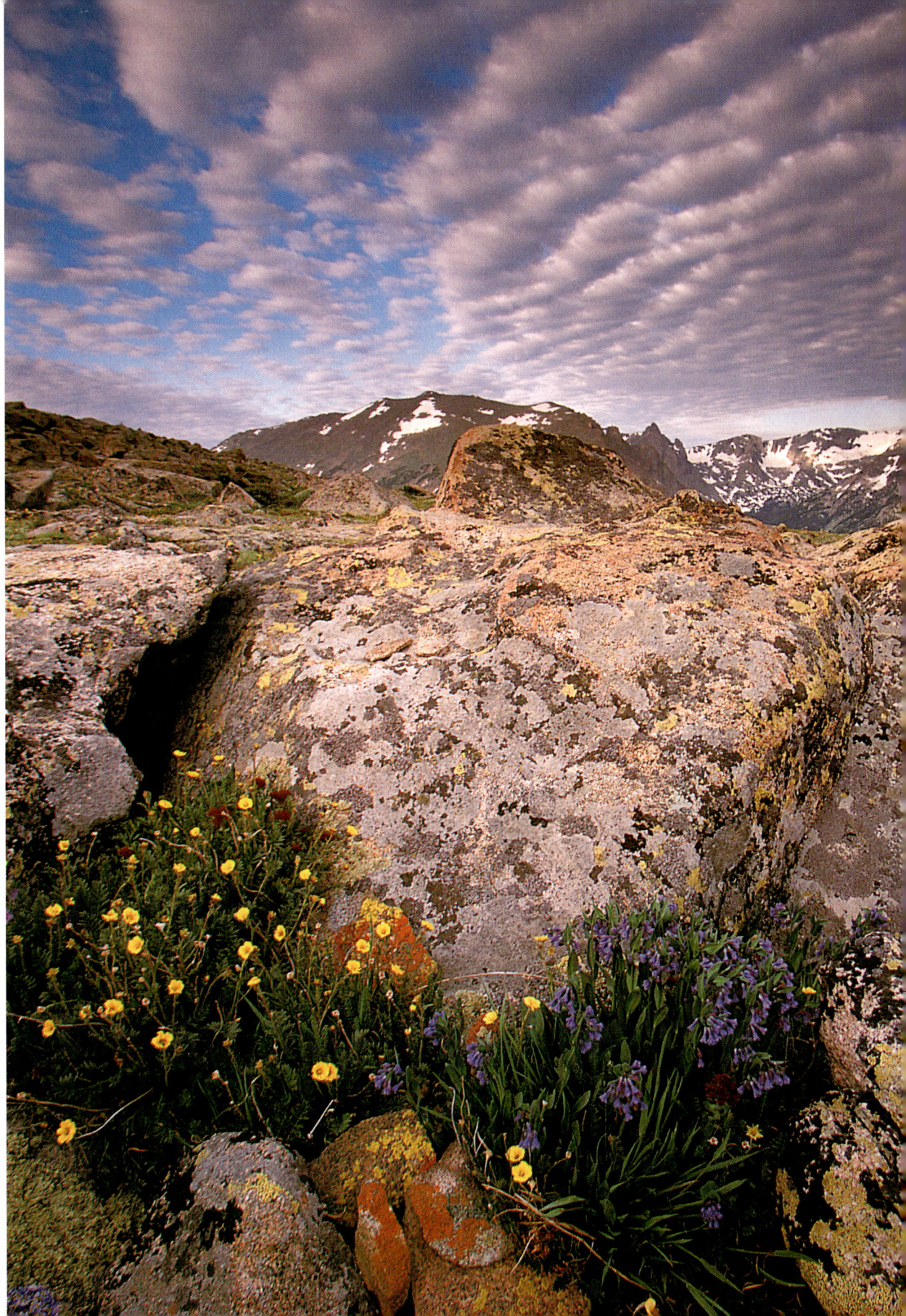

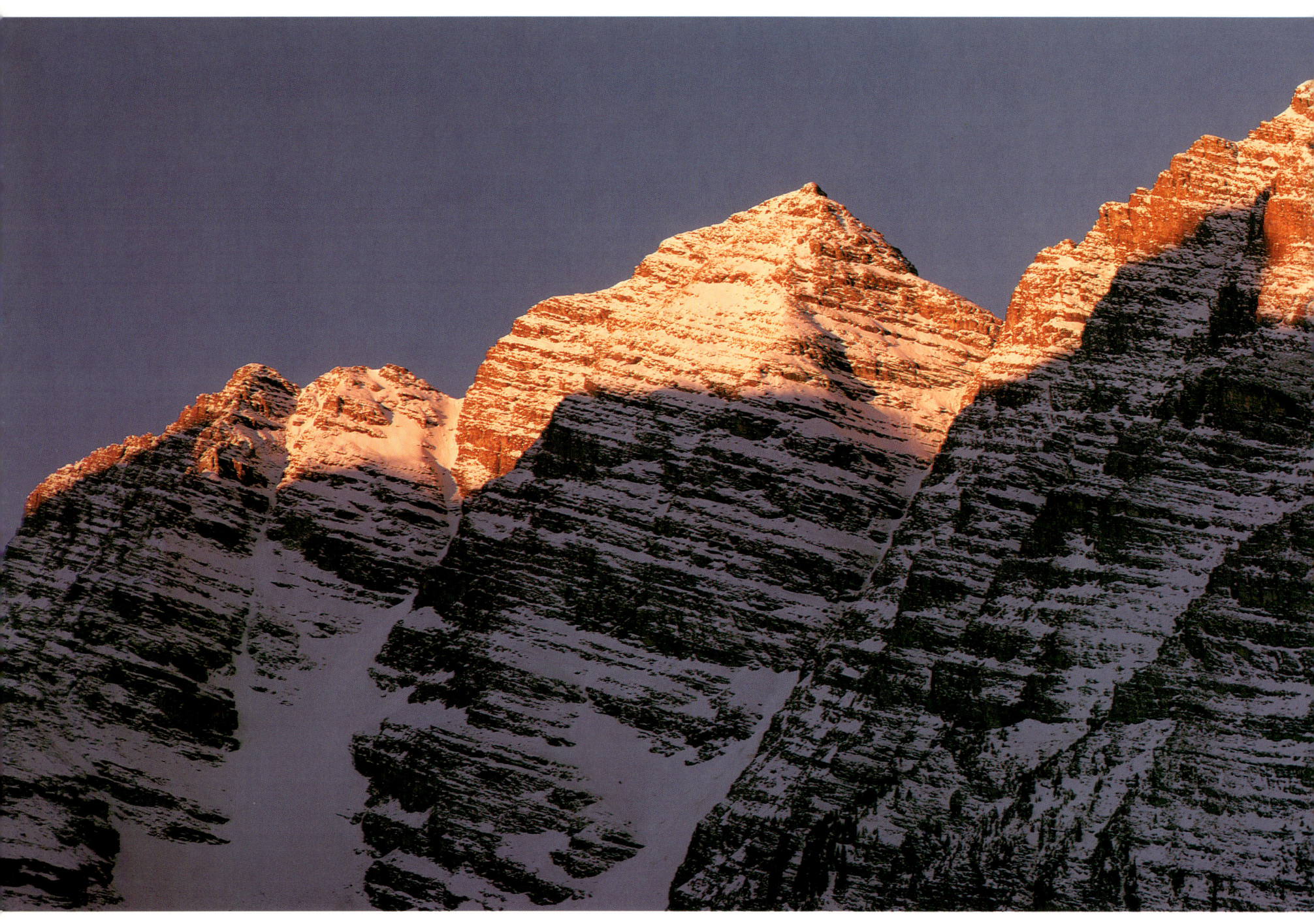

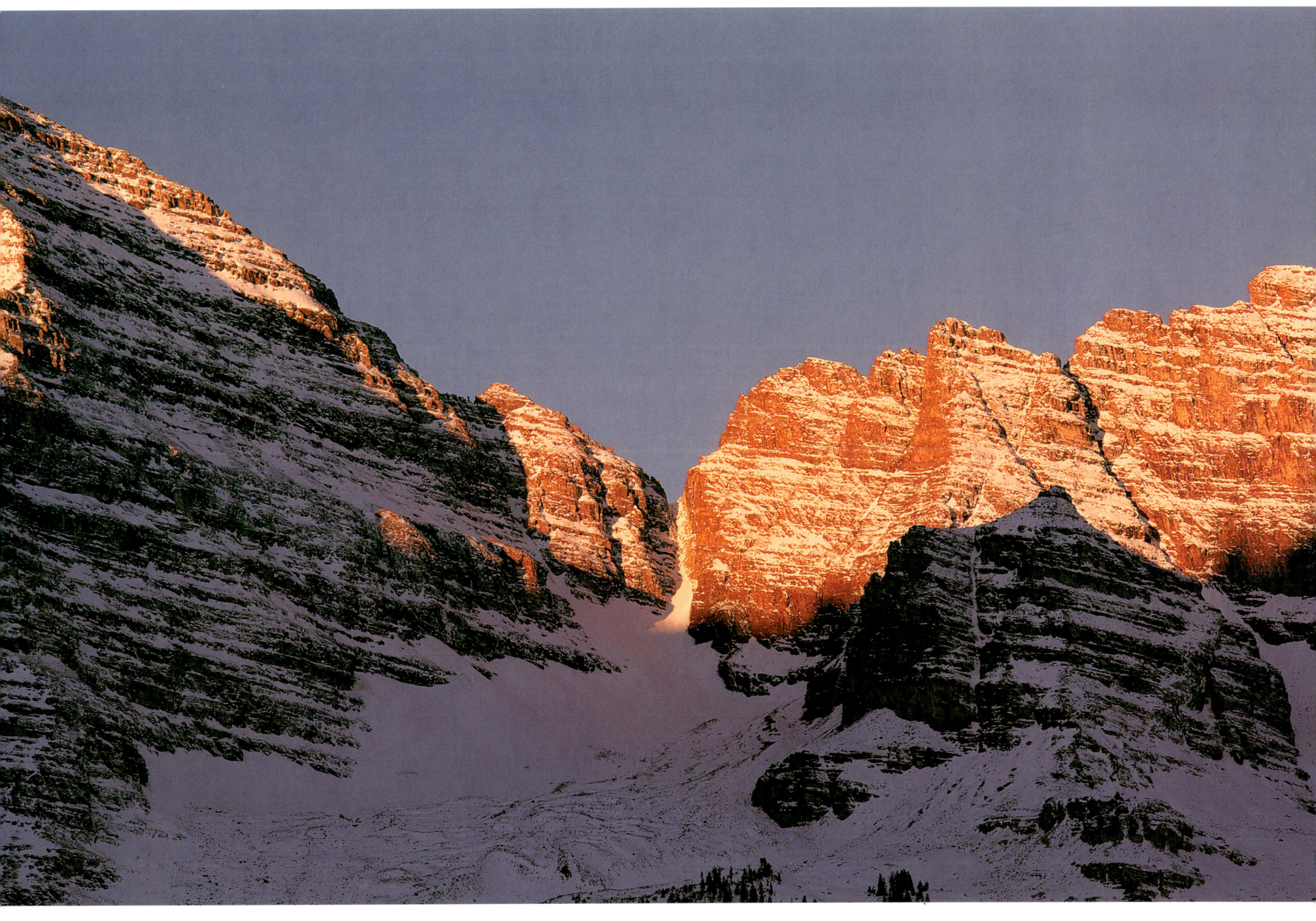

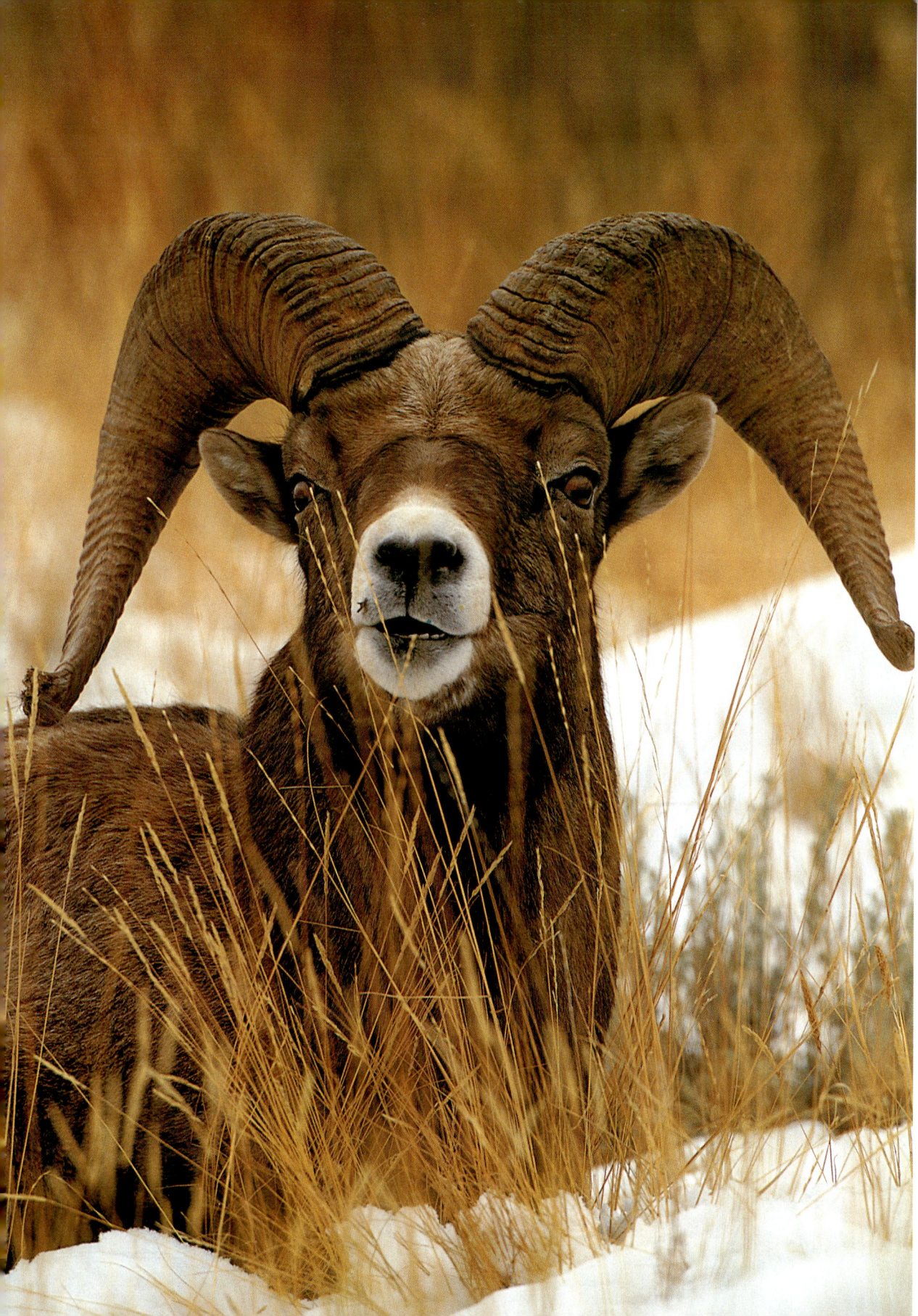

Overleaf: Maroon Bells–Snowmass Wilderness

Left: Rocky Mountain bighorn sheep (*Ovis canadensis*), Mount Evans

Right: Hoary marmot (*Marmota caligata*), Mount Evans

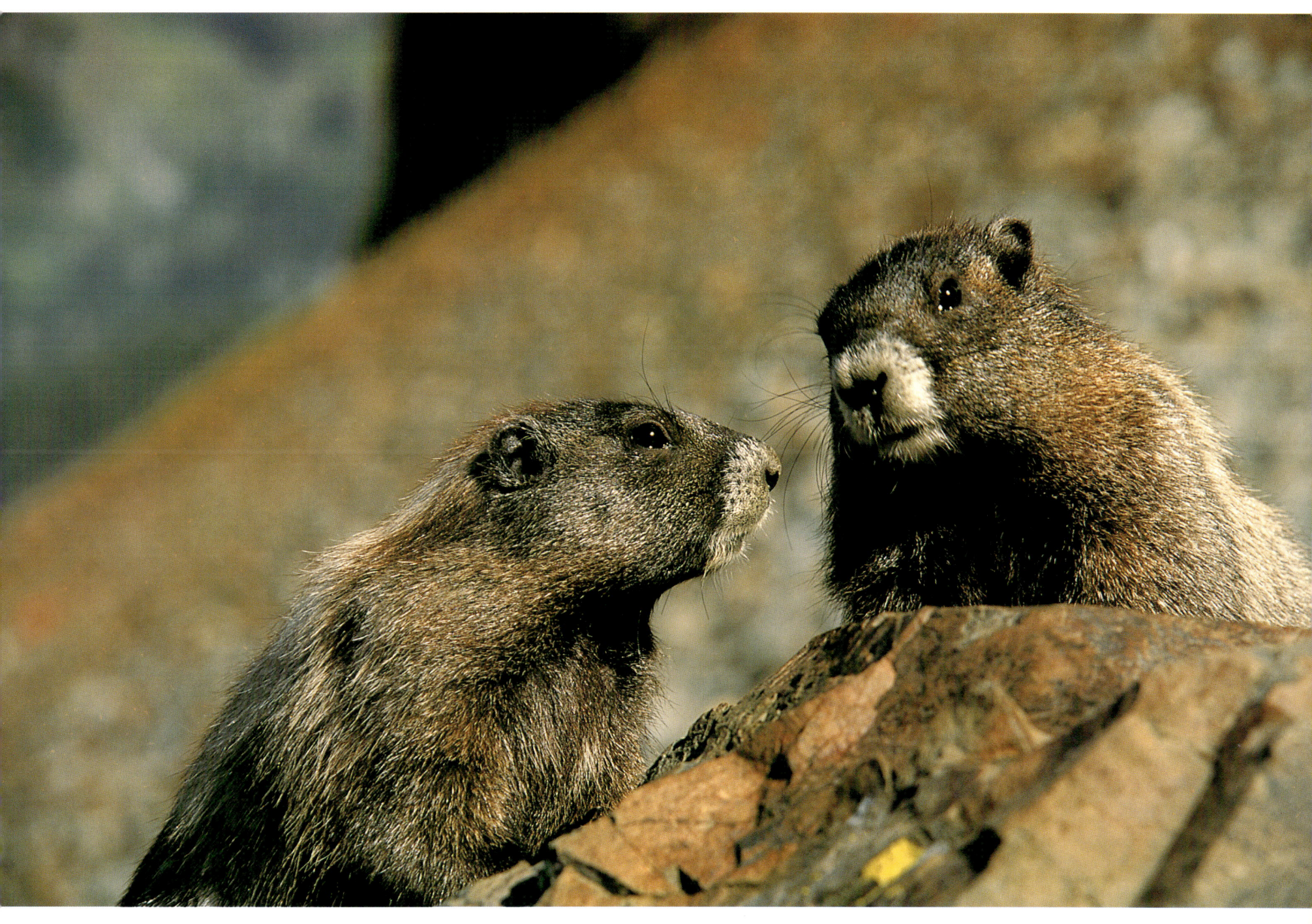

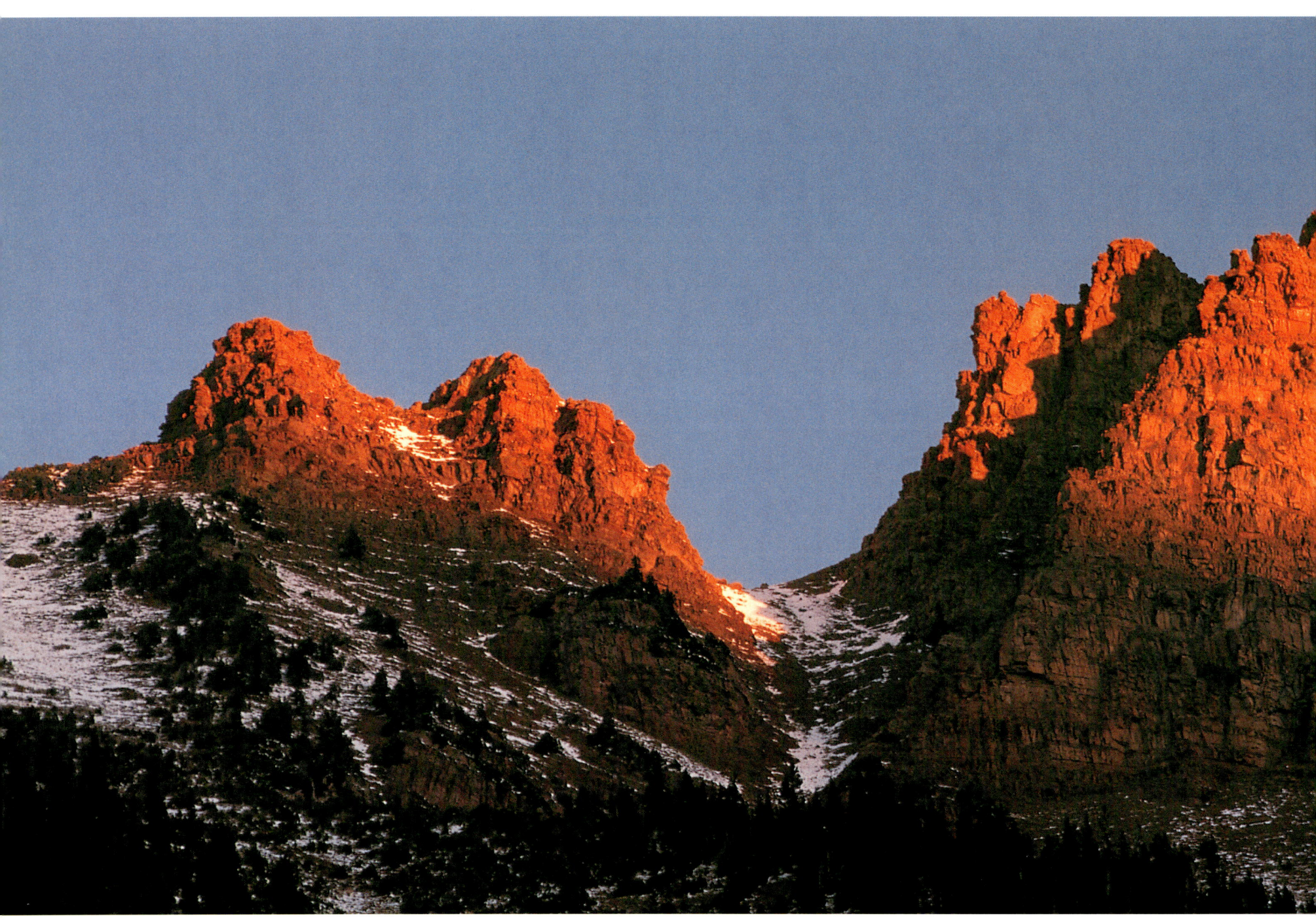

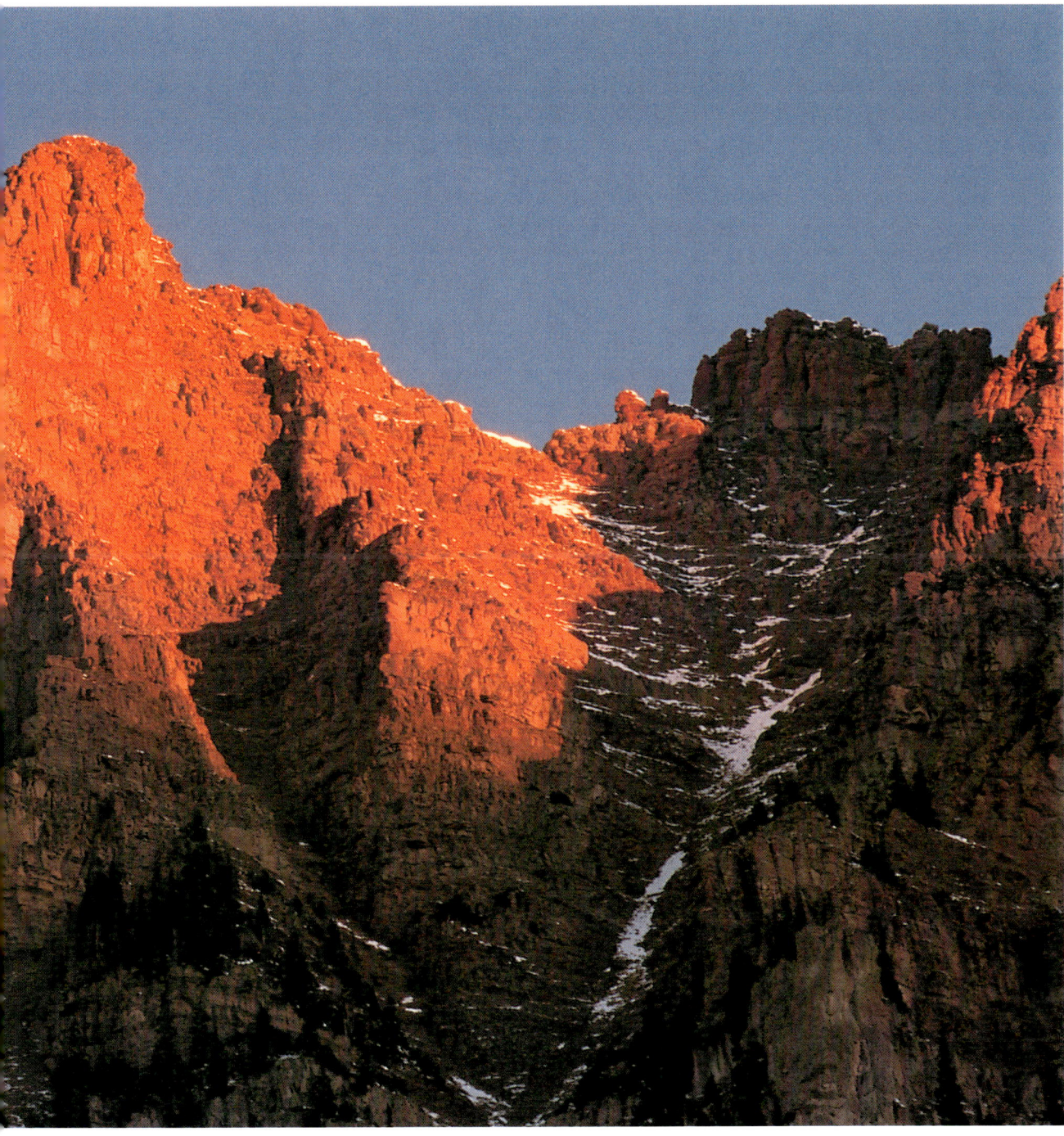

Sievers Mountain, Maroon Bells–Snowmass Wilderness

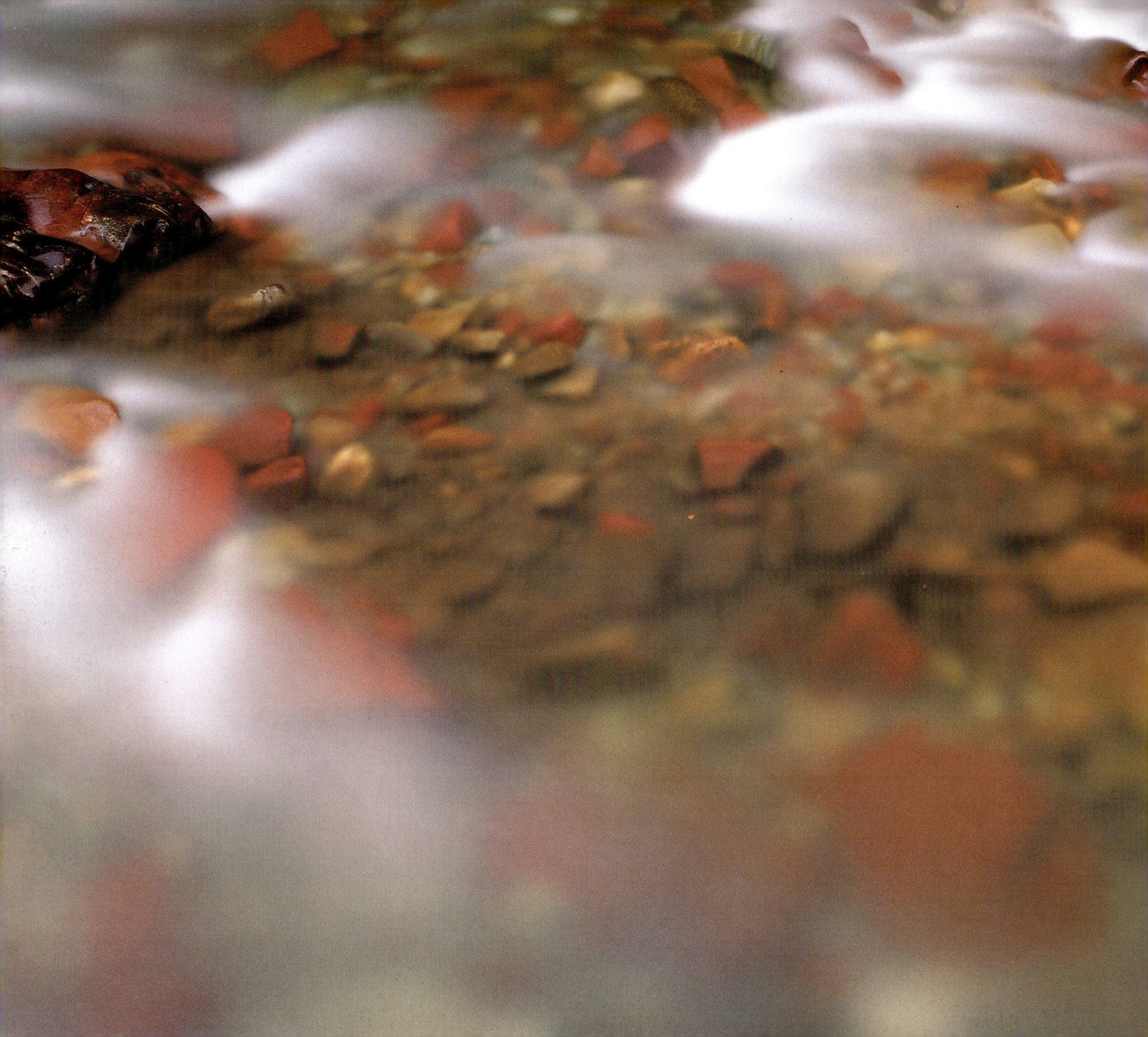

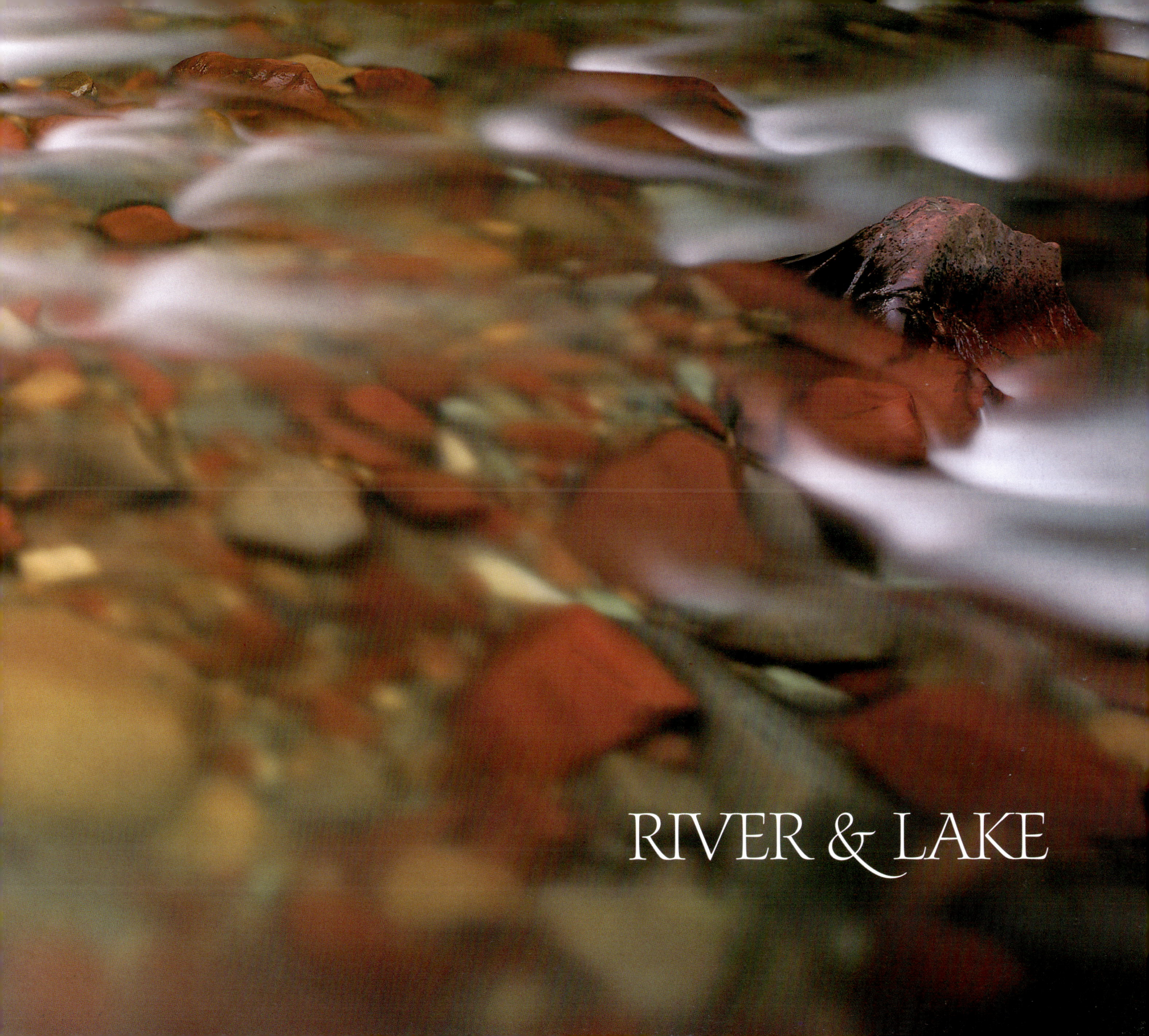

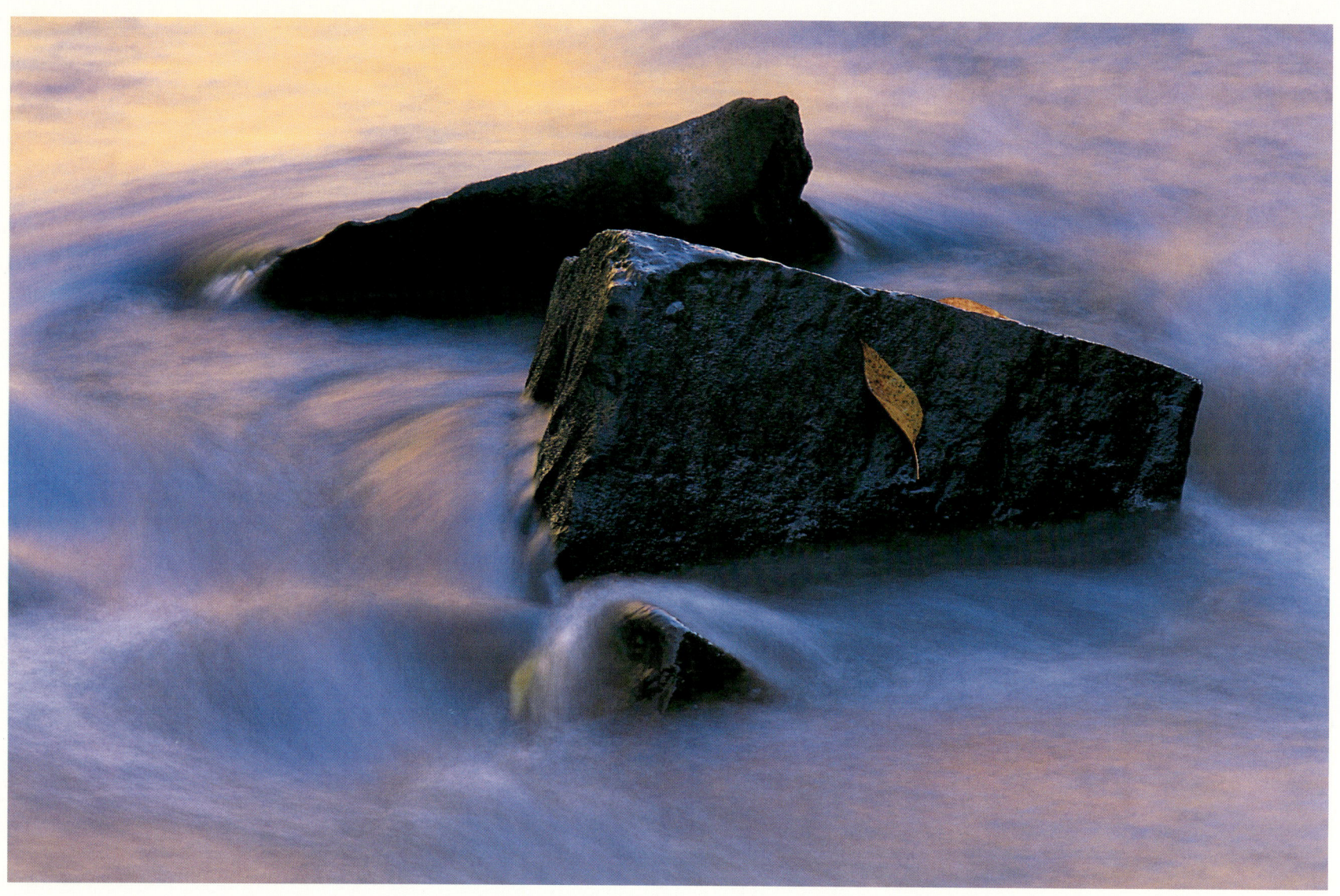

My mother's face aimed at the sun and she said, "thank you, thank you, thank you," to no one I could see. She loves sunshine. We had hiked down an alpine stream together, setting camp in the bottom of a steep valley for a couple of summer nights.

Overleaf: Maroon Creek, MaroonBells-Snowmass Wilderness

Left: Green River

I was down by the water, prying through chest-high blades of grass. In the stream, trout haunted spaces behind rocks where the water was deep. The stream was clear to the bottom, curled and coiled with shadows from the surface, and from the passing of trout. I walked back and assembled my fishing rod, pulling the line through and tying off a fly as I returned to the water.

This stream, called Pool Creek, flows from the mountains, down through a place called Roubideau Canyon. There it adds to the steep, gurgling waters of creeks named Bull, Beach, Long, and Terrible. This water breaks through the alpine forests, gaining volume as it pours along piñon/juniper woodlands and farther to the dry, swept, sage desert, meeting the Gunnison River. The Gunnison is a river of size. I once guided boat trips down this stretch of the Gunnison, through the bloodstain sandstone of Dominguez Canyon, spending countless nights below the cliffs of dry side canyons. The Gunnison flows north, joining the Colorado River as it swings toward Utah. The entire state is a web of communication, water gathering to tell stories of summits and canyons, of distant lands.

My mother found her place on the ground, lying back to admire the warm sun. Grass and the sharp purple flowers of lupine leaned away to mark the outline of her body. I was playing the hunter. I studied the stretch of water, just at a turn where logs had been pushed atop one another leaving sheltered holes and eddies. I saw the trout. I counted four of them. They were motionless against the current. I cast into the calm behind a collection of sticks and alder leaves. The fly was watched by the fish. It changed the activity of several hovering fish, who communicated to each other with turns of their bodies. One swept out and struck.

Here in the high country, at the watershed where rivers are born, the stream was small. The fish didn't have too many places to go. I was able to get it to shore quickly. It was a native cutthroat trout, its back painted with the dark, vermicular squiggles one would expect of beetle-tunneled wood waterlogged in a stream. I kept my hand beneath it so that it was able to float between my fingers. It took its bearings from my hand.

My mother was suddenly at the water, on her knees. "Let me see," she said impatiently.

I moved out of the way so that she could touch the fish. She stroked along its fleshy, white belly. "So beautiful," she said as she examined the trout from every side, continuing to stroke its soft skin. "So, so beautiful." She was talking directly to the fish. When I let it free, too small for eating, she marveled at its skill of motion and graciously complimented it.

I cast again, caught again. In about ten minutes of working this one turn in the creek I caught seven trout. They rose and contemplated the fly before either taking it or darting into obscurity. Probably they had never encountered an artificial fly. It was, after all, a tributary to a tributary to a tributary. A secret fishing hole. I picked the one trout I wanted and if another came for the fly, I would pull my line from the water before the strike. I would try again until the right fish took. None were big enough. This was too high in the watershed, the trout were too young. Winter had been so relentless this year that this August creek was still running with April's cold snow water.

In the evening I went out looking for fish for a meal. Larger fish were needed. We planned to cook trout with salt and dandelion leaves on an alderwood fire. My mother gathered the wood and I walked downstream with my rod.

Downstream, the creek was no longer simple for fishing. It had the design of a train wreck. Everything boxed on itself, mangy with spruce and fir trees, hardly a spot to get a fishing line through. No room for the back cast, no room for the forward cast.

I found gashes in the vegetation through which I could stick one arm and a rod. The fishing was, as before, plentiful. Trout were hungry, as hungry as they were small. They were each returned to the water because of their size.

There were so many fallen trees that I couldn't get a fly into the water. I kept walking, swinging legs over, looking for the place to cast. It only thickened. Finally, I stopped and set the rod against a ragged stump. Wedges of low sunlight struck small waterfalls, lighting humpbacked rocks soft with moss. There were elaborately shaped monkeyflowers and ghostly pale Indian pipes growing along the water. Piles of leaves a hundred years deep grew darker and wetter toward the bottom until they became dirt. Mayflies hung over the creek like stars.

Right: Rocky Mountain National Park

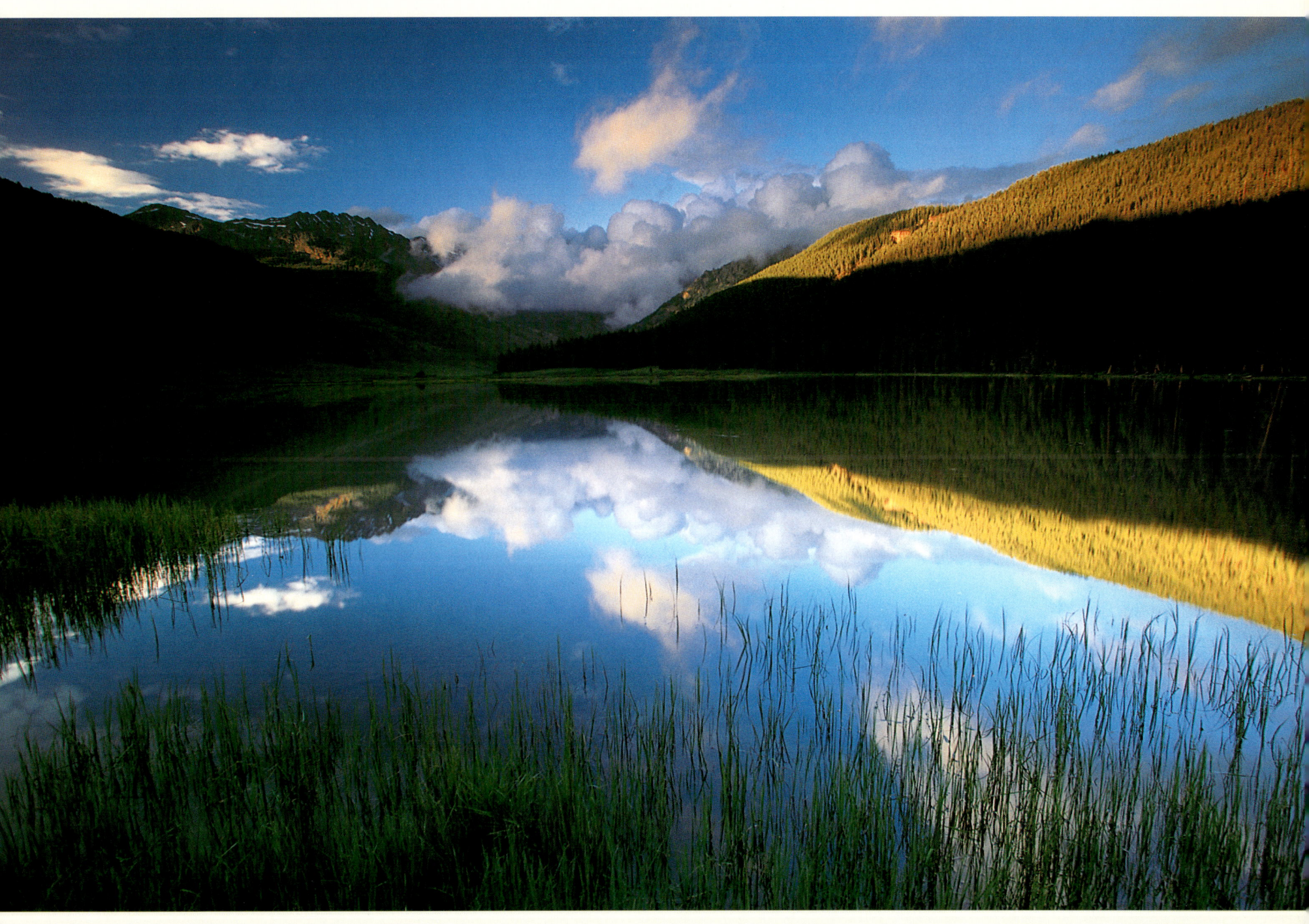

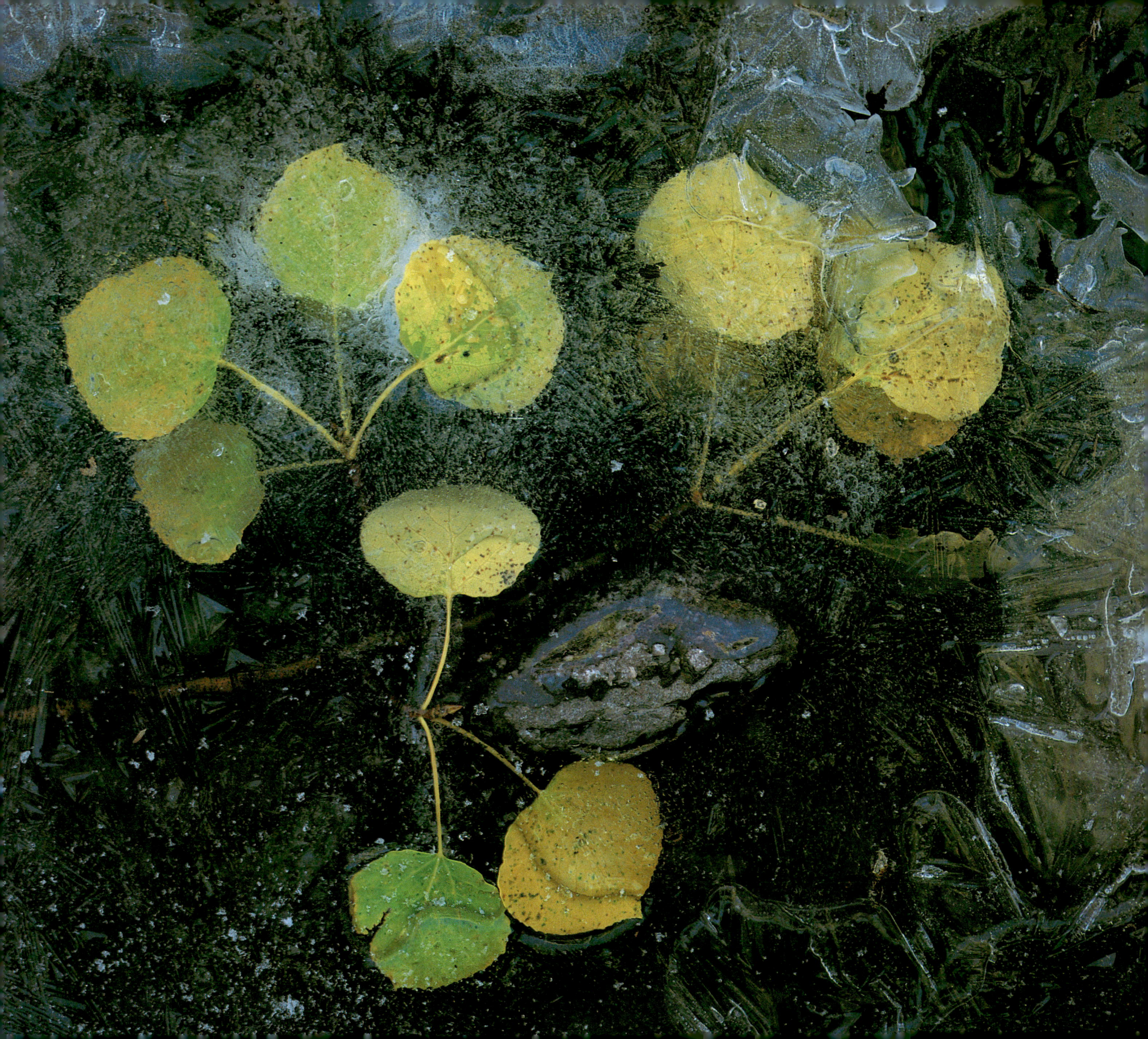

Left: Rocky Mountain National Park

Right: Stream, Great Sand Dunes National Monument

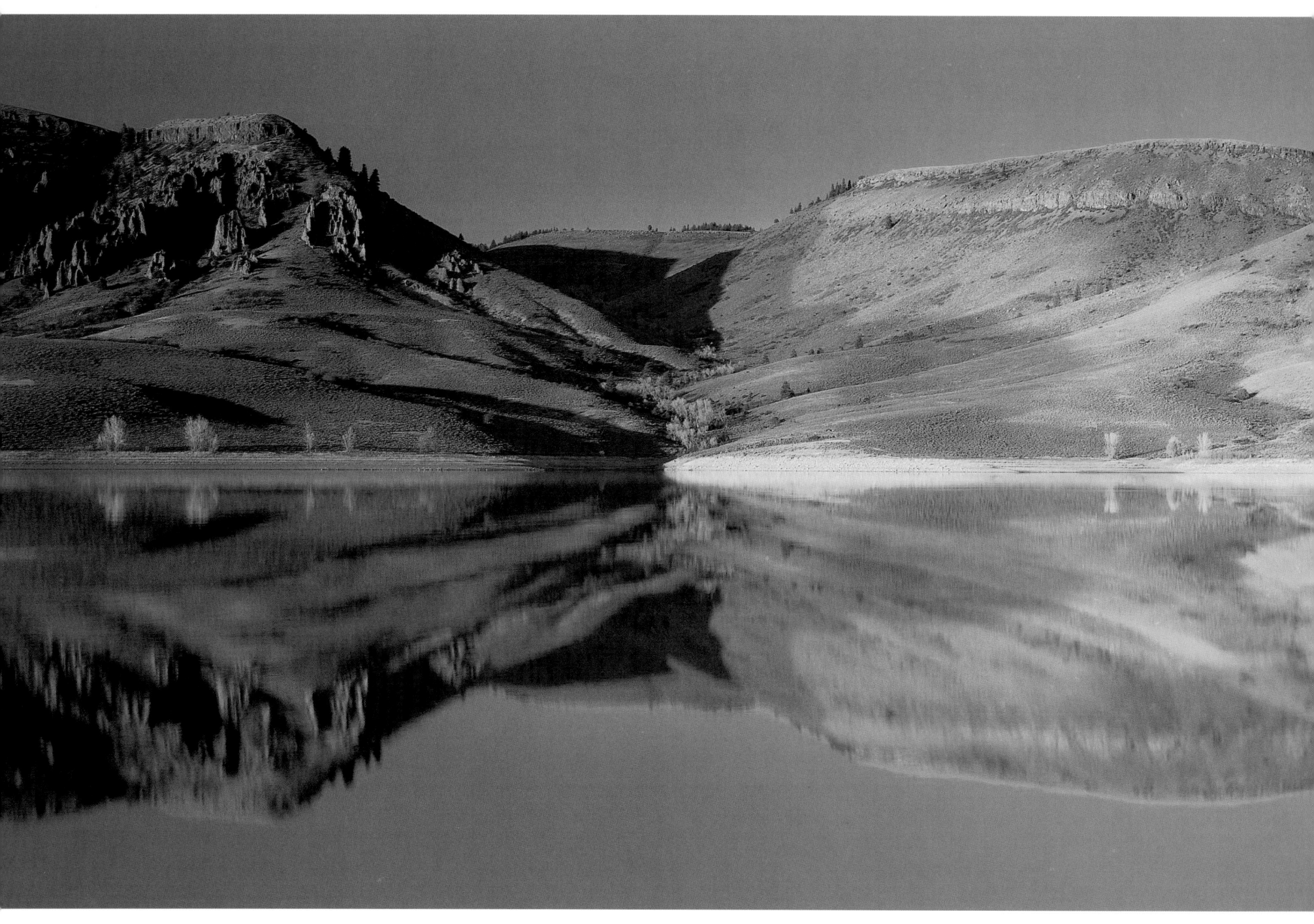

Dillon Pinnacle reflection, Gunnison River

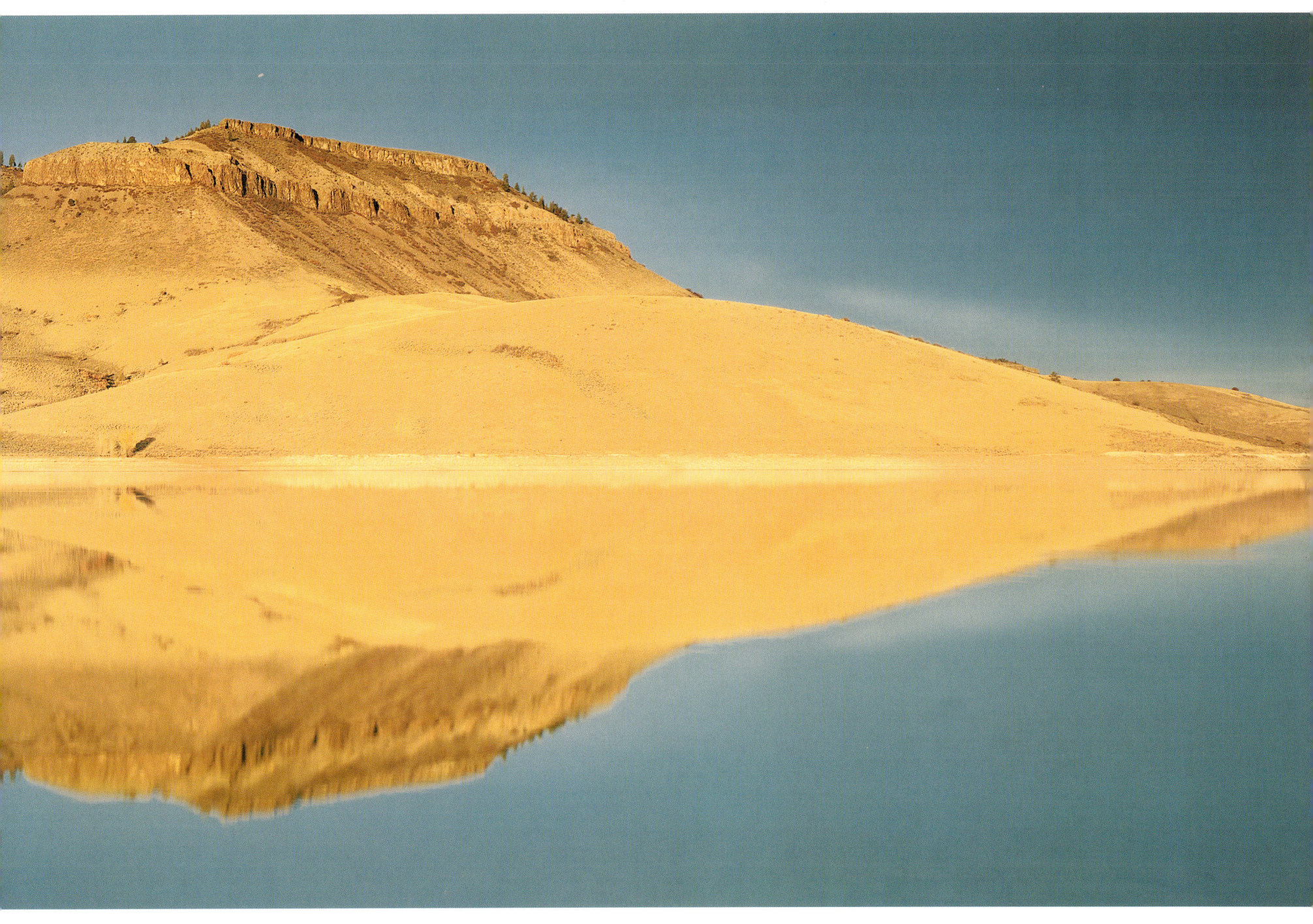

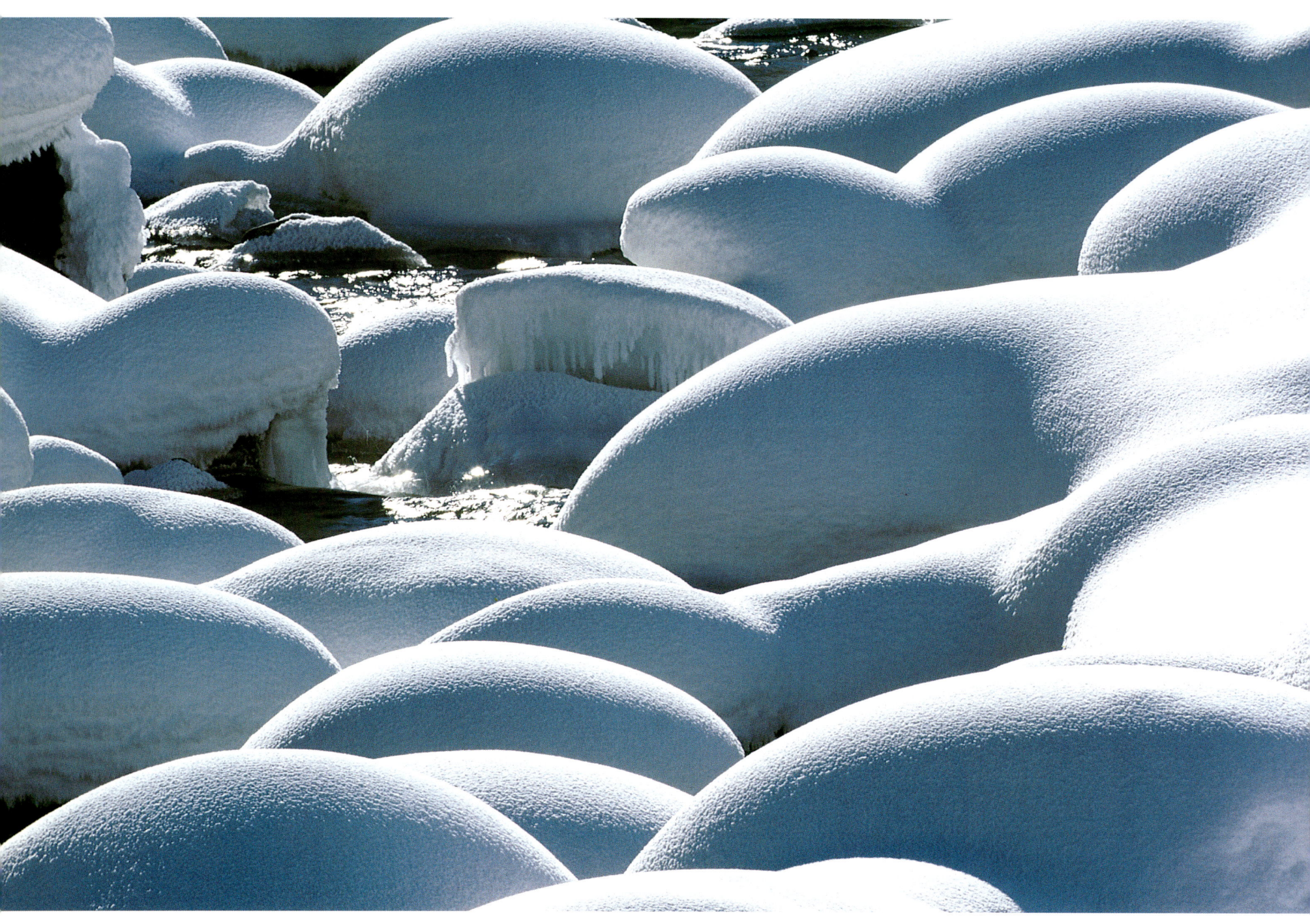

Left: Snow-covered rocks, Taylor River

Below: Mule deer (*Odocoileus hemionus*), South Platte River

Right: Snow-covered rocks, Taylor River

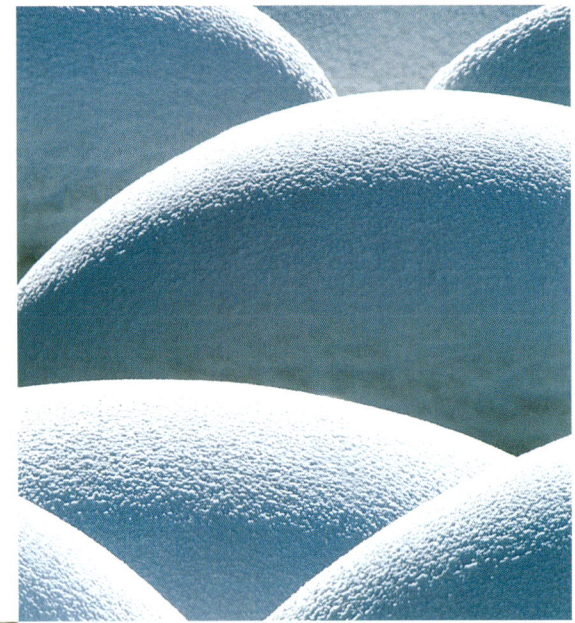

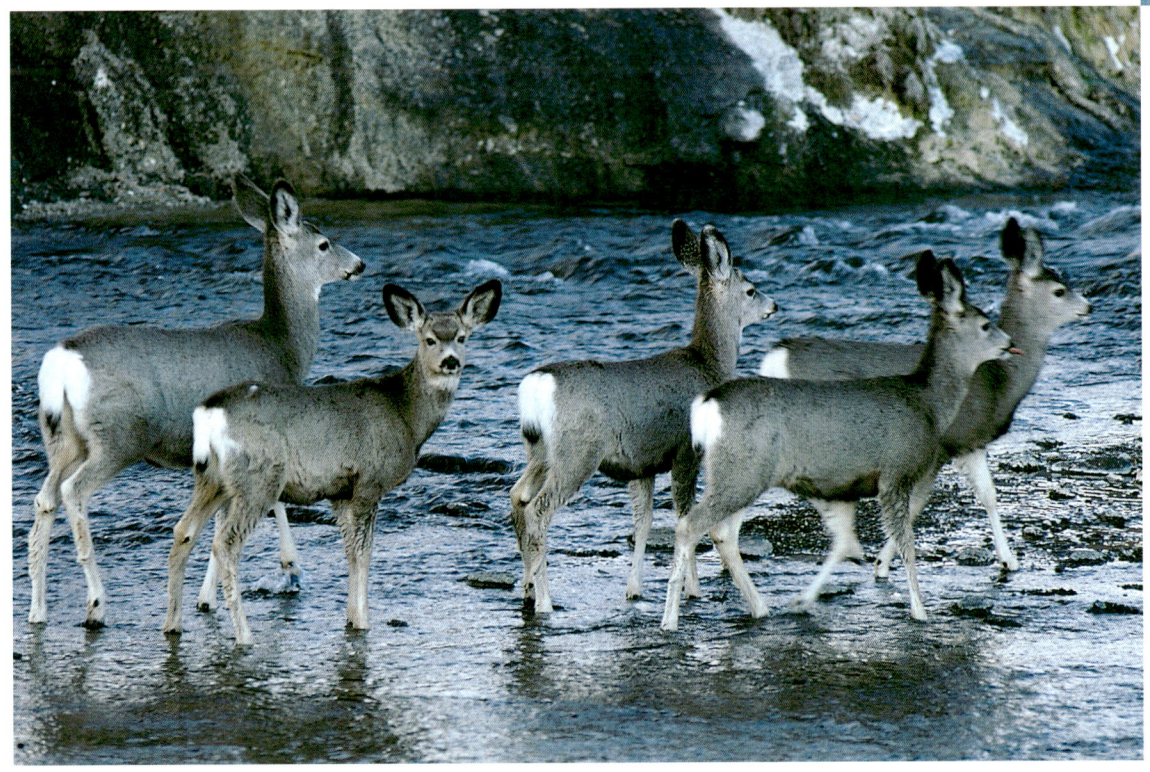

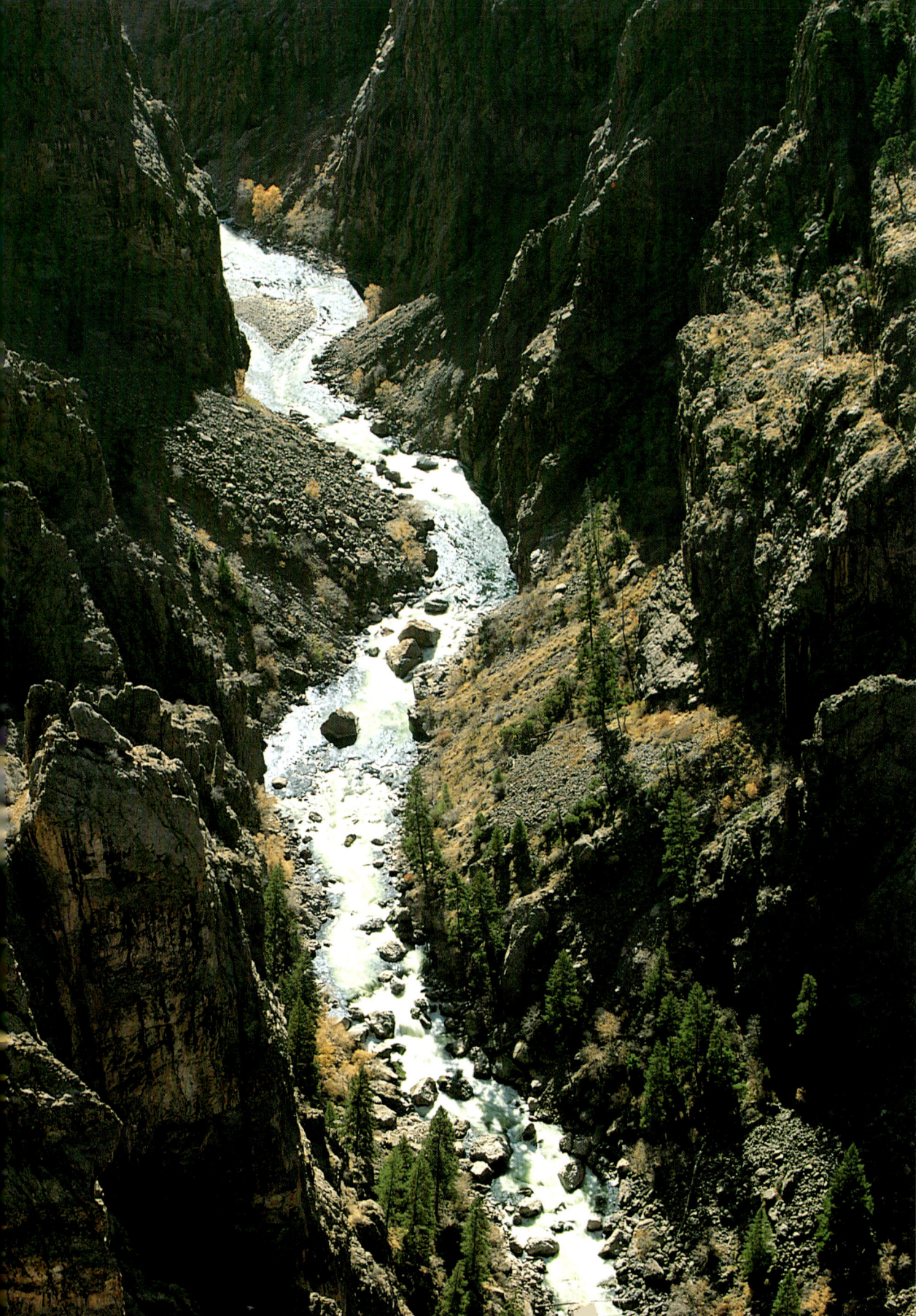

Left: Black Canyon of the Gunnison National Park

Right: Black bear (*Ursus americanus*), Buckskin Creek

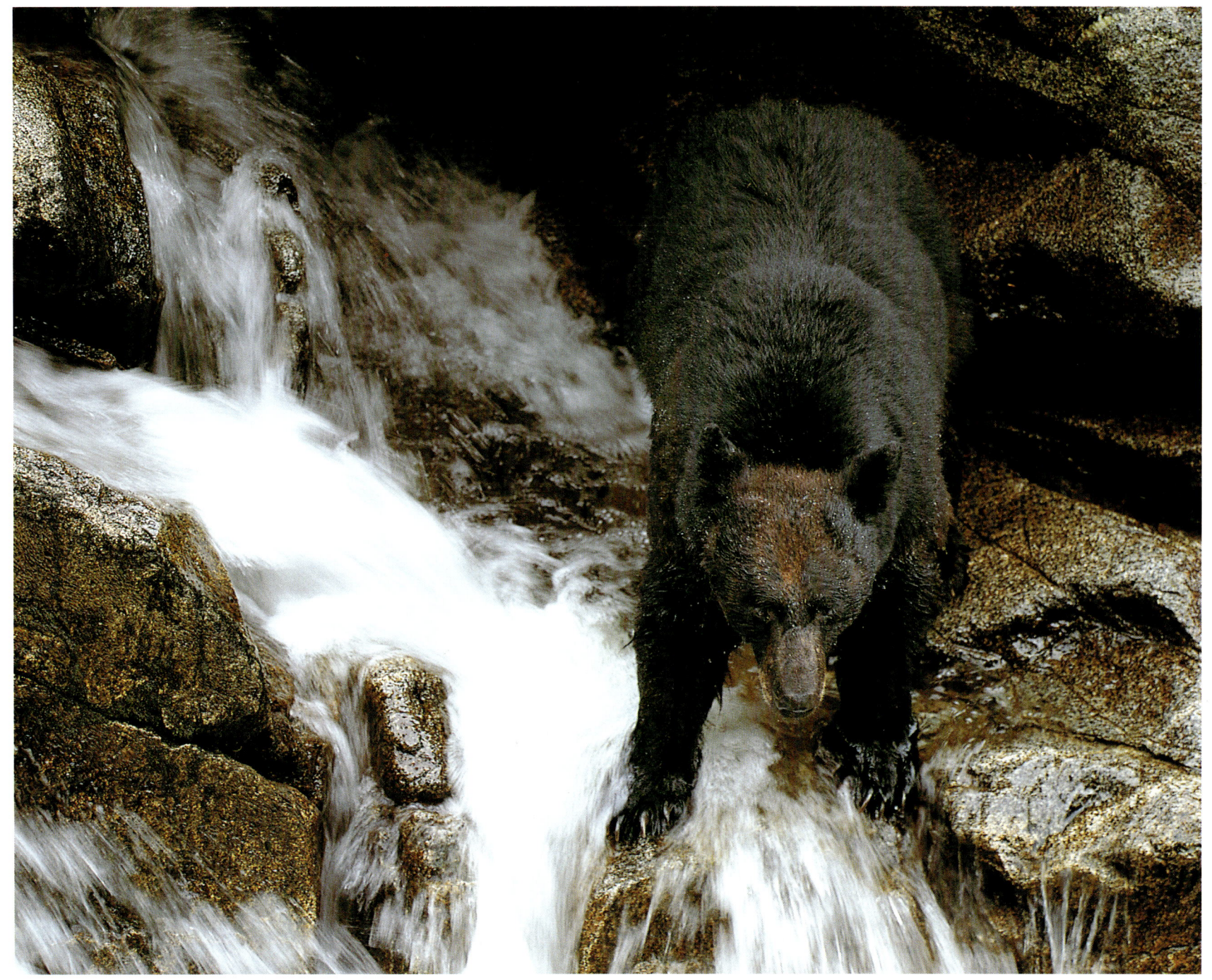

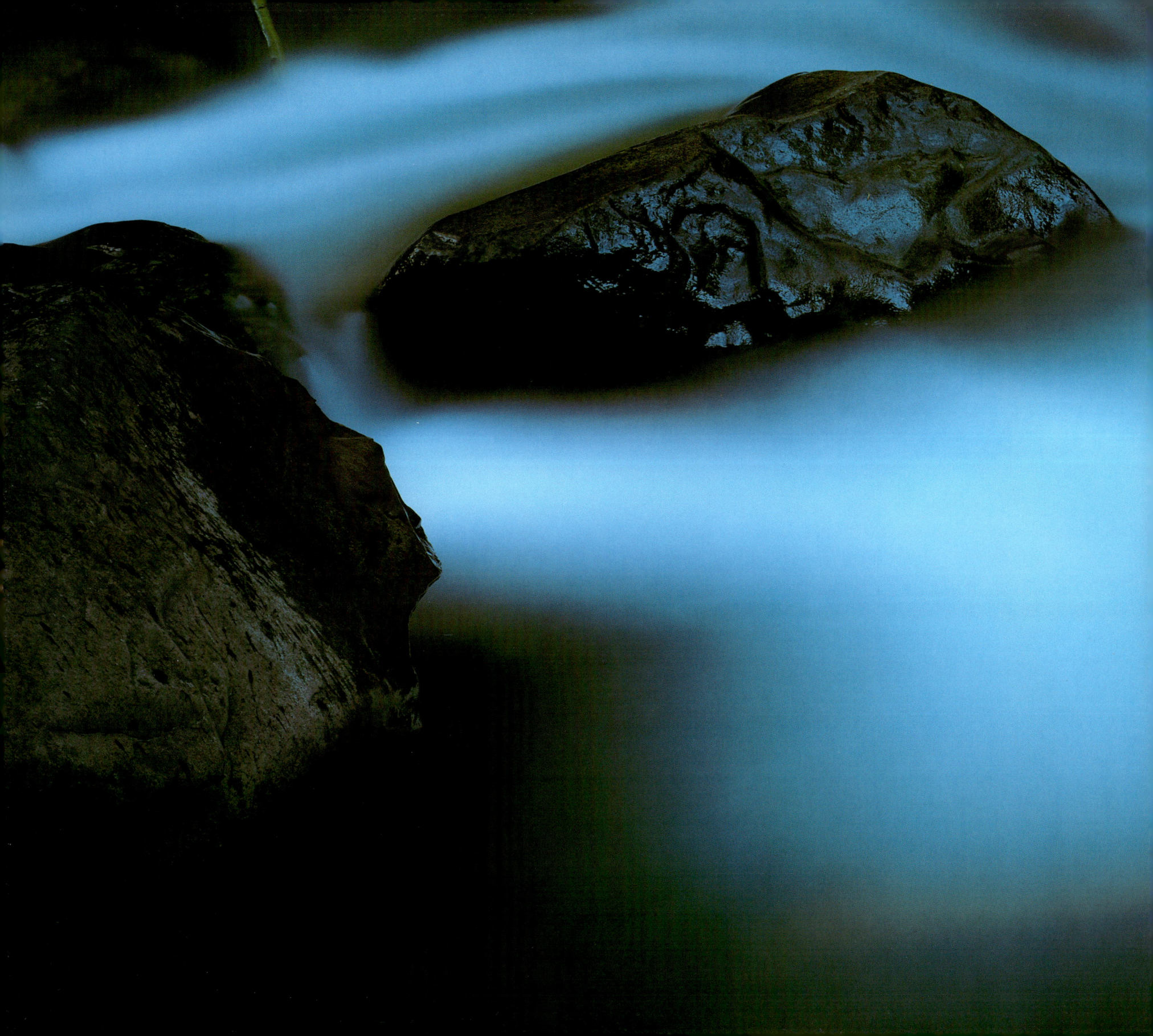

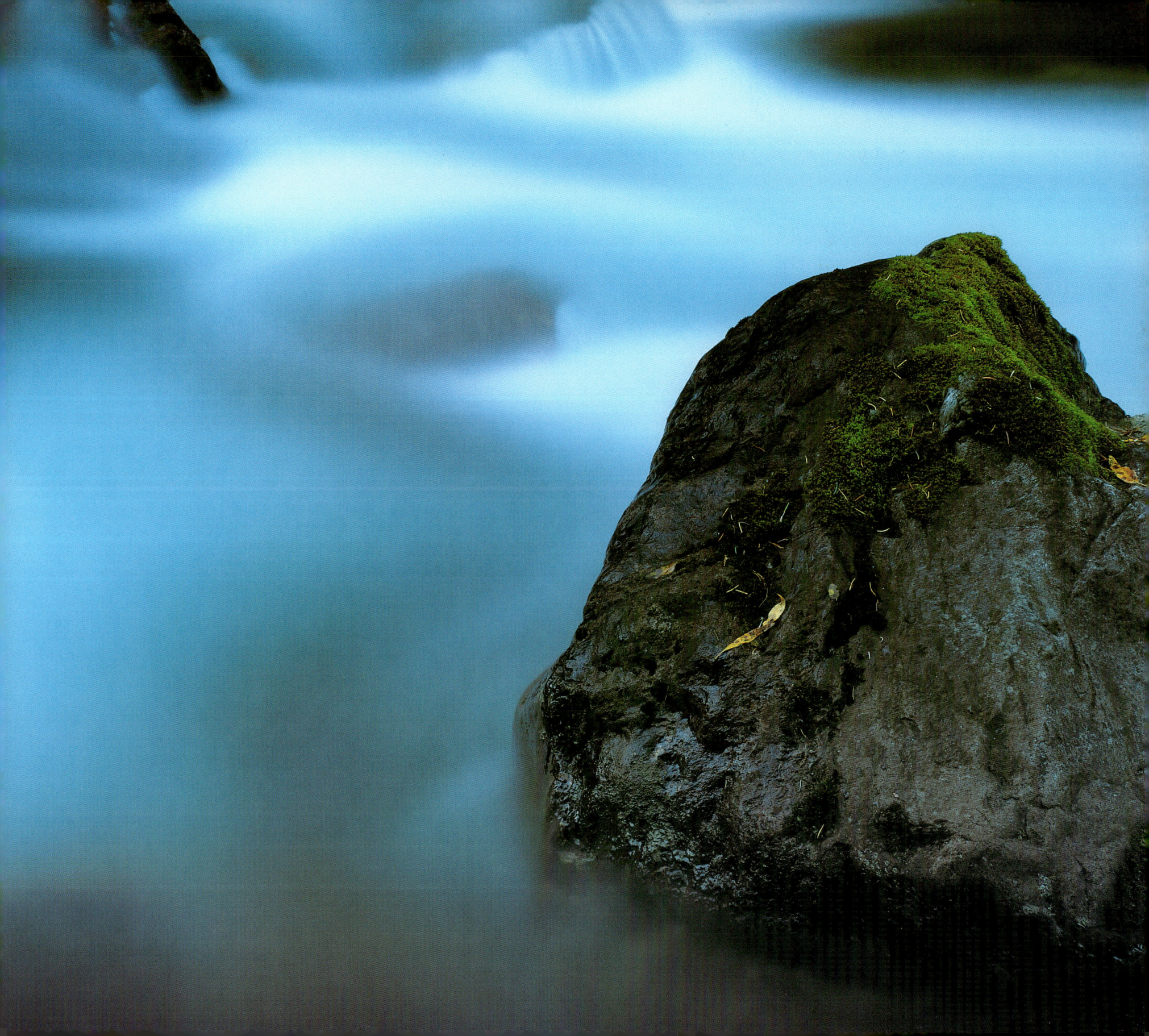

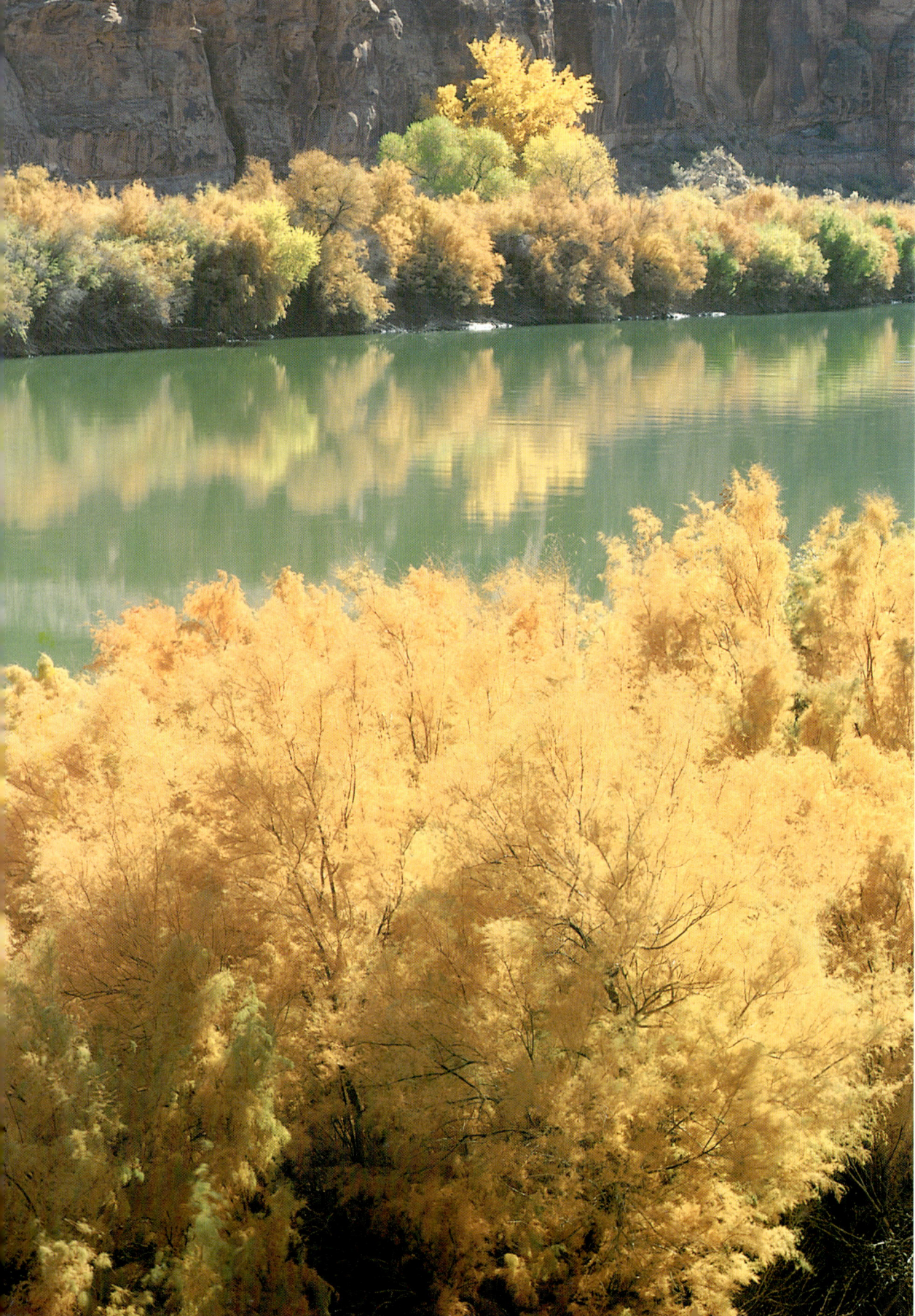

Overleaf: Maroon Creek, Maroon Bells-Snowmass Wilderness

Left: Colorado River, Ruby Canyon

Right: Yampa River Canyon, Dinosaur National Monument

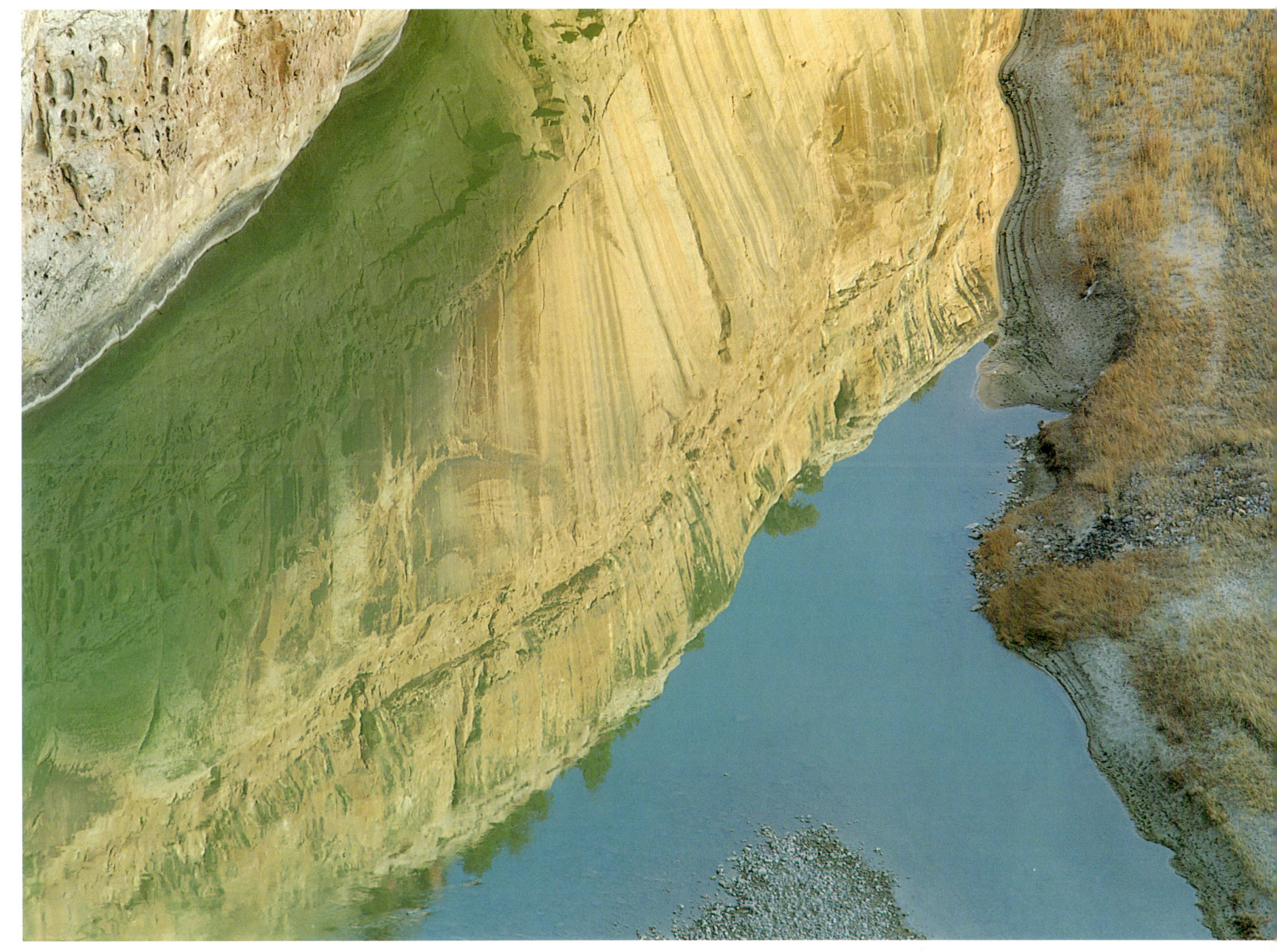

RIVER & LAKE

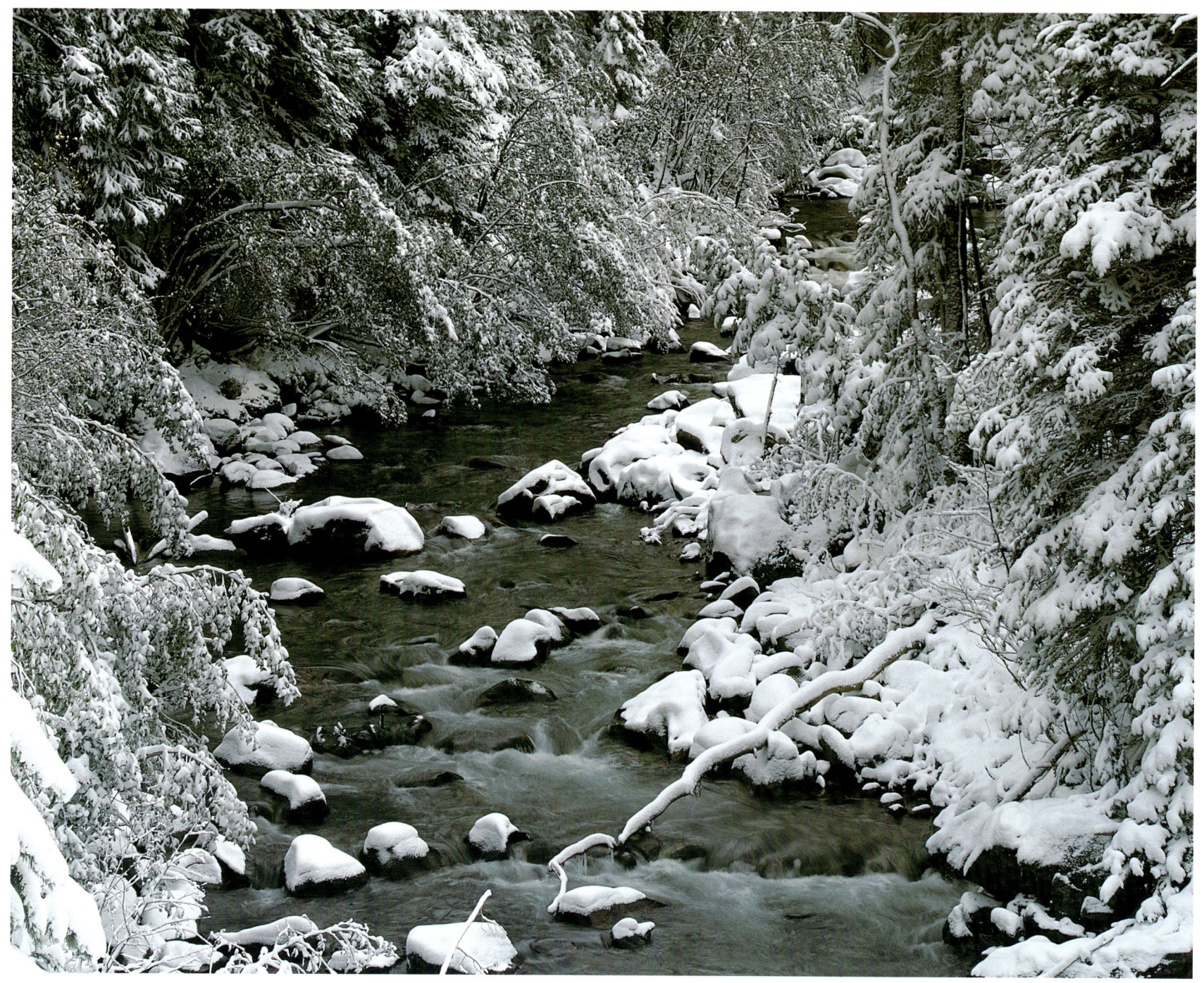

Roaring Fork River, Maroon Bells-Snowmass Wilderness

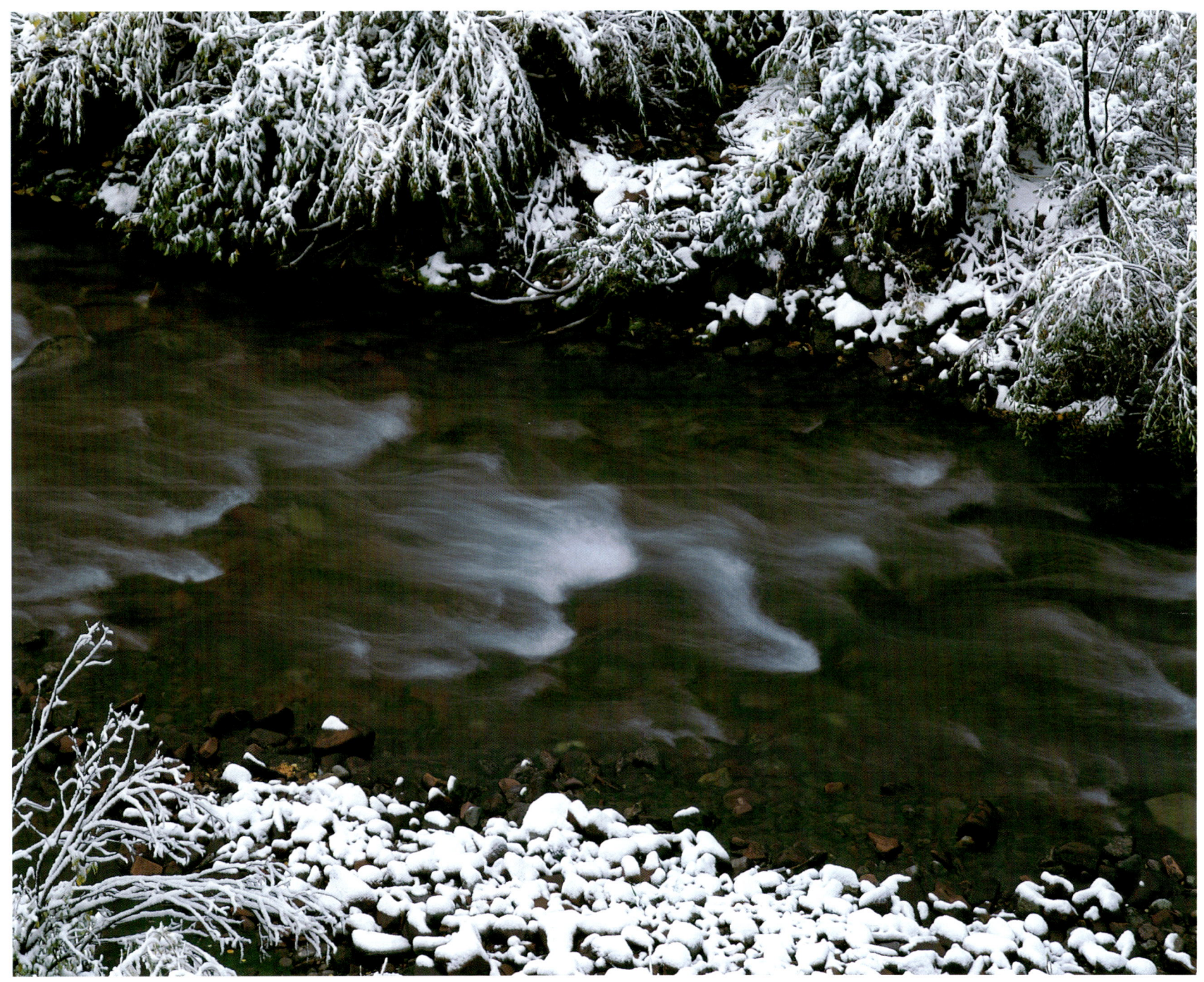
Roaring Fork River, Maroon Bells-Snowmass Wilderness

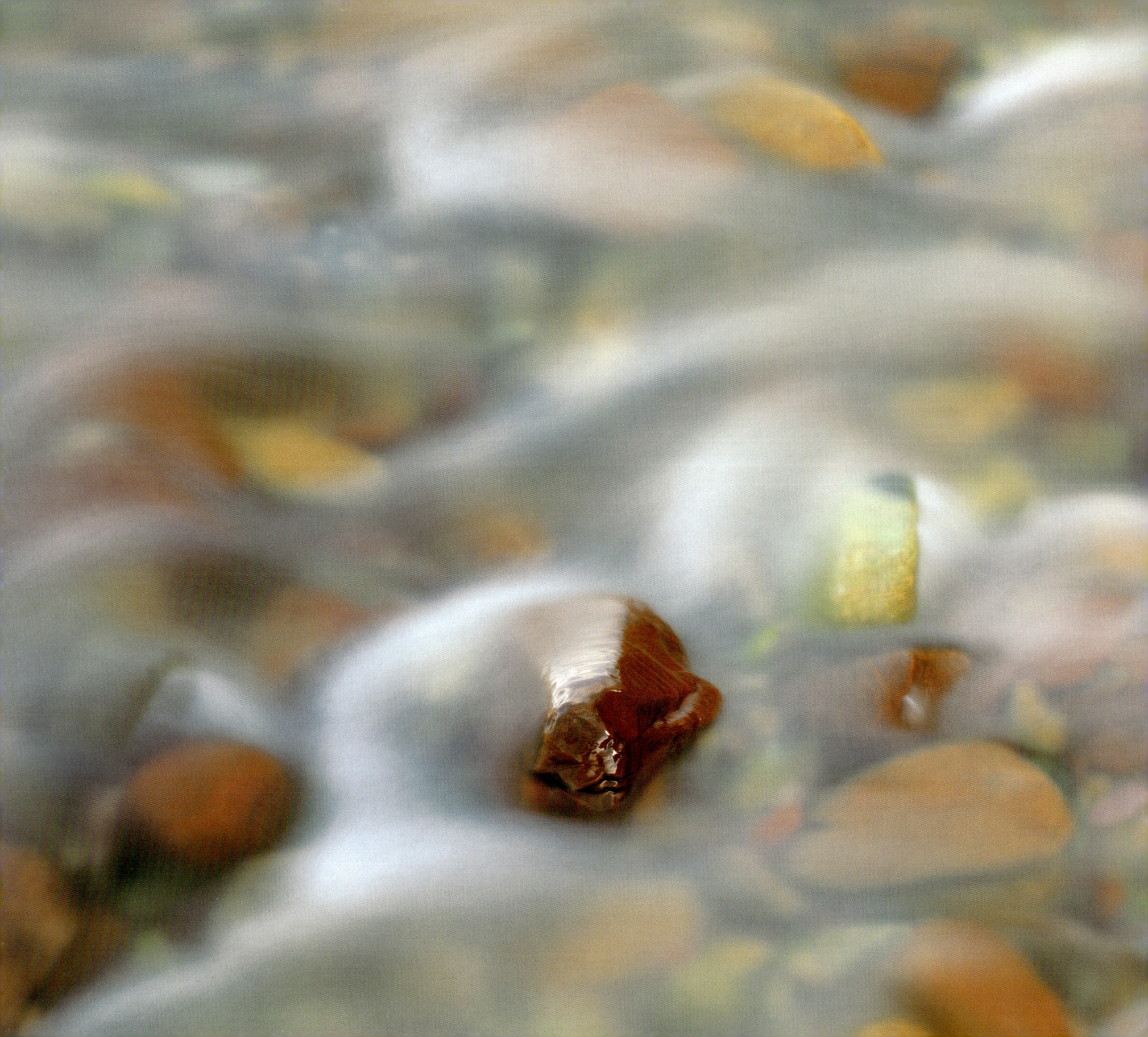

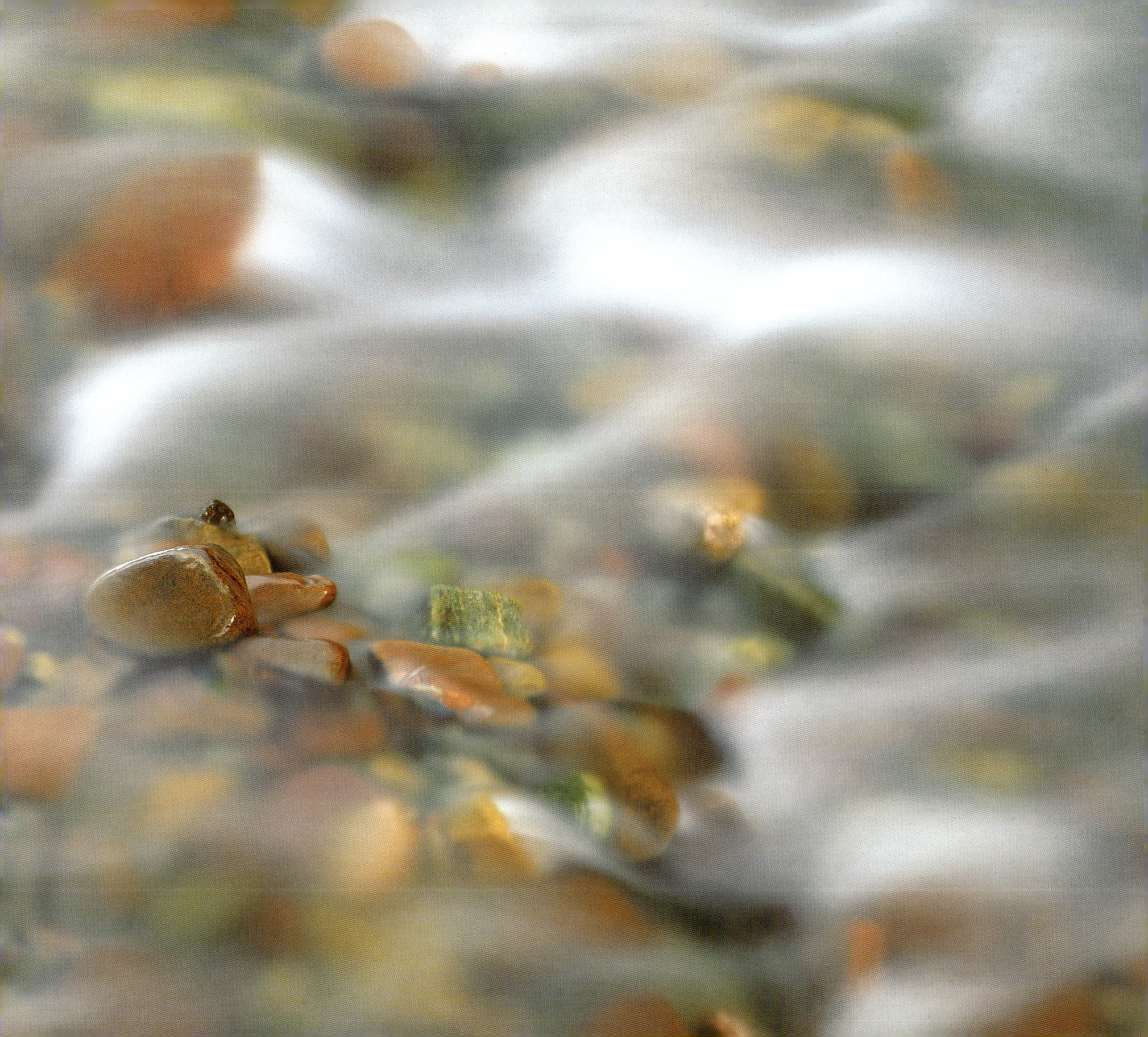

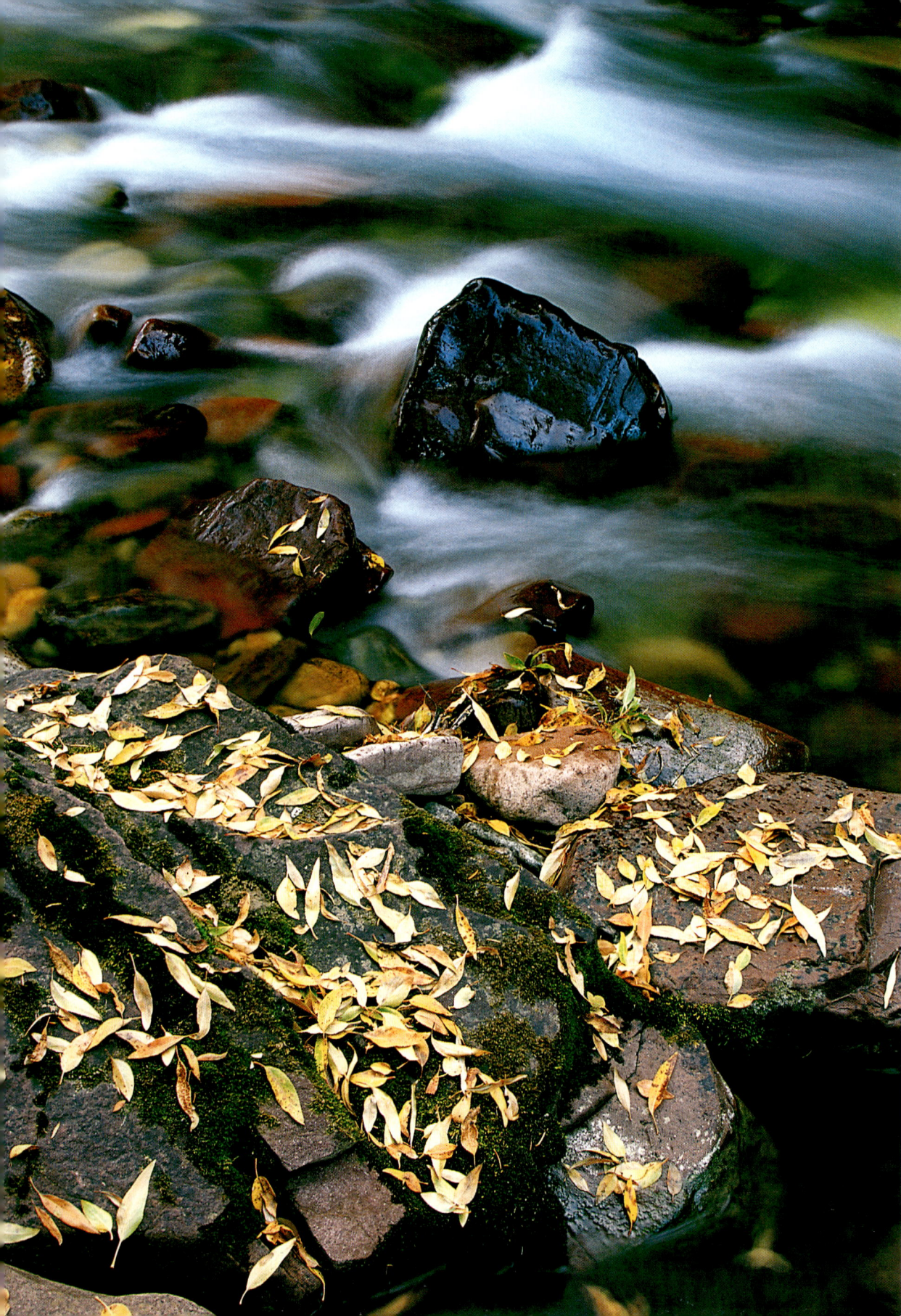

Overleaf: San Miguel River

Left: Roaring Fork River, Maroon Bells-Snowmass Wilderness

Right: San Miguel River

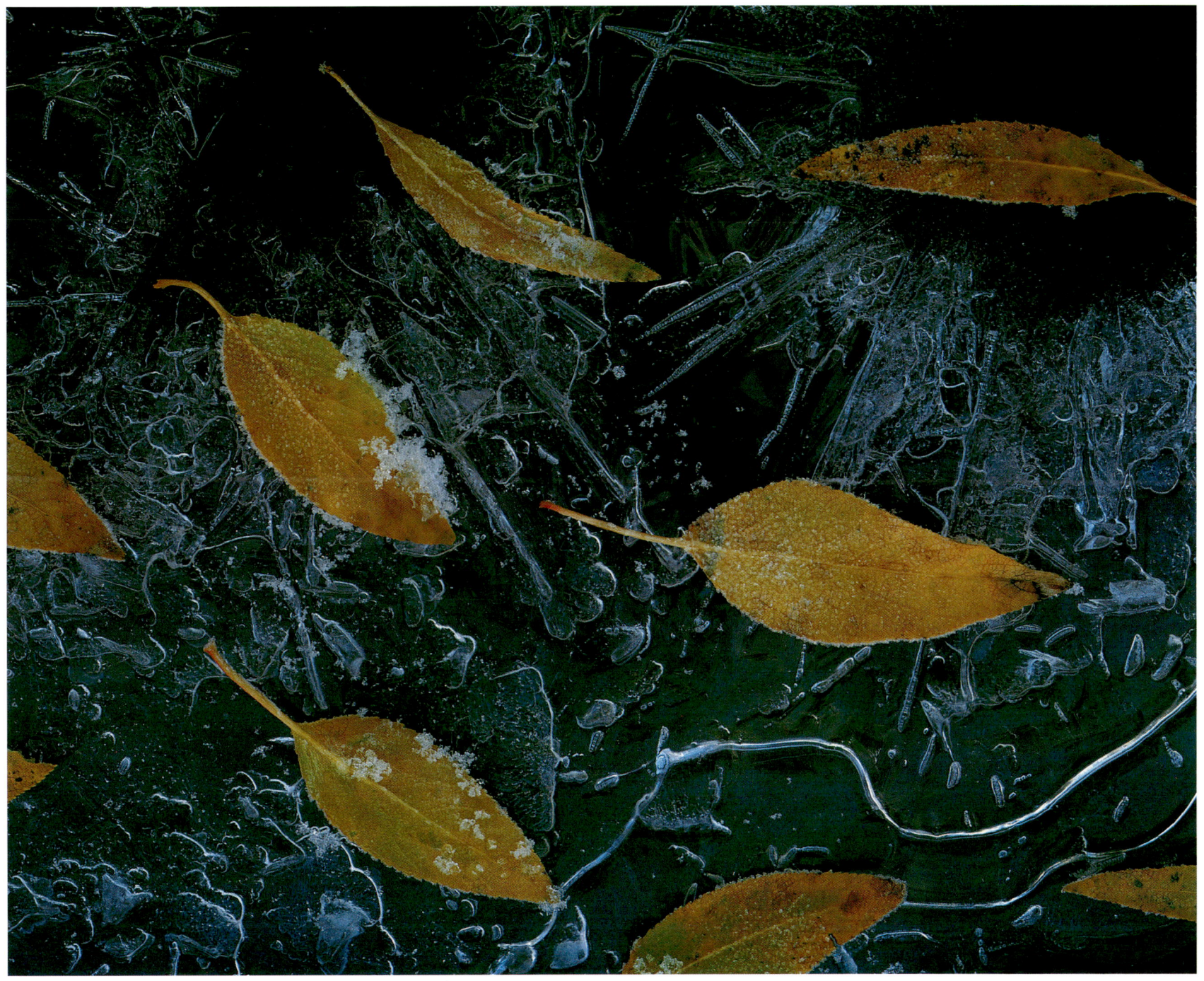

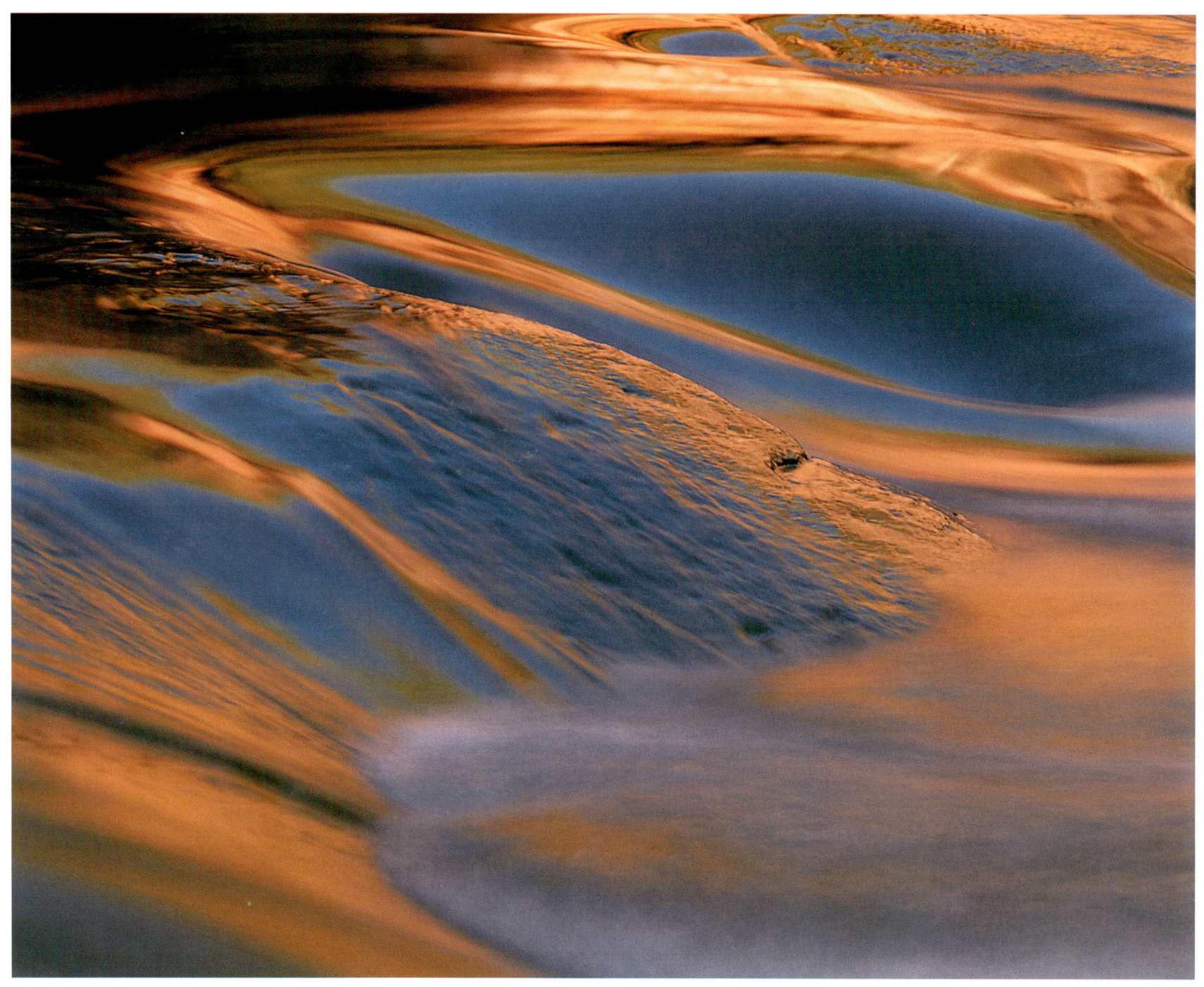

West Salt Creek, Colorado National Monument

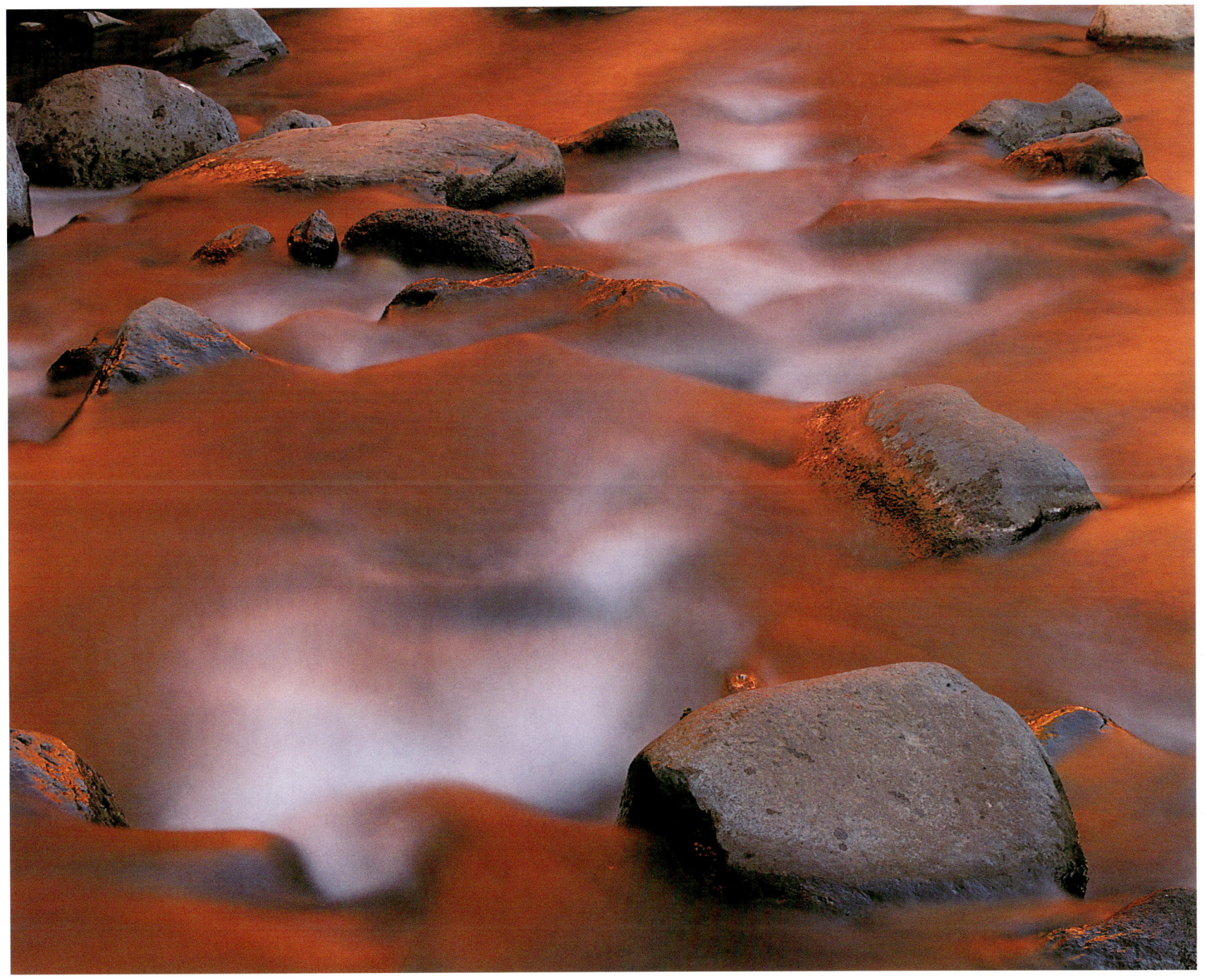

West Salt Creek, Colorado National Monument

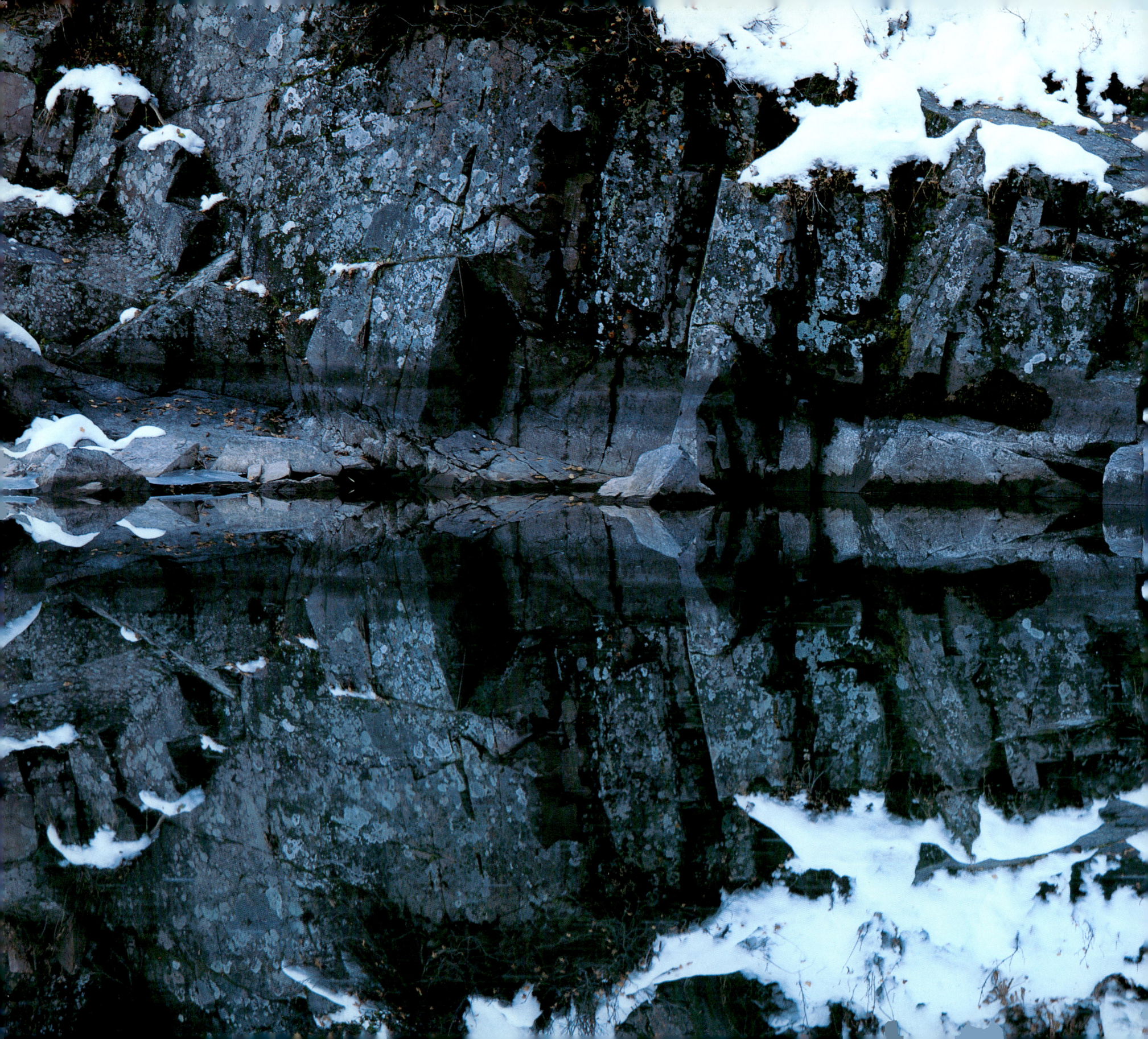

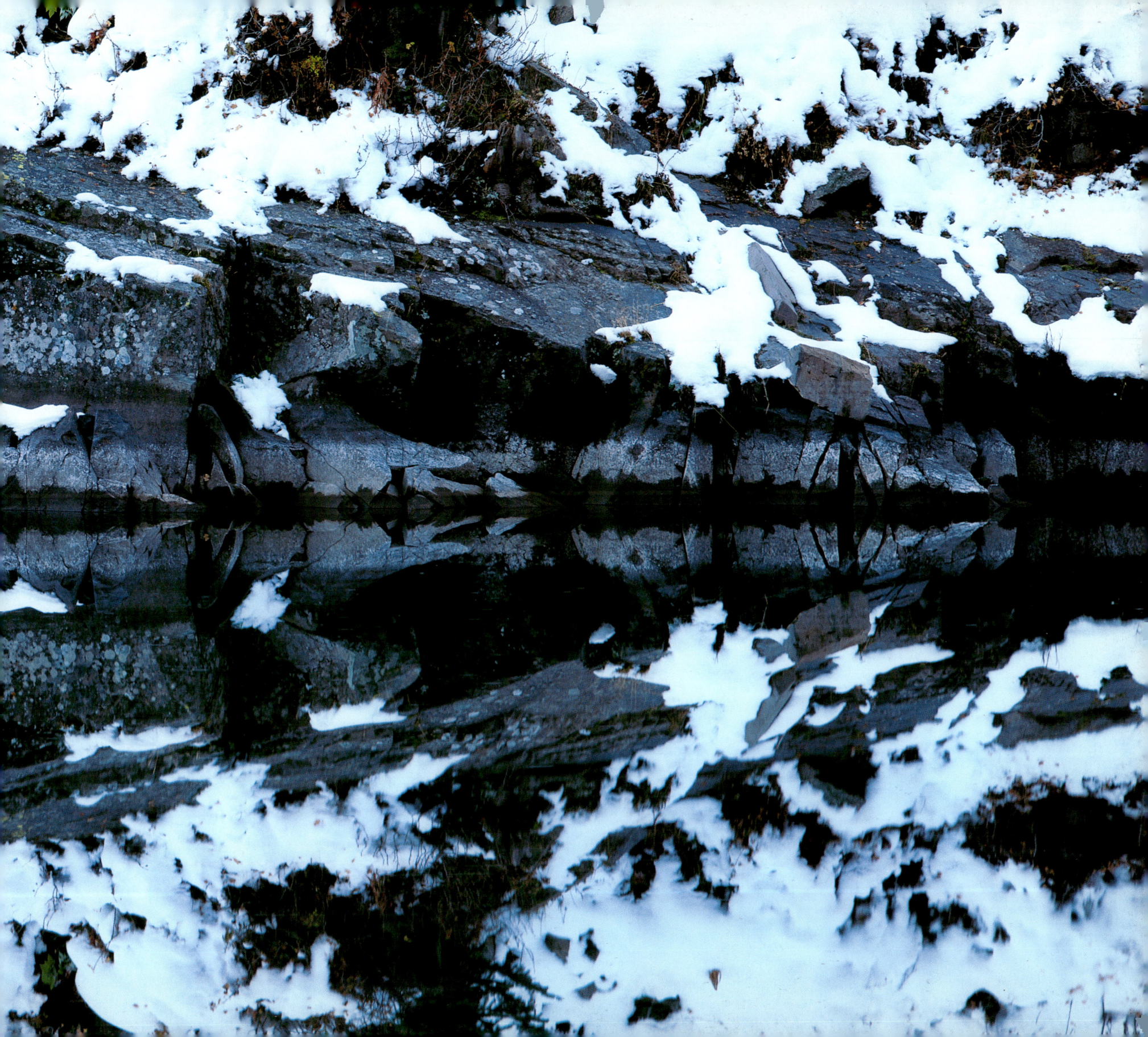

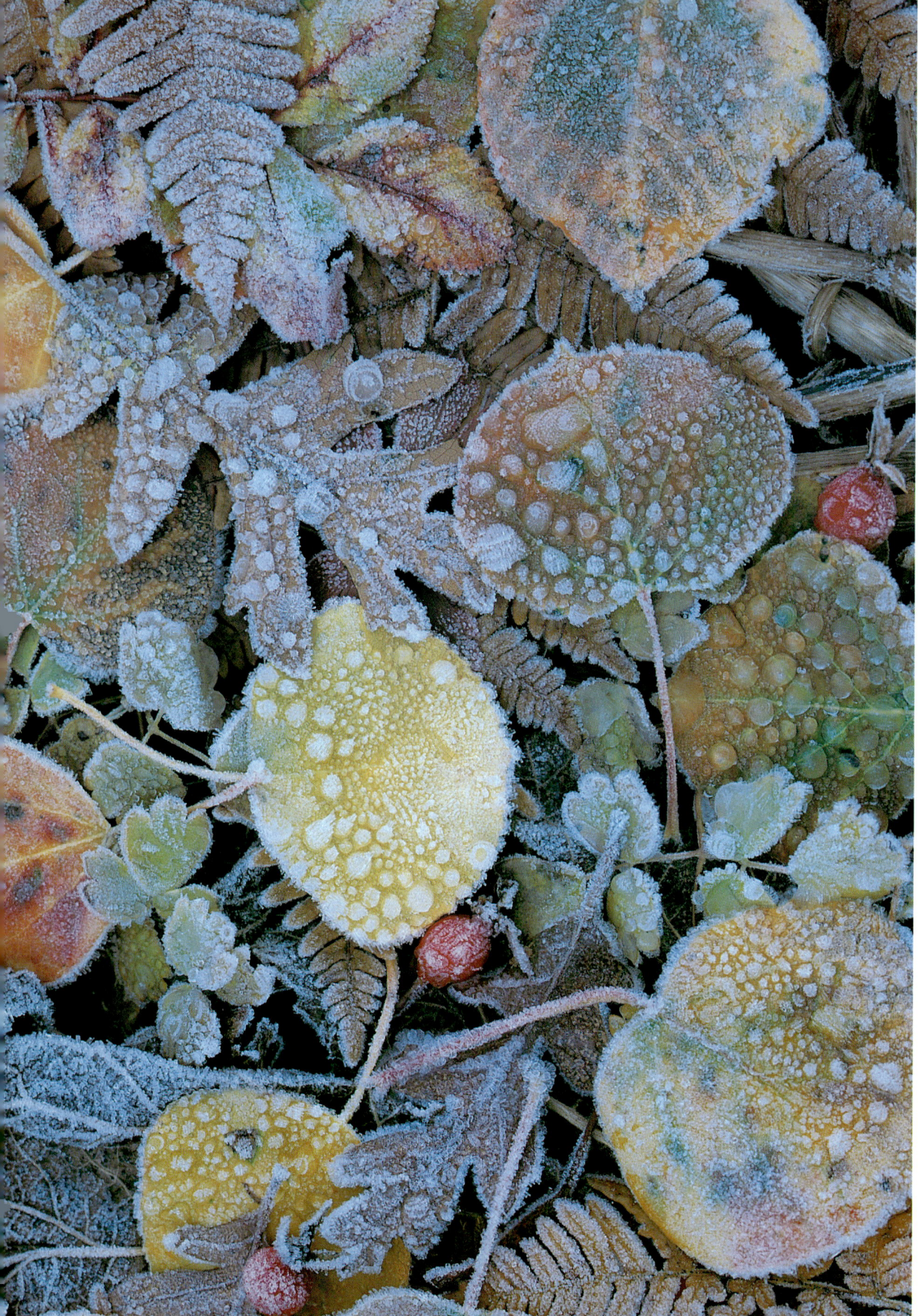

Overleaf: Maroon Lake, Maroon Bells-Snowmass Wilderness

Left: Maroon Bells-Snowmass Wilderness

Right: Roaring Fork River, Maroon Bells-Snowmass Wilderness

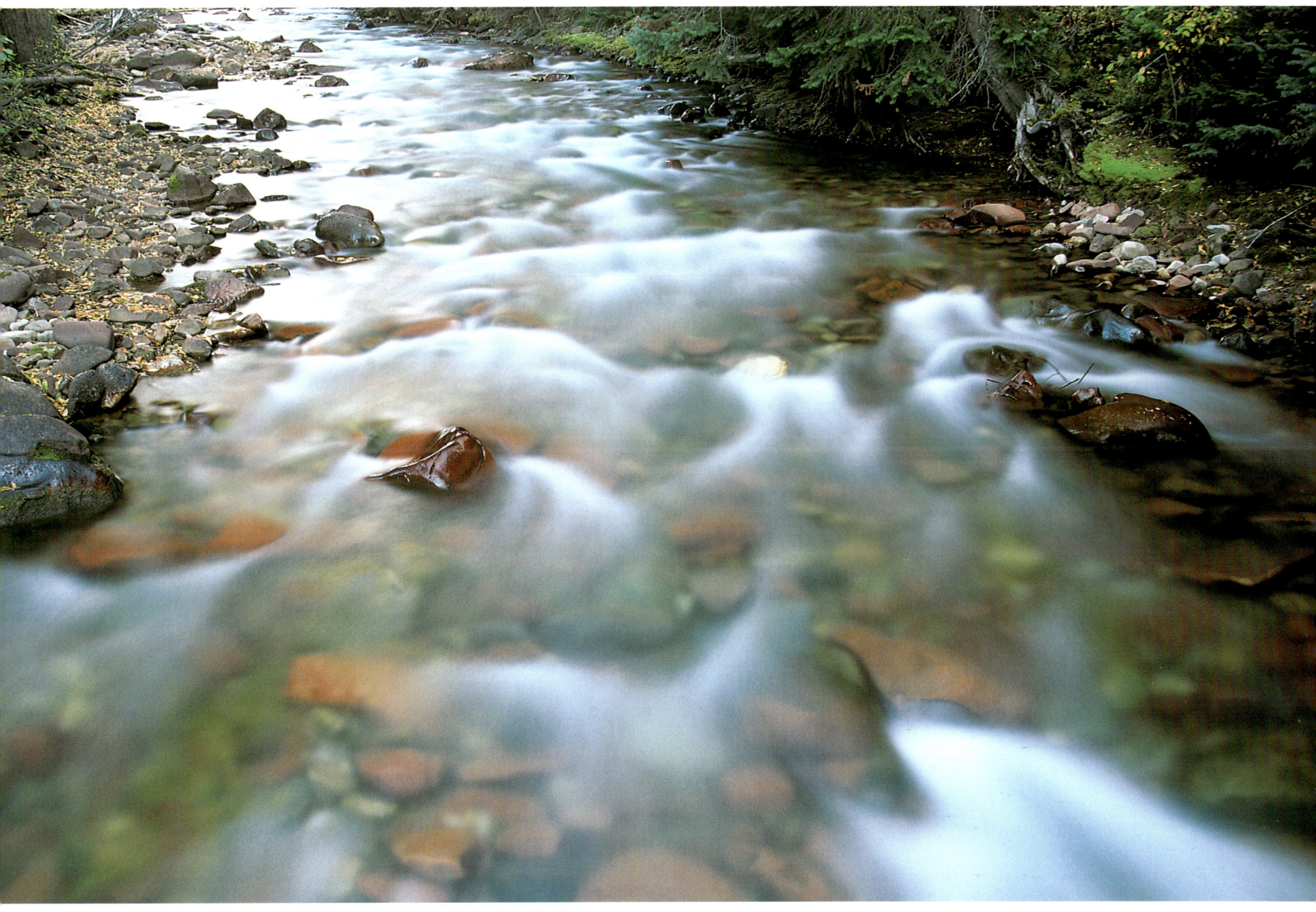

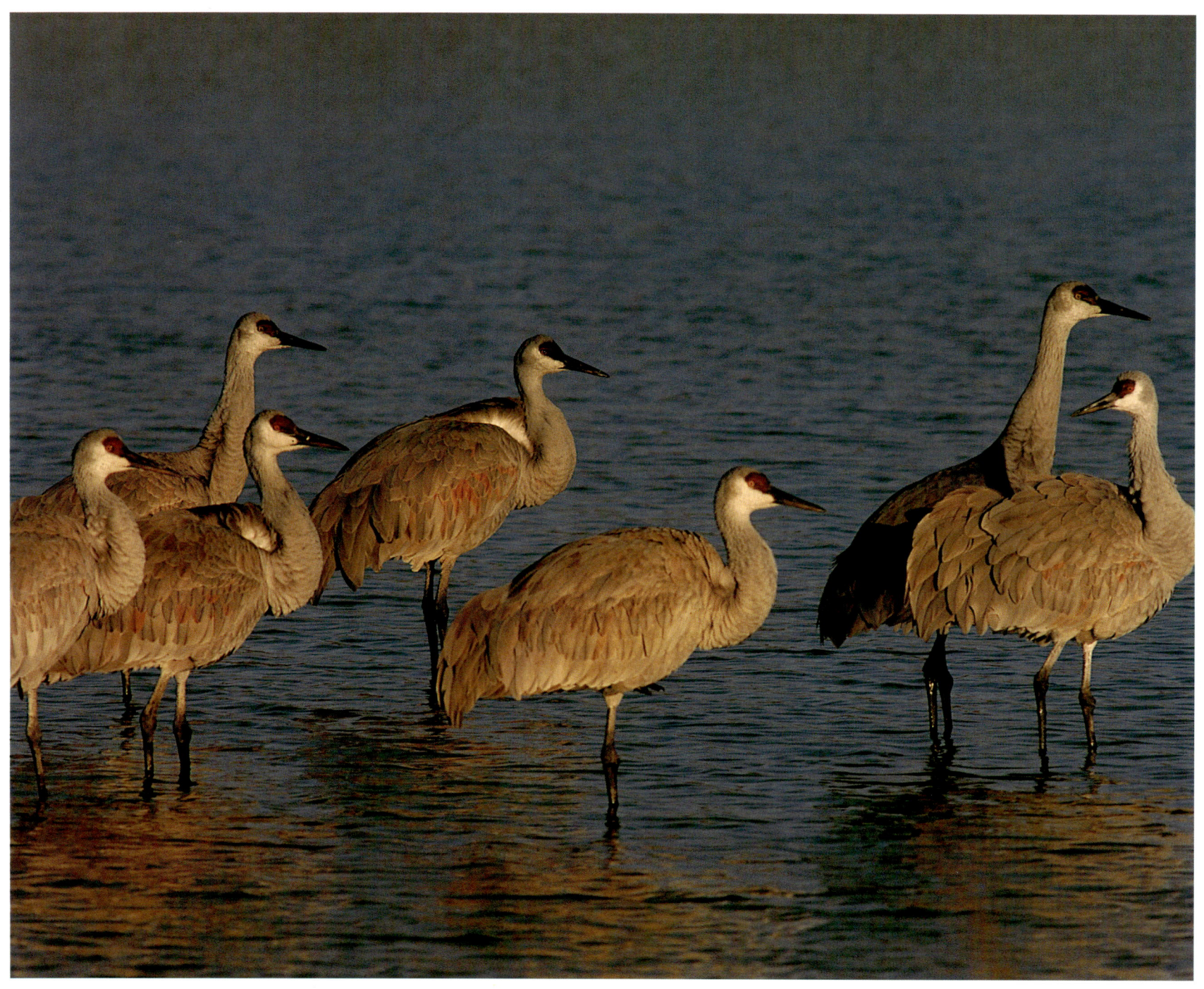

Left: Sandhill cranes (*Grus canadensis*), South Platte River

Right: Black Canyon of the Gunnison National Park

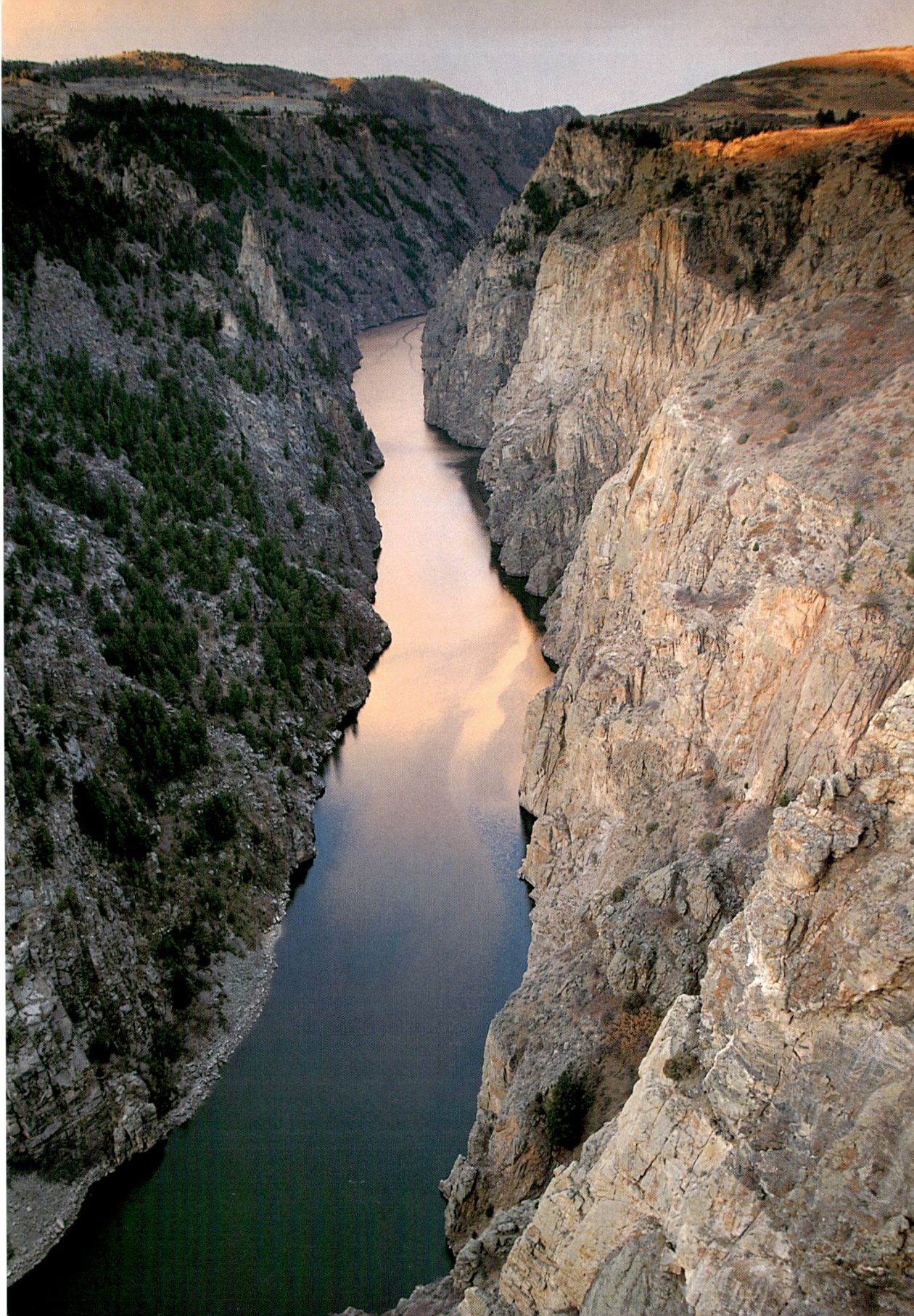

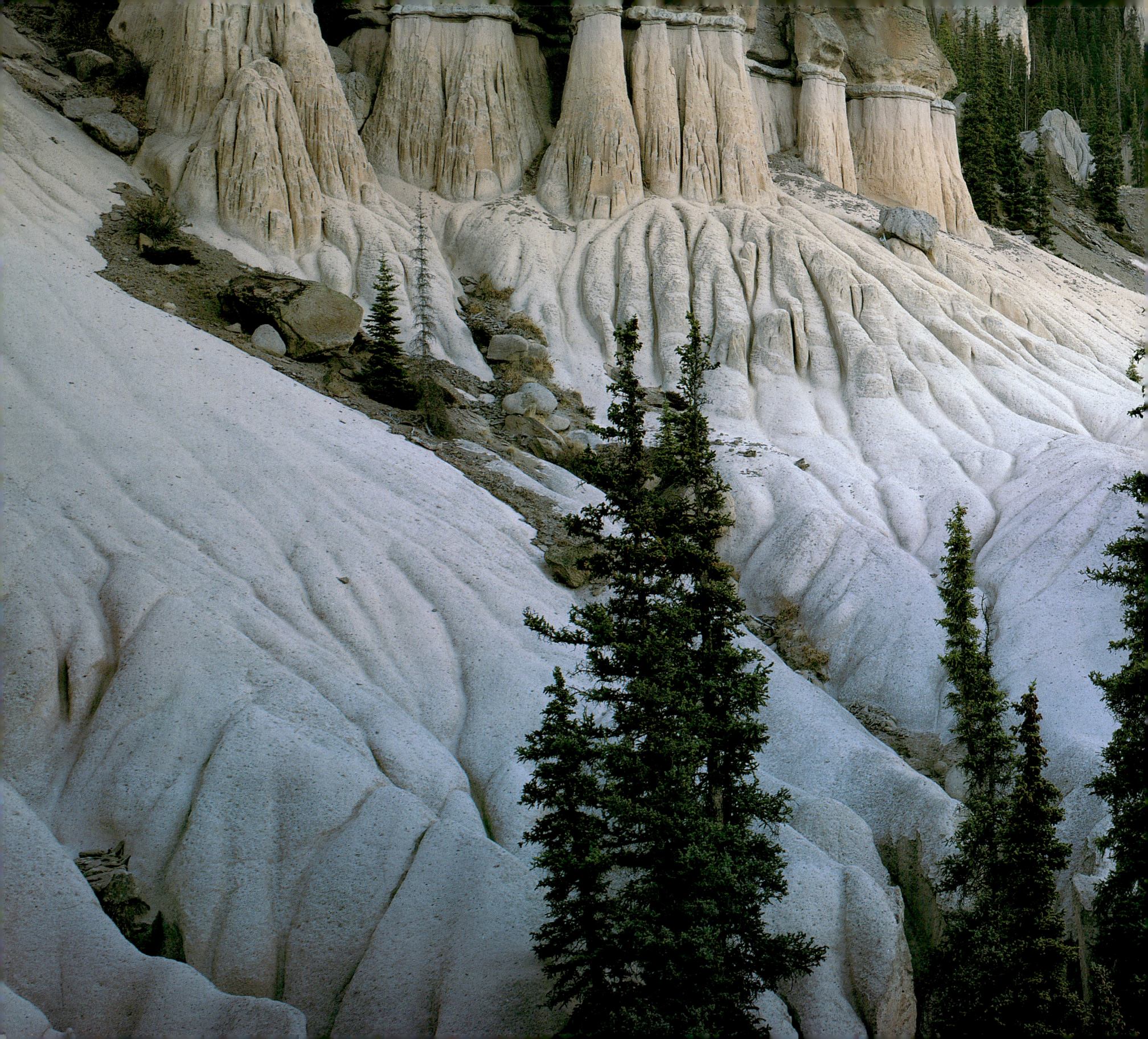

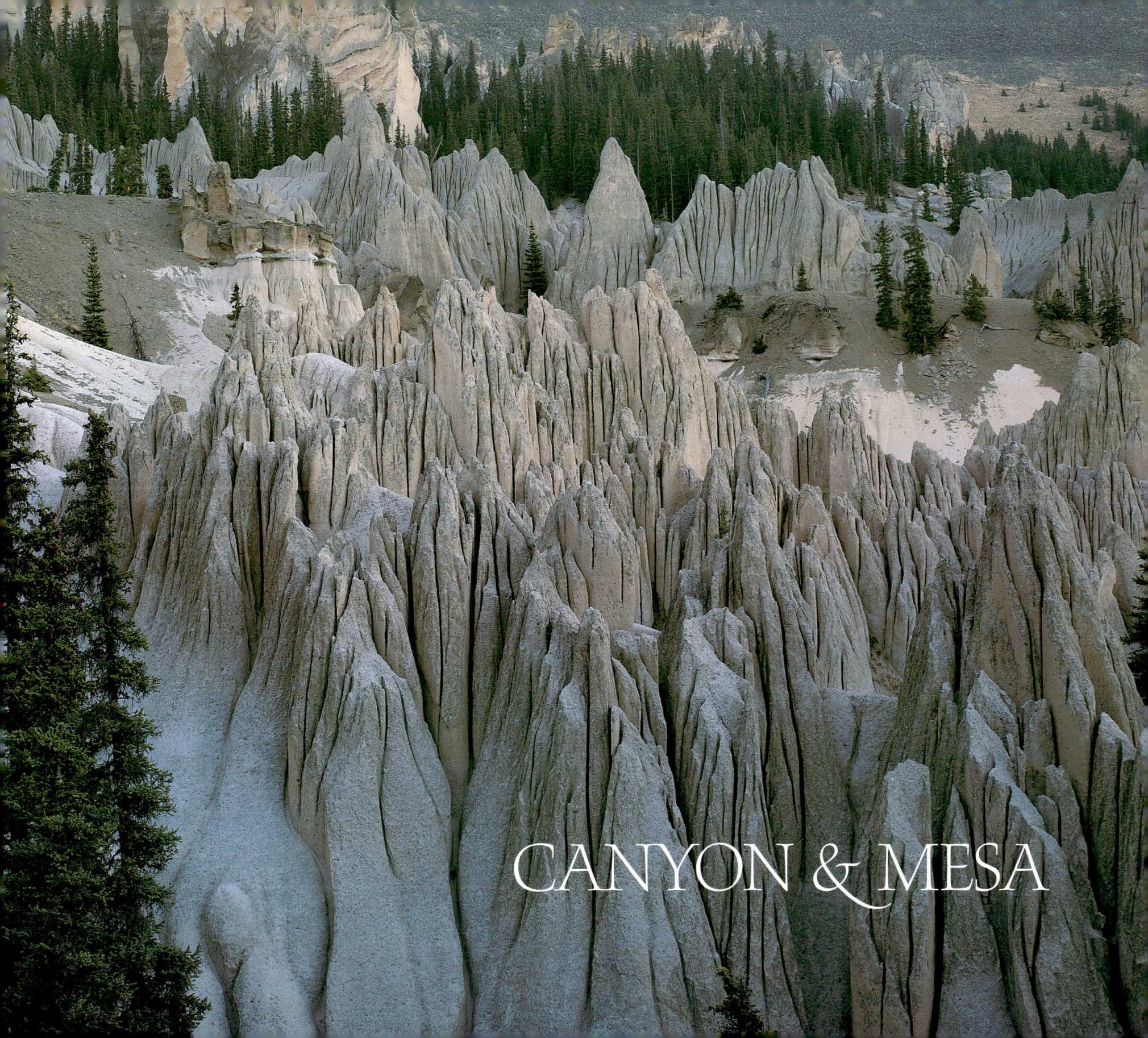
CANYON & MESA

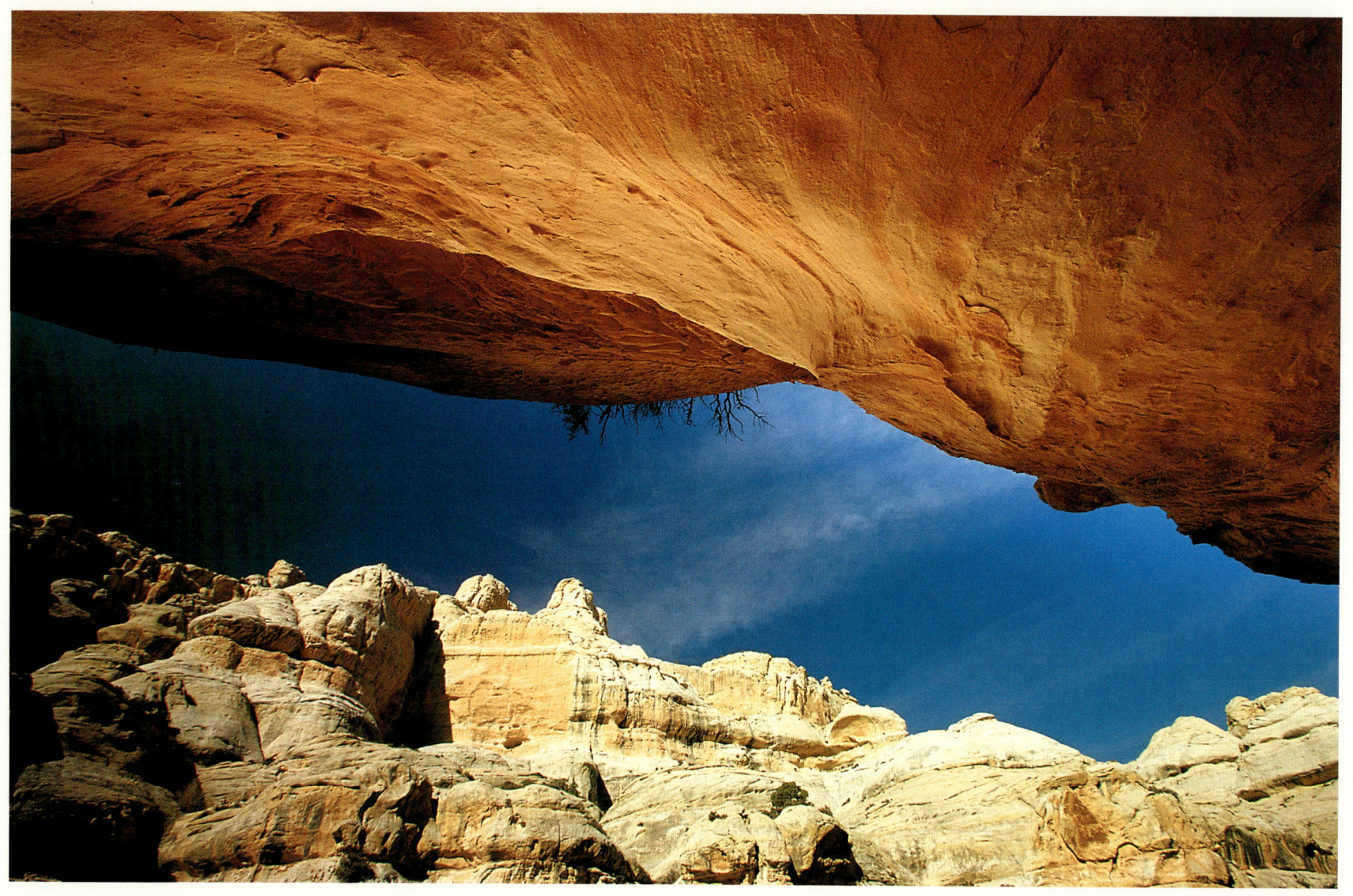

At 8,000 feet, where aspens finger into the ponderosa pines, I drove my truck into the summer grass. The mesa here is a smooth platform among mountains and desert. Everything around is made of cragged, snow-covered pinnacles or of steep-walled, stone canyons, while

Overleaf: Wheeler Monument

Left: Rattlesnake Canyon, Black Ridge region

Right: Coyote (*Canis latrans*), Dinosaur National Monument

the mesa suspends between them flat as a kitchen table.

I stopped the truck on a dirt two-track, wild blue flax grown high in the centerline, and walked from there. Fields commonly visited by elk spanned in all directions, ending in dry forests. The elk prefer to stand at the edge, just between the open grass of meadows and the shade of trees. That boundary is where I have stood on winter nights, snowshoes strapped to my feet, moonlight in the meadow showing the sly motions of a coyote sniffing grouse from beneath the snow. I know why the elk like this place. It is protecting.

Into the forest I walked, following these patchy islands of pines surrounded by oceanic meadows. Each tree was familiar: the crooked one, the tall one with the cropped top, the five seedlings now grown two feet tall. I had once lived on this mesa. My home had been a canvas tipi with long, slender poles made of lodgepole pine. Over twenty feet in diameter, the tipi stood in a tight grove of ponderosa pines. The

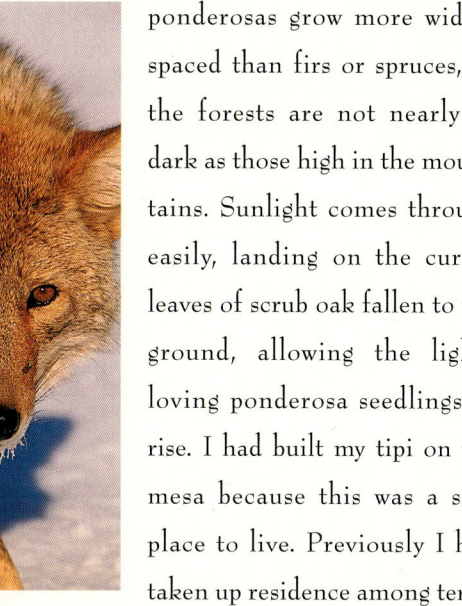

ponderosas grow more widely spaced than firs or spruces, so the forests are not nearly as dark as those high in the mountains. Sunlight comes through easily, landing on the curled leaves of scrub oak fallen to the ground, allowing the light-loving ponderosa seedlings to rise. I had built my tipi on the mesa because this was a safe place to live. Previously I had taken up residence among terrifying peaks and avalanches and long, arduous routes in the San Juan Mountains. I came to this mesa so I could breathe easily. So I could spread my arms and inhale the sky.

A mesa is a lifted, flat-topped chunk of earth that is wider than it is tall (compared to a butte, which is taller than it is wide). In Spanish, the word means "table," an apt name for pieces of ground that are often the only smooth objects in the territory. Their tops are decorated with scrubby forests of piñon and juniper, or with thick webs of high-elevation coniferous forests peppered with lakes and marshy meadows, ringed by sudden drops to the land thousands of feet below.

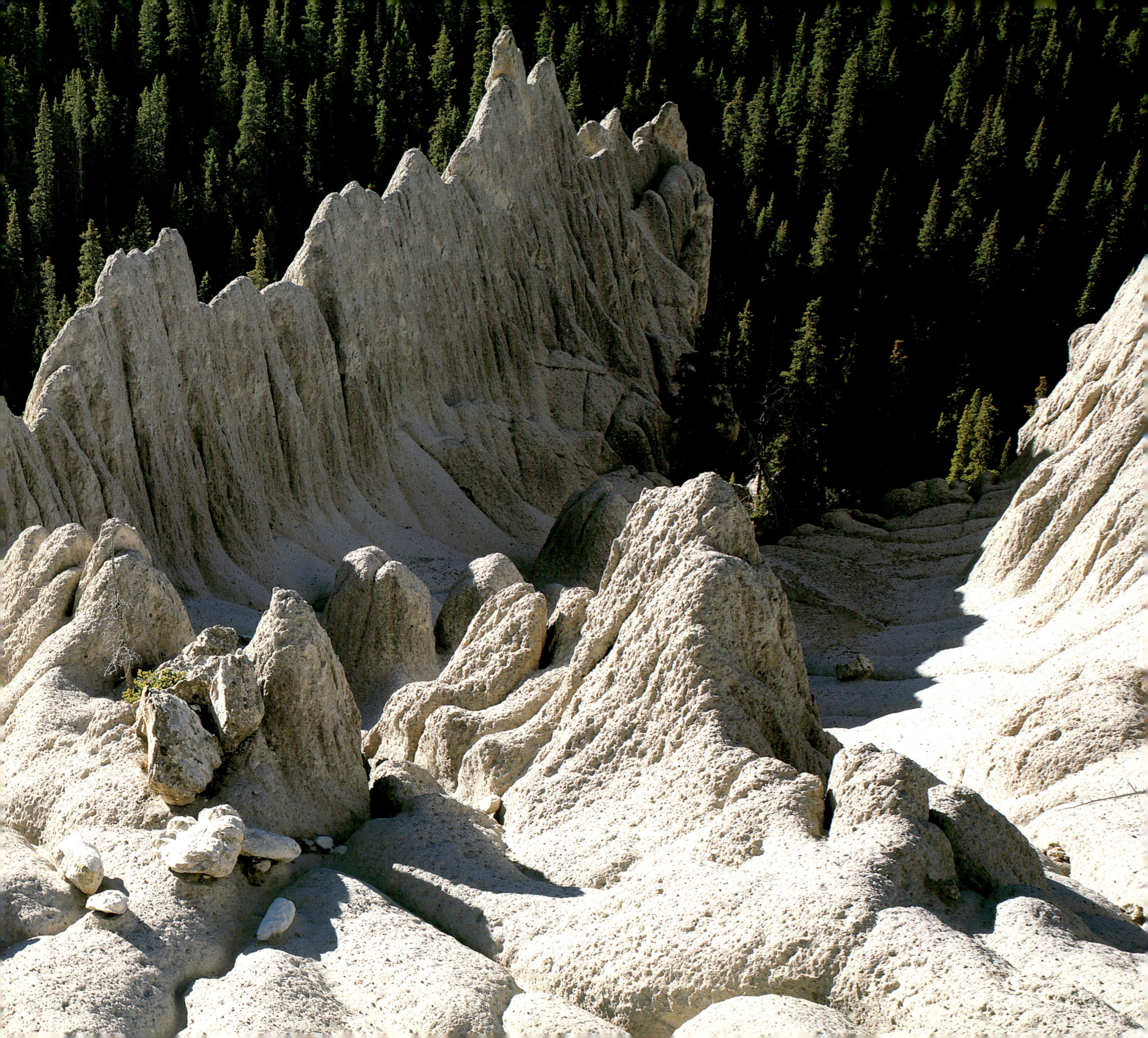

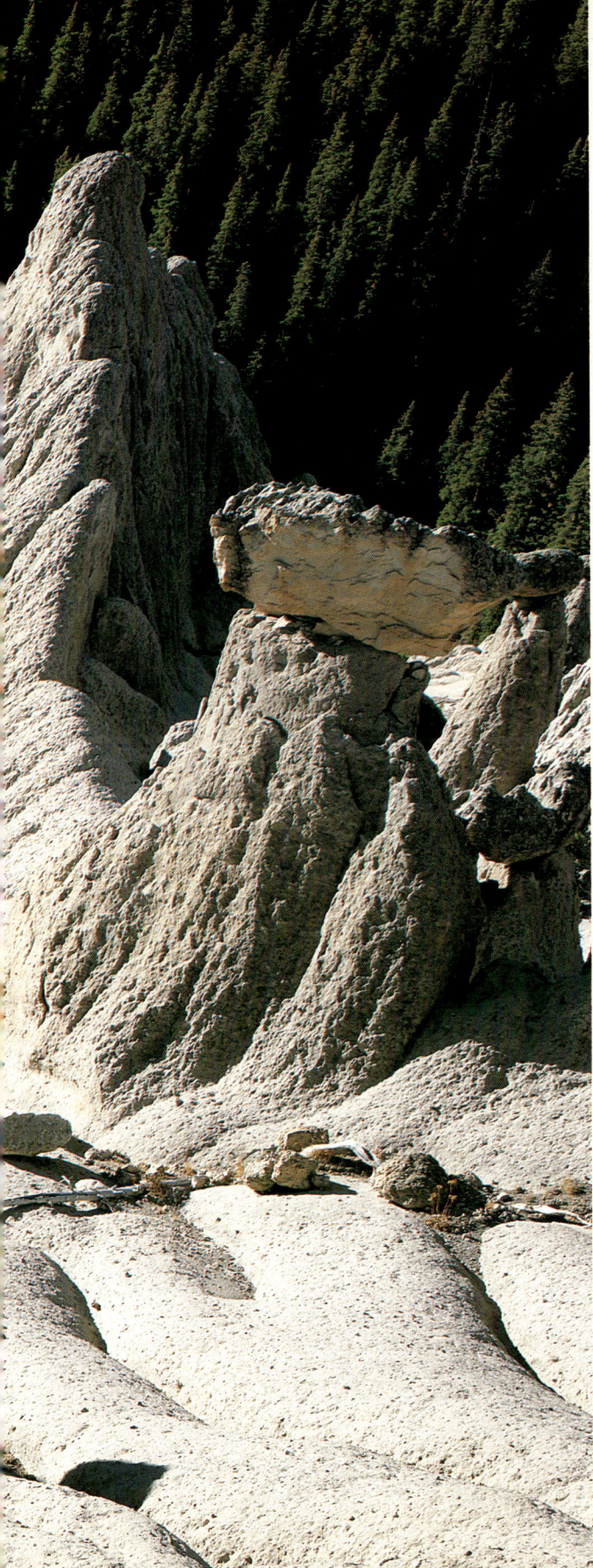

Wheeler Monument

This mesa's edges crumble into canyons like piecrust breaking away. Wildcat Canyon comes down from a small cattle ranch a couple of miles north of here, opening up cliffs and blocks of volcanic rock. Dolores Canyon, its name derived from a Latin word for "sorrows," runs immediately south of Happy Canyon.

It is a half-day's walk from some mesa tops thick with spruce and fir trees down to a pure, stone, dry desert. Palisades of sandstone geologically related to those of Monument Valley are exposed from the eroding walls and slopes. The desert is too low in elevation to reach the passing clouds, while the high mesas drag and scrape against the sky, grabbing the rain and snow. There is a bold sense of irony and contradiction when deserts rub shoulders with forests. Mesas gather water, tumbling it down in small, silver creeks, which run through the desert like dreams. Few places on the planet show such stark opposition.

It had been some time since I was a year-round resident of this mesa. Often I lectured myself about taking the tipi down someday, hauling away my belongings to place in storage somewhere, but whenever I came to do the deed, I ended up opening the smoke flaps at night and falling asleep under blankets of stars.

I walked into the next grove west and there stood the tipi. The sun had seared the canvas to tearing. The entire south side had caved in, ripped at the seams, left hanging with streamers and scraps. I touched the fabric. It was brittle. I had patched it before, but if I tried again, the material would only shred around my stitches. I understood that I no longer had a home.

This time I would do it. Pulling out a pair of leather gloves, I went to work, first freeing the twenty-foot-tall smoke flap poles. A gentle curve had warped into each pole, memory from standing here for seven years. Studiously I moved my few belongings outside: a collection of animal skulls gathered from the area—those of a black bear, coyote, weasel, and a small cat; the ceramic pitcher and basin used as both a shower and bath; pieces of string carefully tied and stored for future use; a box of matches.

Afternoon storms built as I worked. Thunder rattled through the pine grove. The air turned damp and heavy with smells. I made unceremonious gestures, calmly removing the pieces of my sanctuary, a place that had offered refuge from storms and had given me a place to sleep. I recalled the winter nights, the firelight on the walls, how I would lie under my covers and watch the animated ochre. This place had the memory of wisdom, and sadness, and the splitting of firewood with an iron maul until I was so tired I fell asleep wherever I sat. There were January nights when I buried myself in the fluff of down blankets, the temperature inside the tipi reaching 27 below zero.

One of the thunderstorms approached with its lightning and its velvet heart. Then the rain came with force.

Limp, unbuttoned canvas hung on the lodgepoles the way a coat drapes on an old man's shoulders. I came in from the rain, taking shelter in the remains of the tipi. One last time. The sound was so utterly kind—rain on canvas. I had heard this sound many times, nearly as soft as snow on canvas.

The wind came. The grass outside folded and whispered. Parts of the canvas blew forward. The tipi closed itself around me, in the manner of someone offering a blanket in comfort.

It was the final sweet gesture and I closed my eyes.

Right: Yampa River Canyon, Dinosaur National Monument

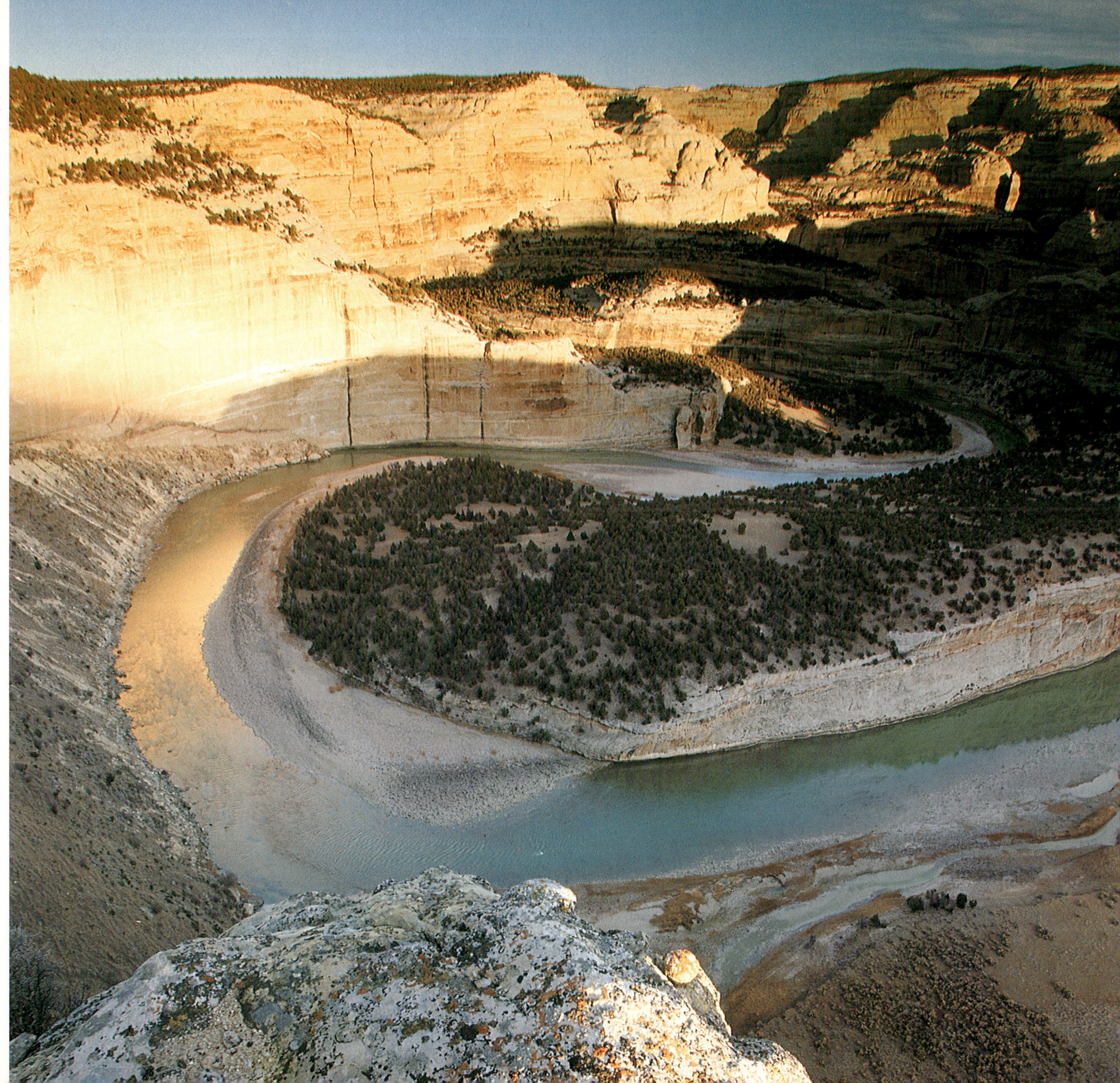

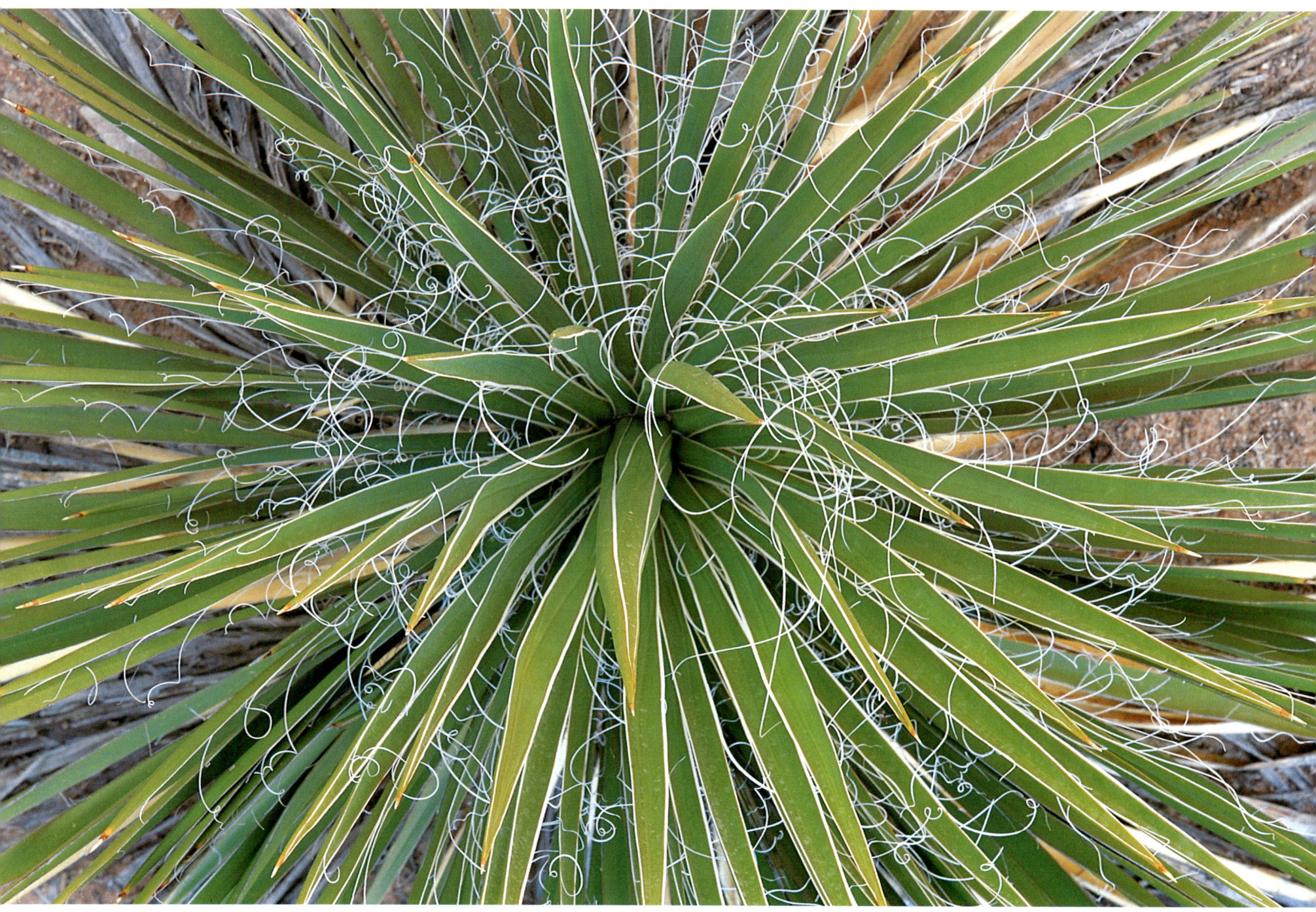

Left: Yucca (*Yucca* sp.), Black Ridge region

Below: Ruffed grouse (*Bonasa umbellus*), Dinosaur National Monument

Right: Golden-mantled ground squirrel (*Spermophilus lateralis*), Dinosaur National Monument

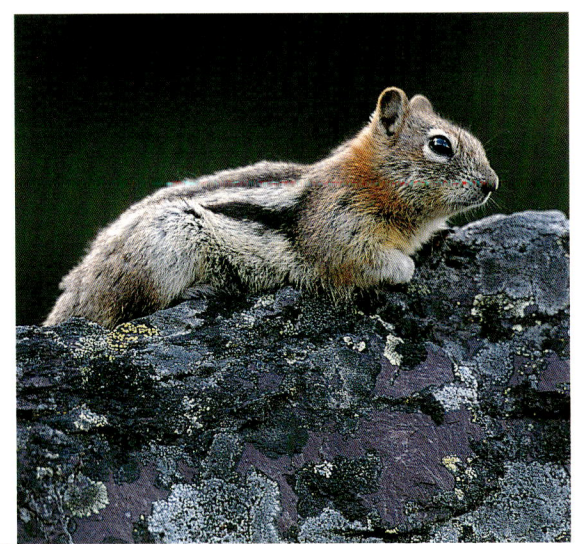

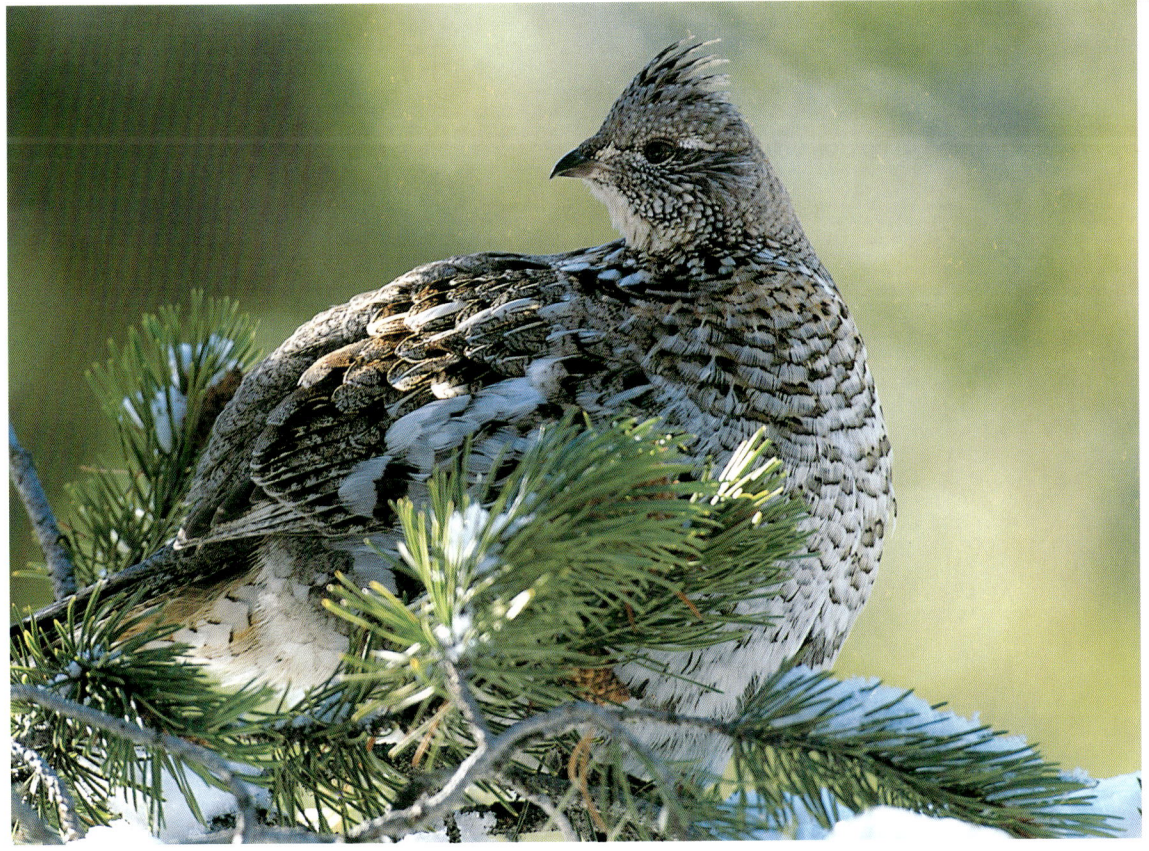

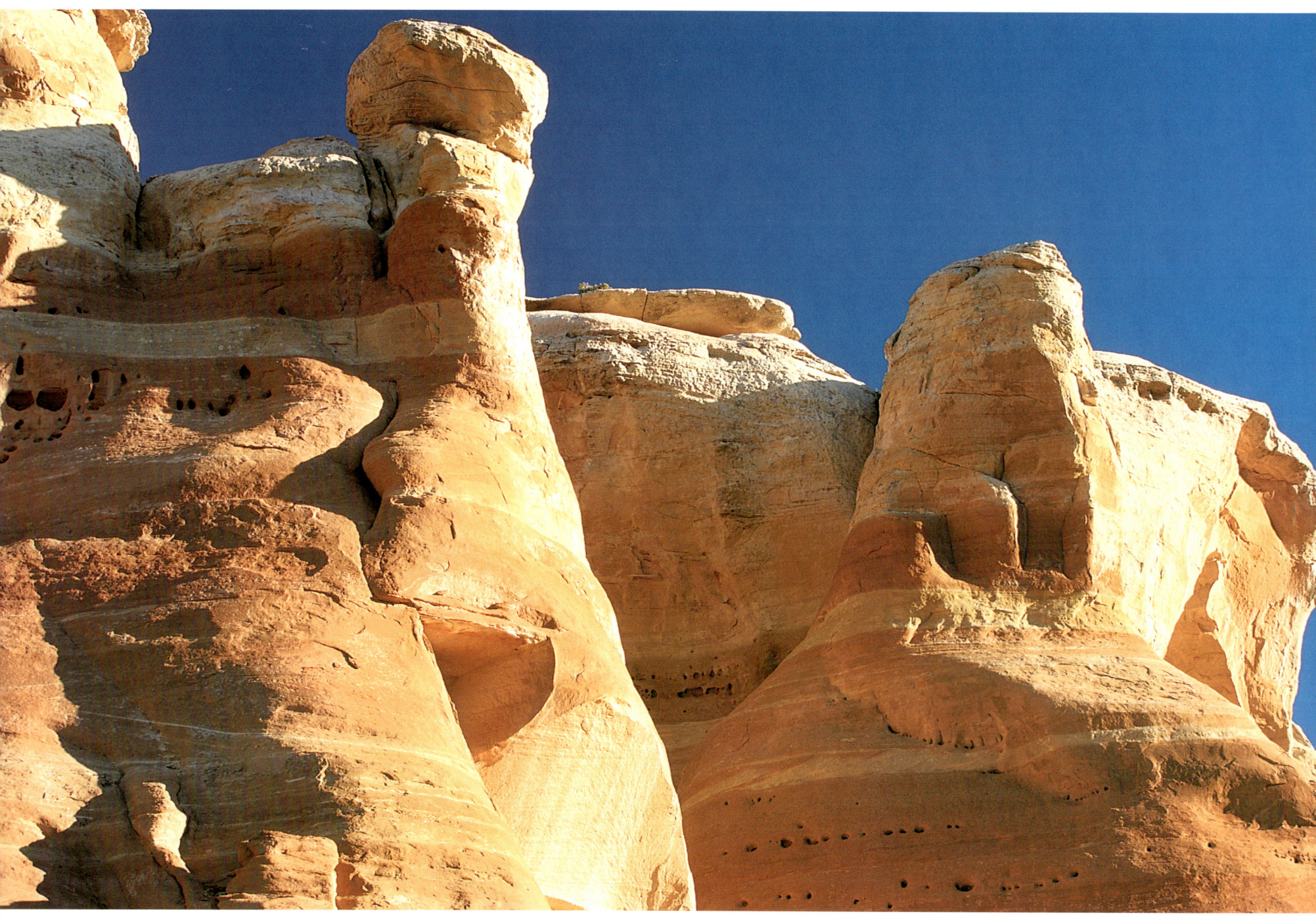

Left: Rattlesnake Canyon, Black Ridge region

Right: Yampa River Canyon, Dinosaur National Monument

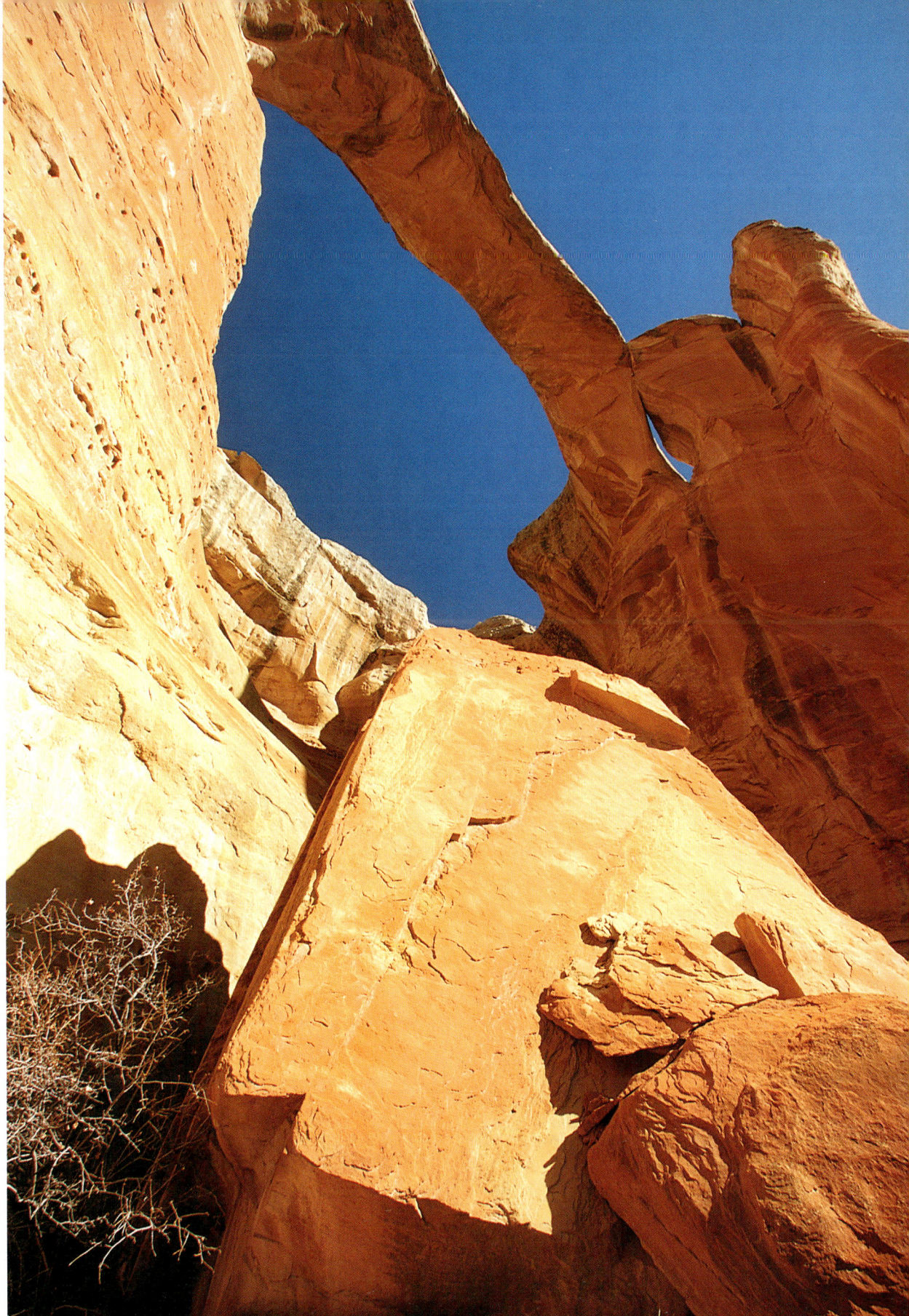

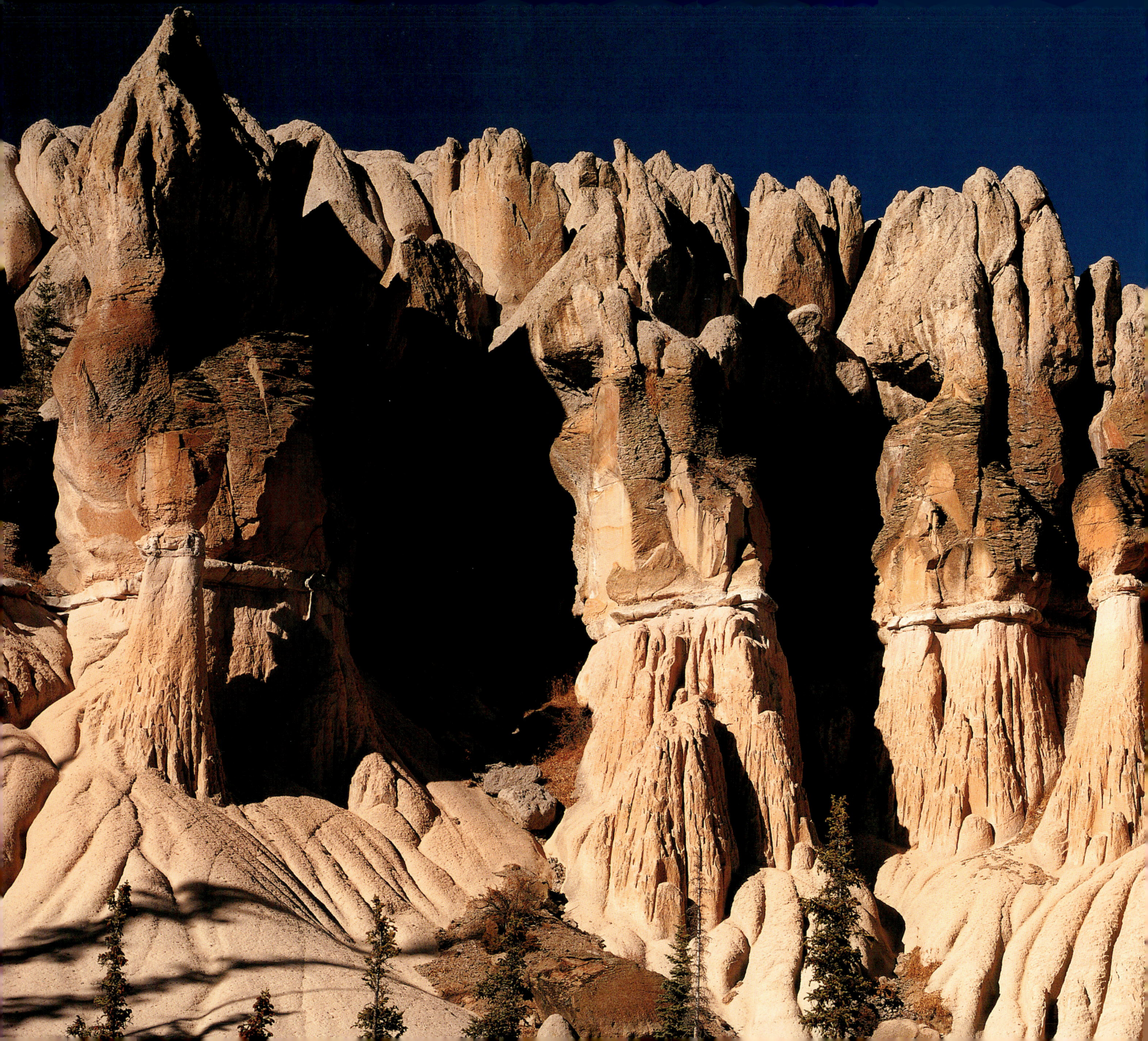

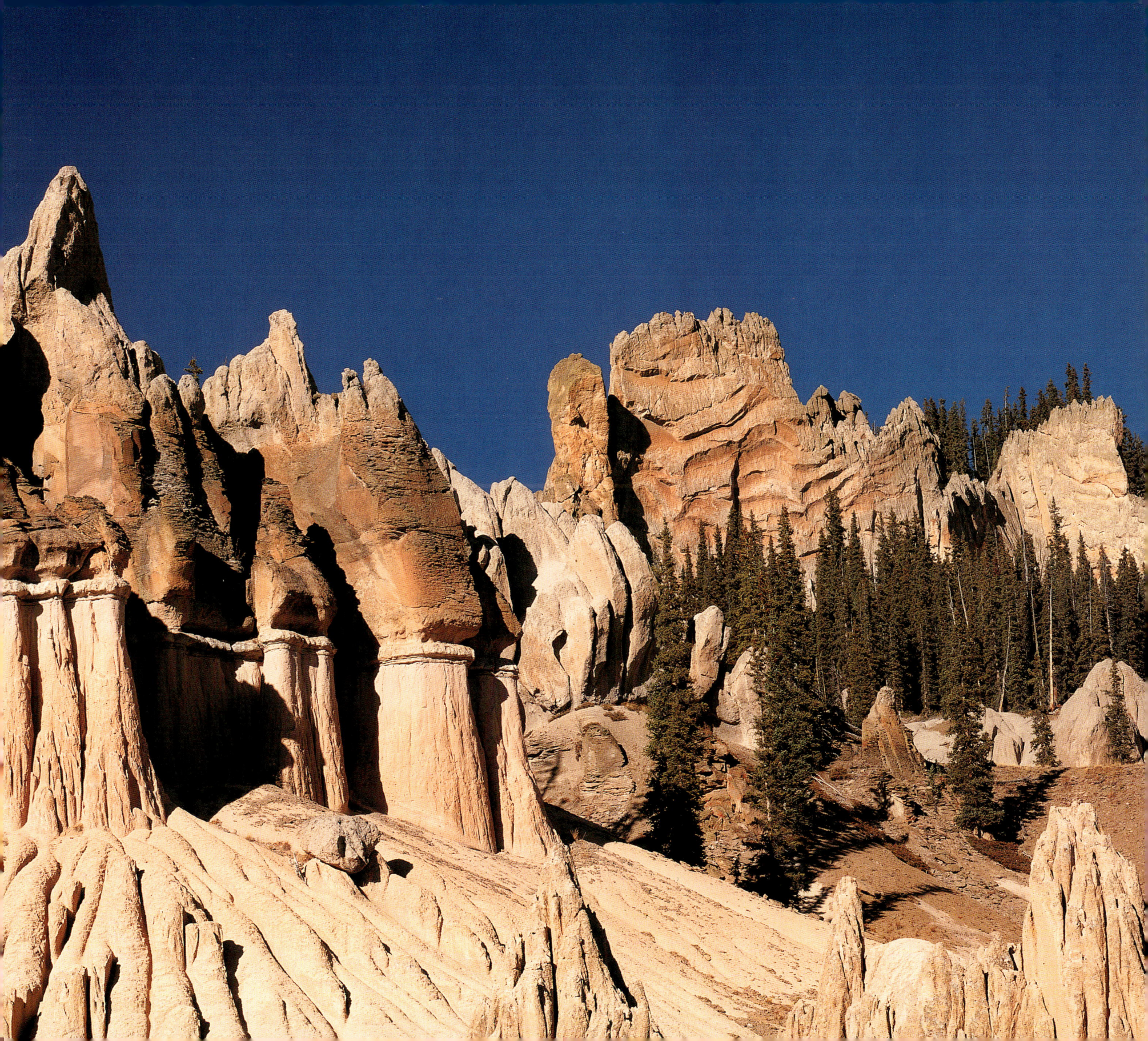

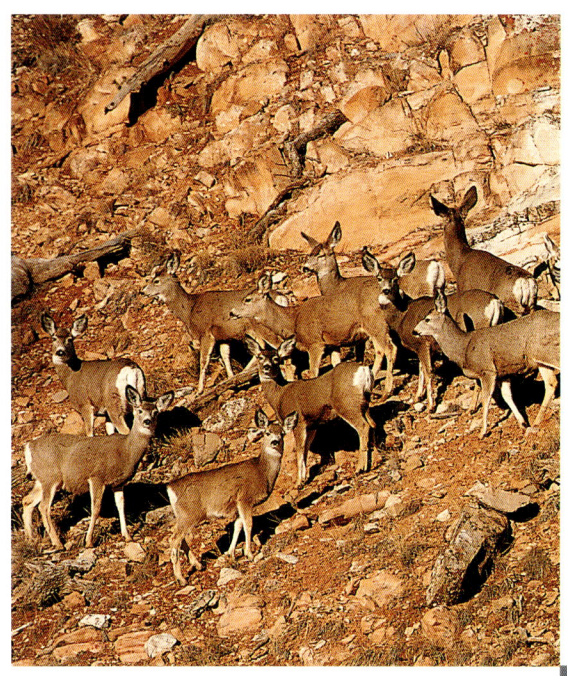

Overleaf: Wheeler Monument

Left: Mule deer (*Odocoileus hemionus*), Dinosaur National Monument

Below: Elk (*Cervus elaphus*), Rocky Mountain National Park

Right: Elk (*Cervus elaphus*), Dinosaur National Monument

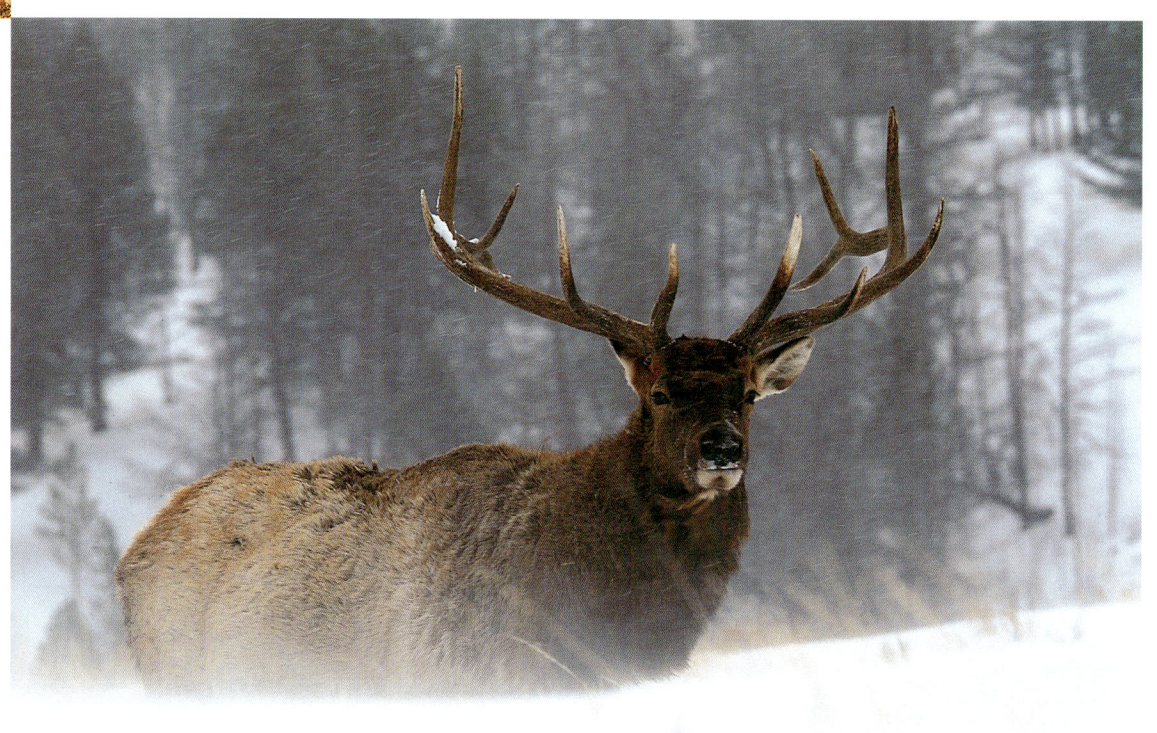

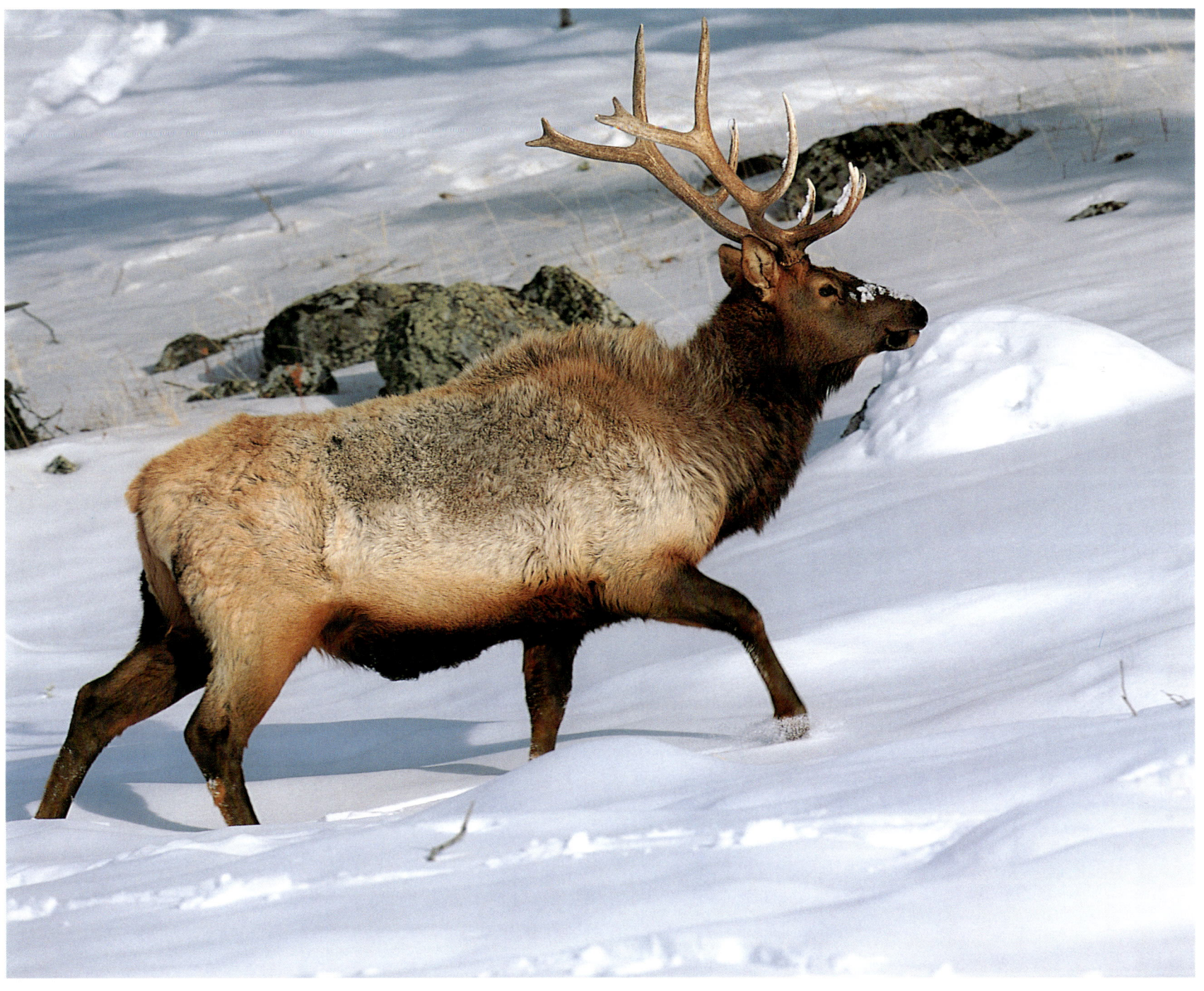

87

CANYON & MESA

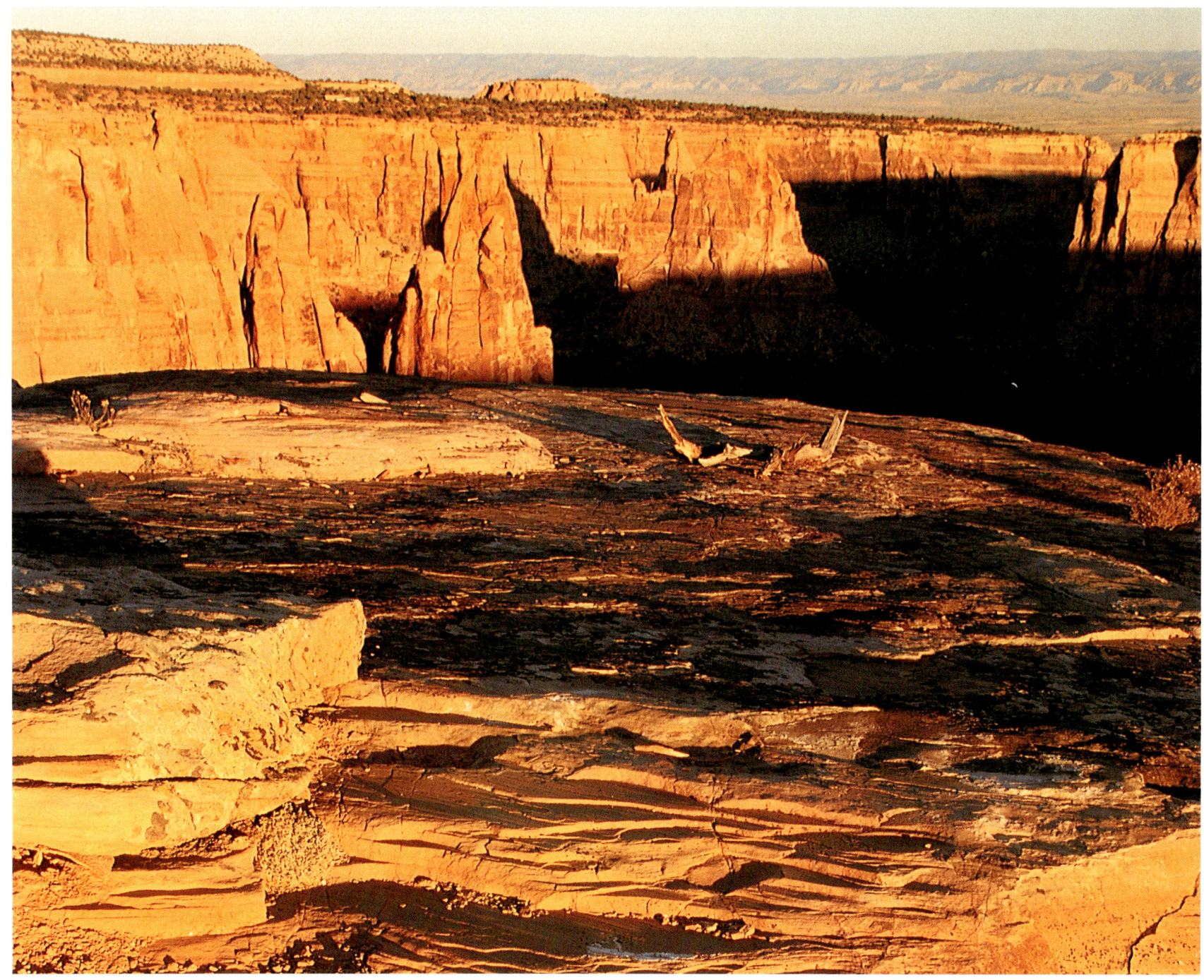

Colorado National Monument

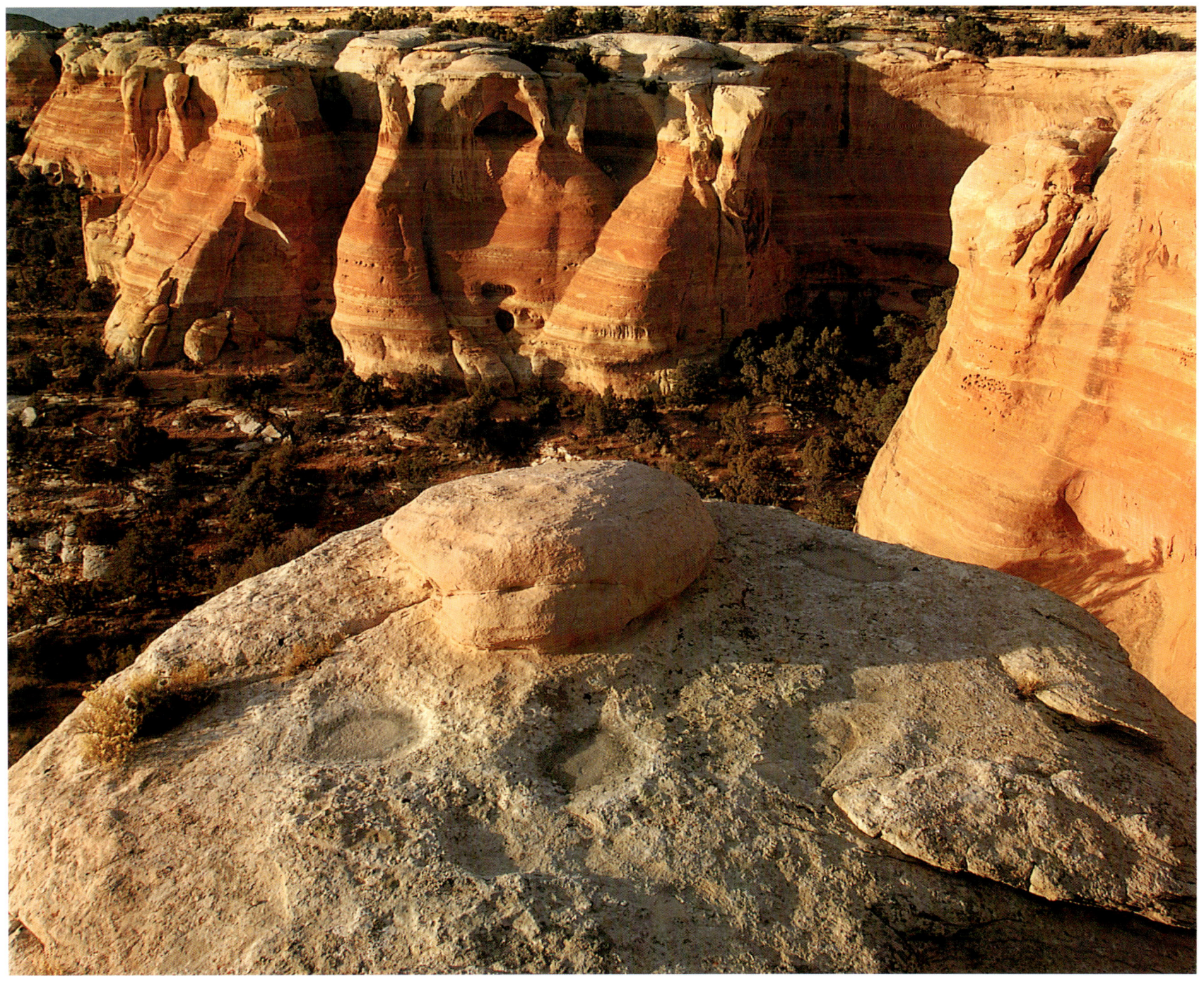

Rattlesnake Canyon, Black Ridge region

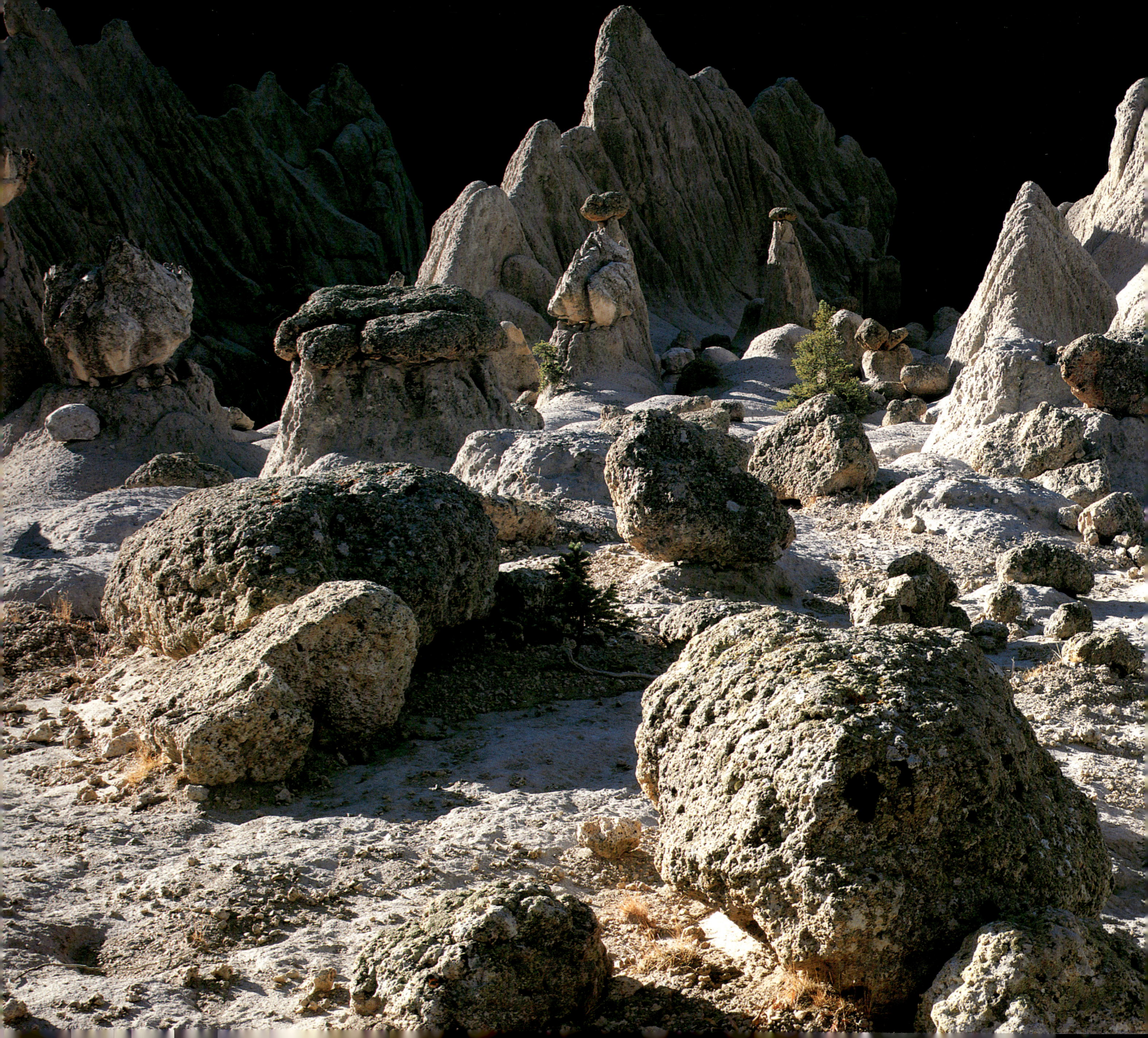

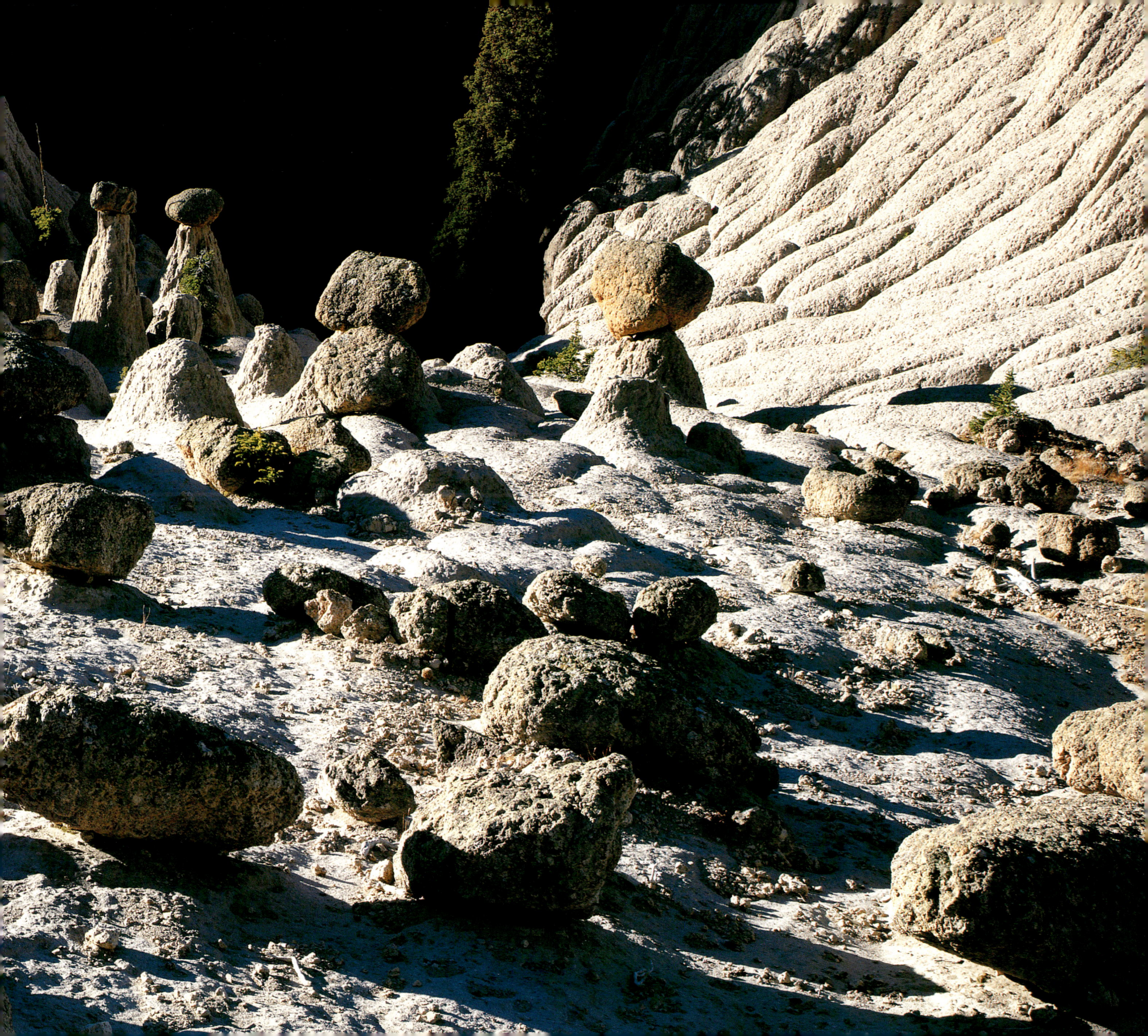

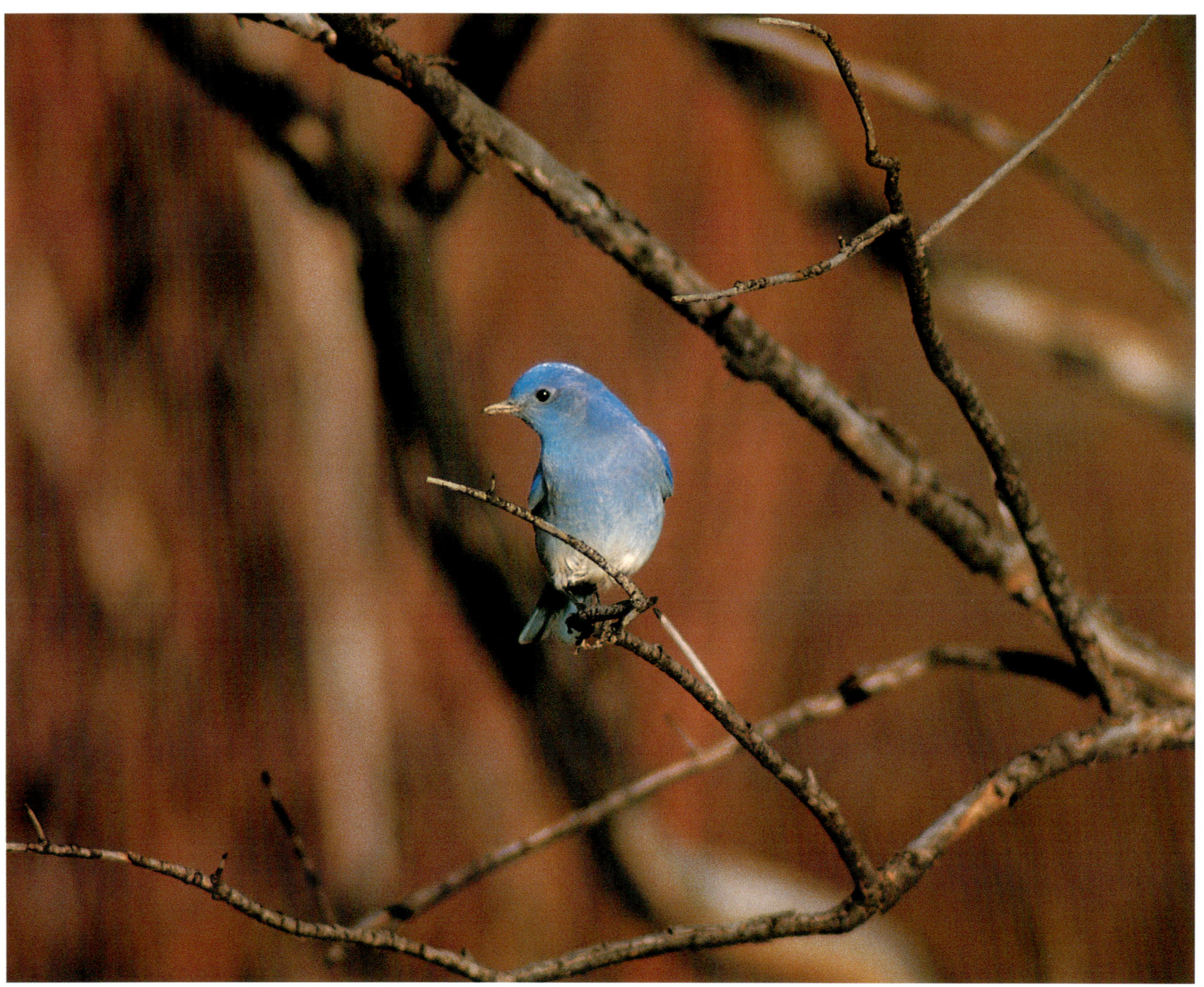

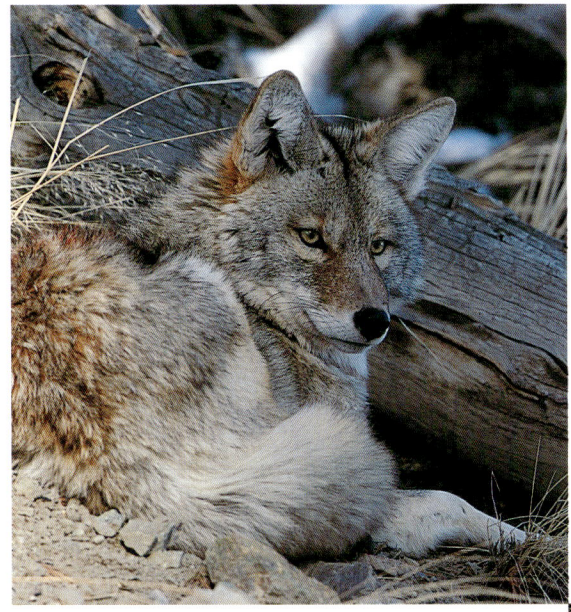

Overleaf: Wheeler Monument

Far left: Mountain bluebird (*Sialia currucoides*), Dinosaur National Monument

Left: Coyote (*Canis latrans*), Dinosaur National Monument

Below: Red foxes (*Vulpes vulpes*), Browns Park National Wildlife Refuge

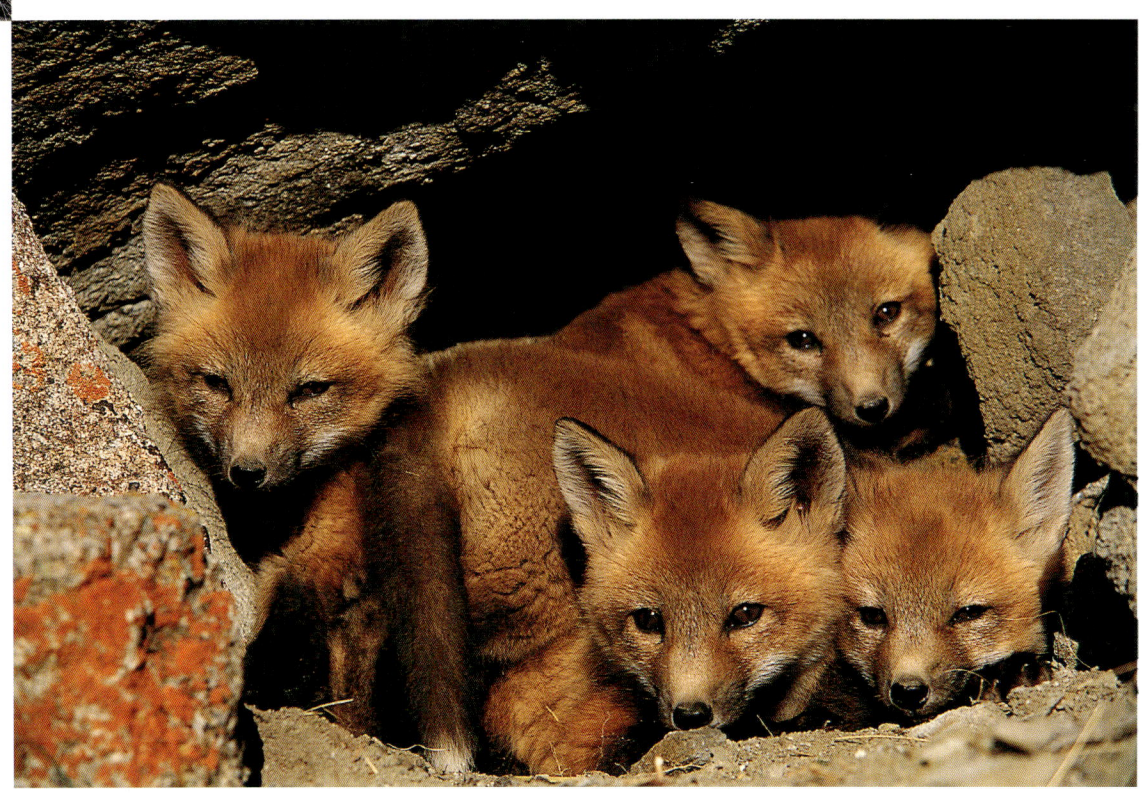

CANYON & MESA

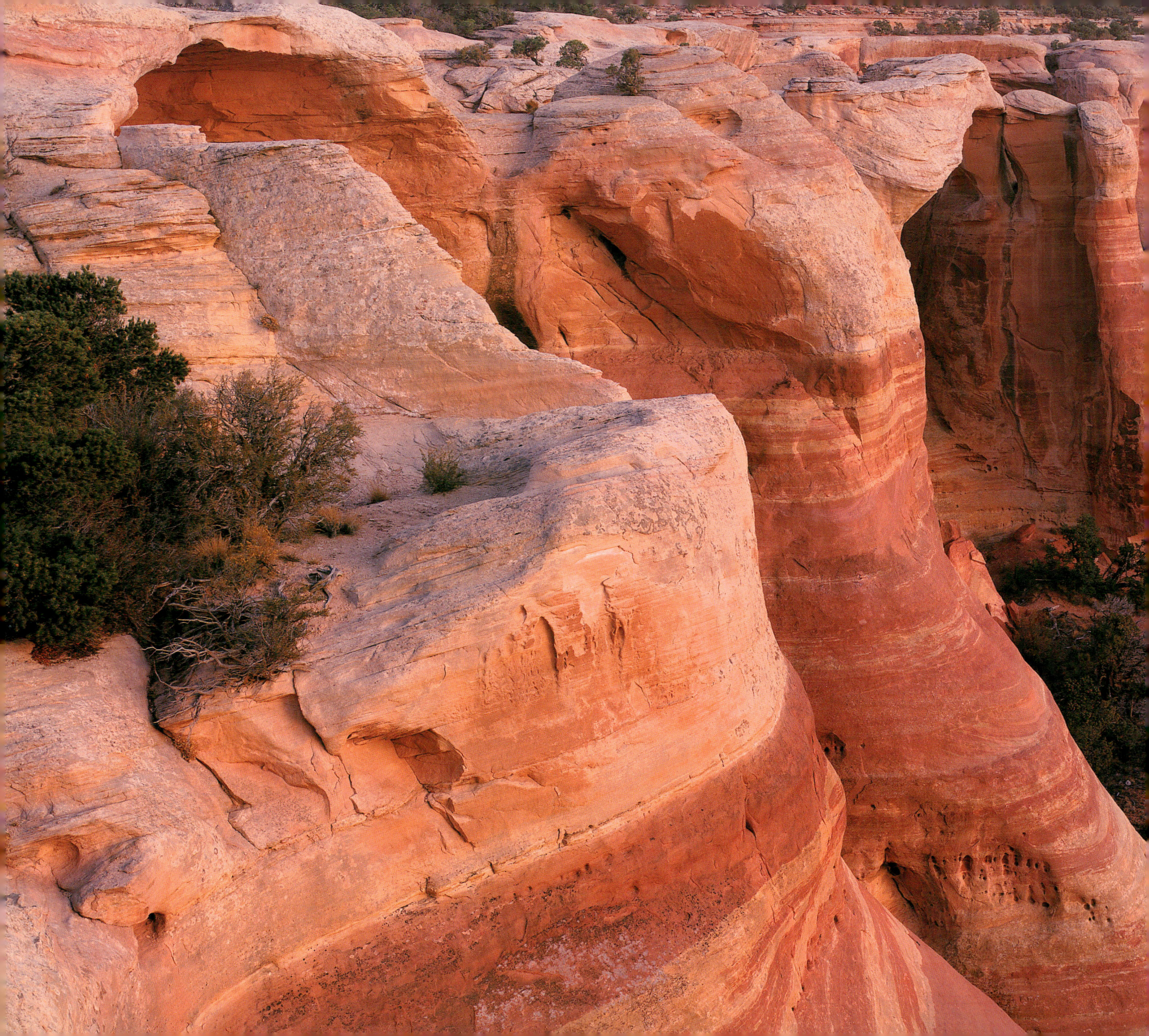

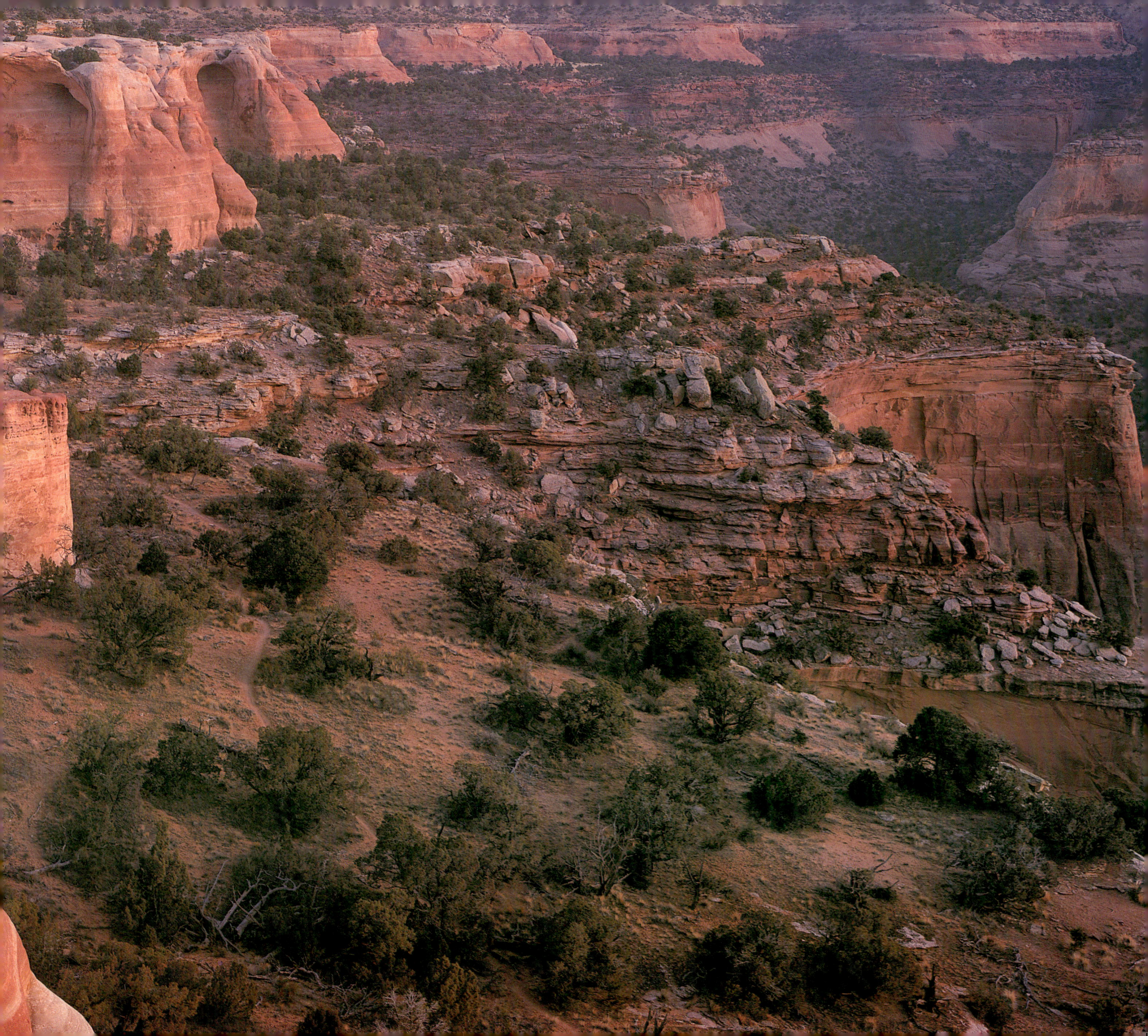

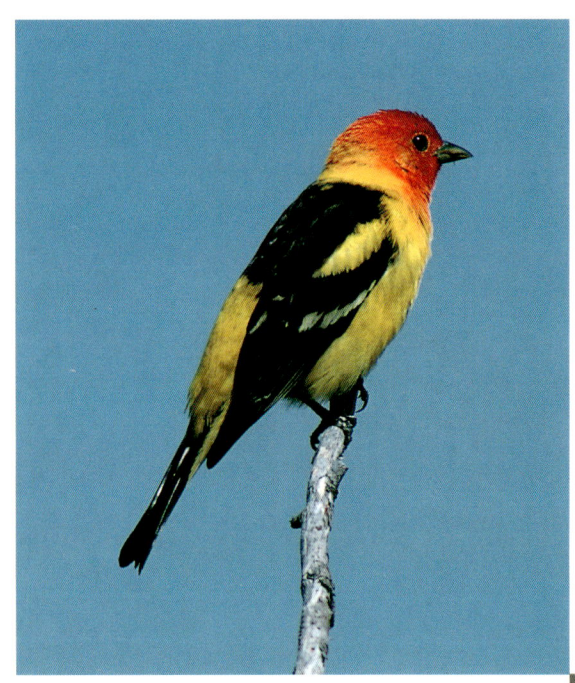

Overleaf: Rattlesnake Canyon, Black Ridge region

Left: Western tanager (*Piranga ludoviciana*), Dinosaur National Monument

Below: Scrub jay (*Aphelocoma coerulescens*), Dinosaur National Monument

Right: Elk (*Cervus elaphus*), Blue Mountain, Dinosaur National Monument

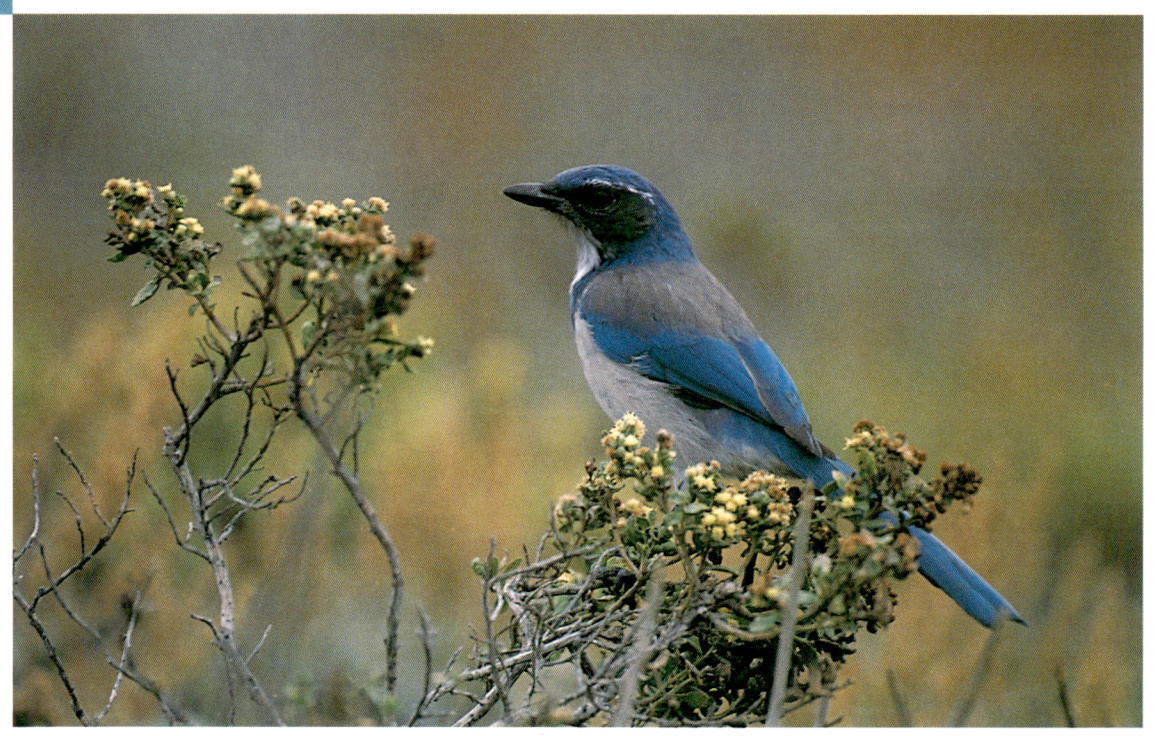

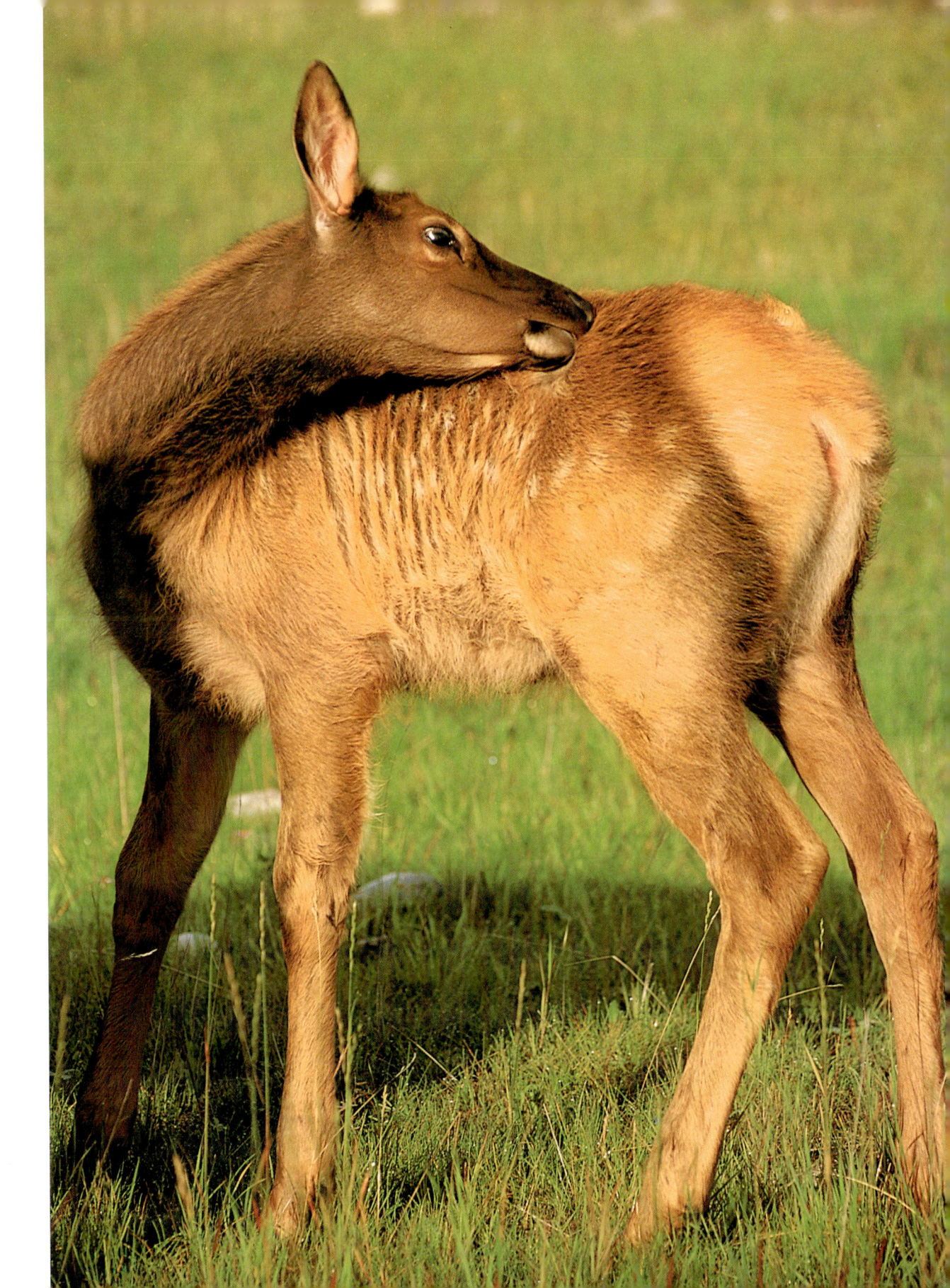

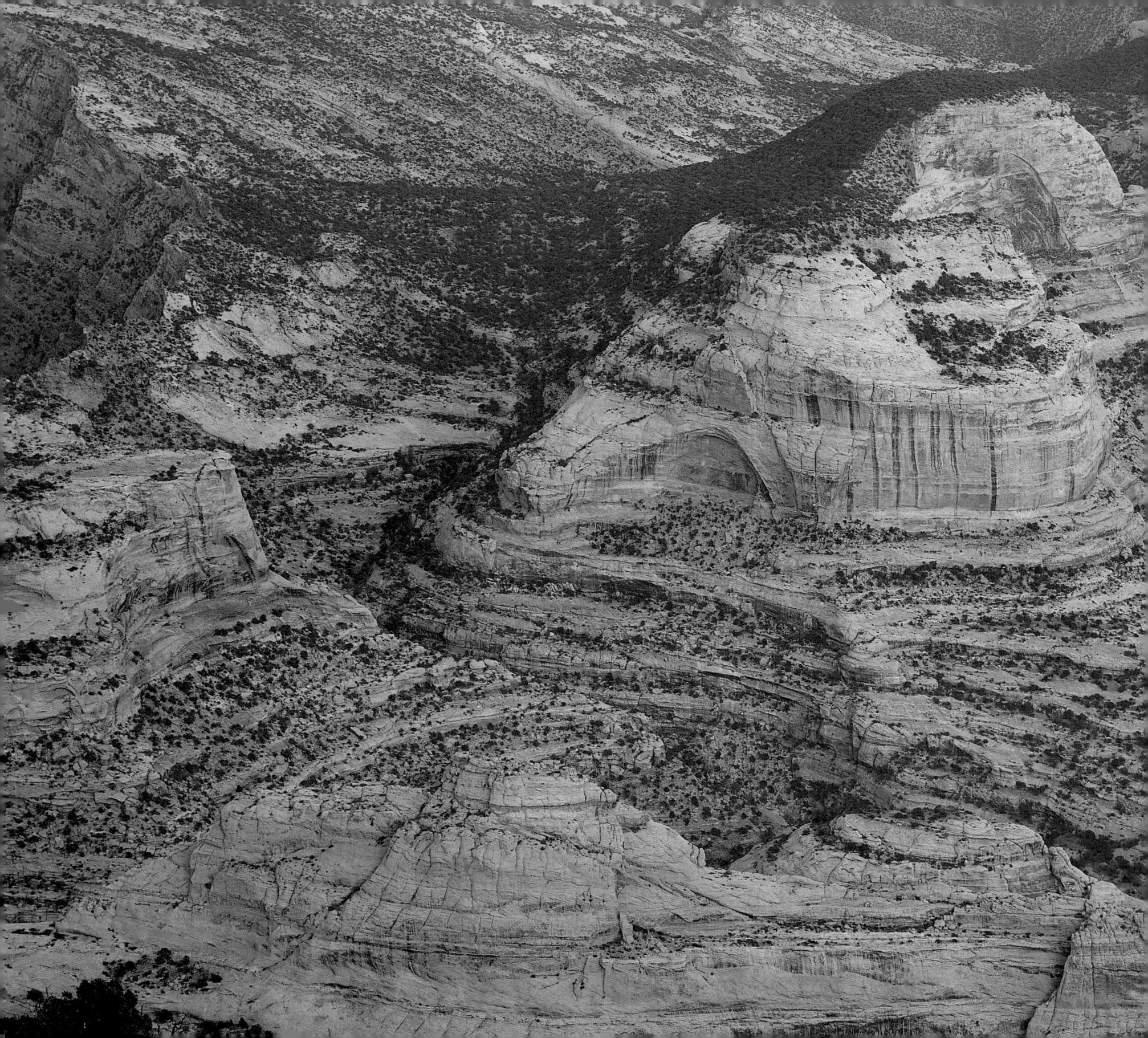

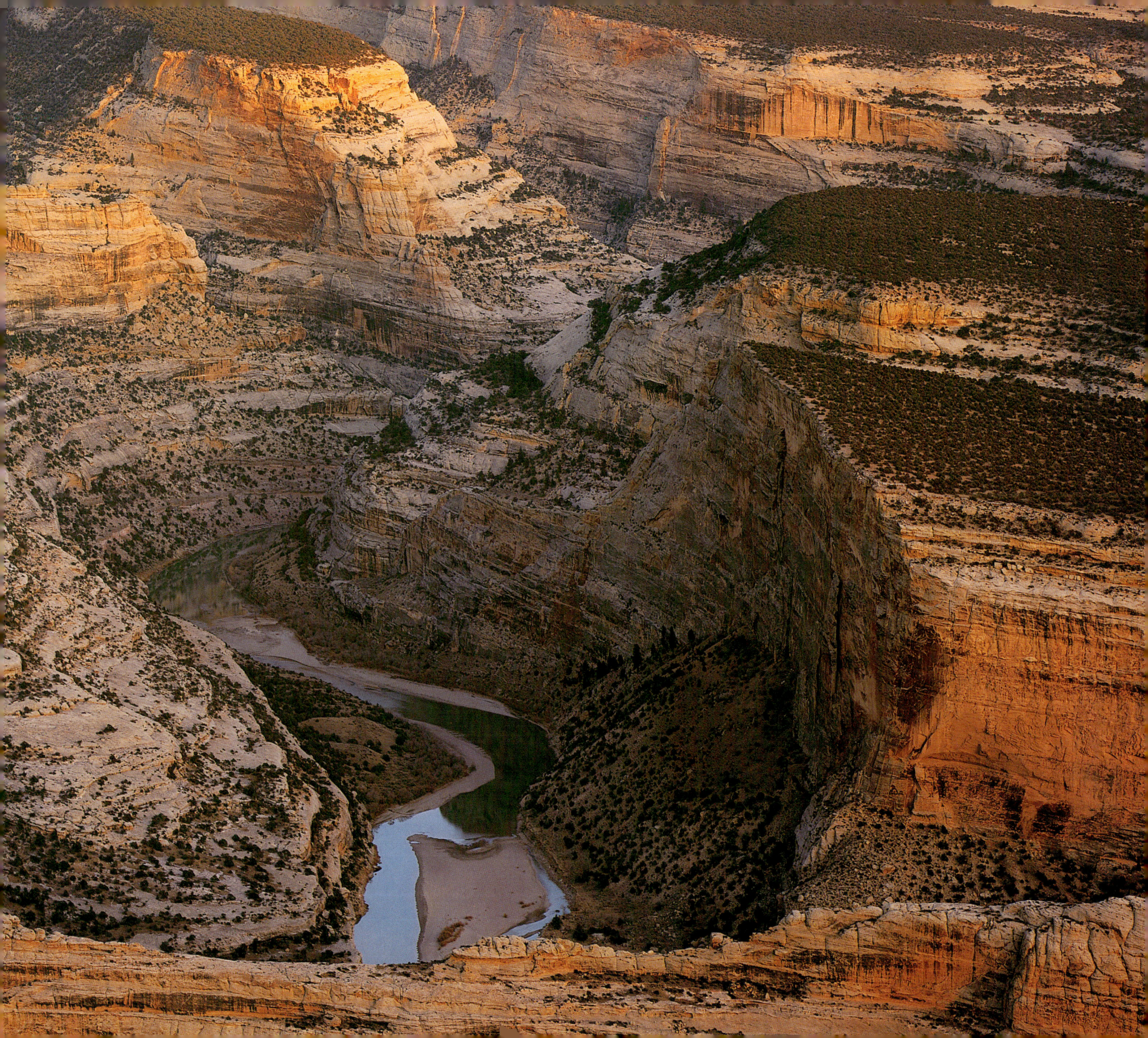

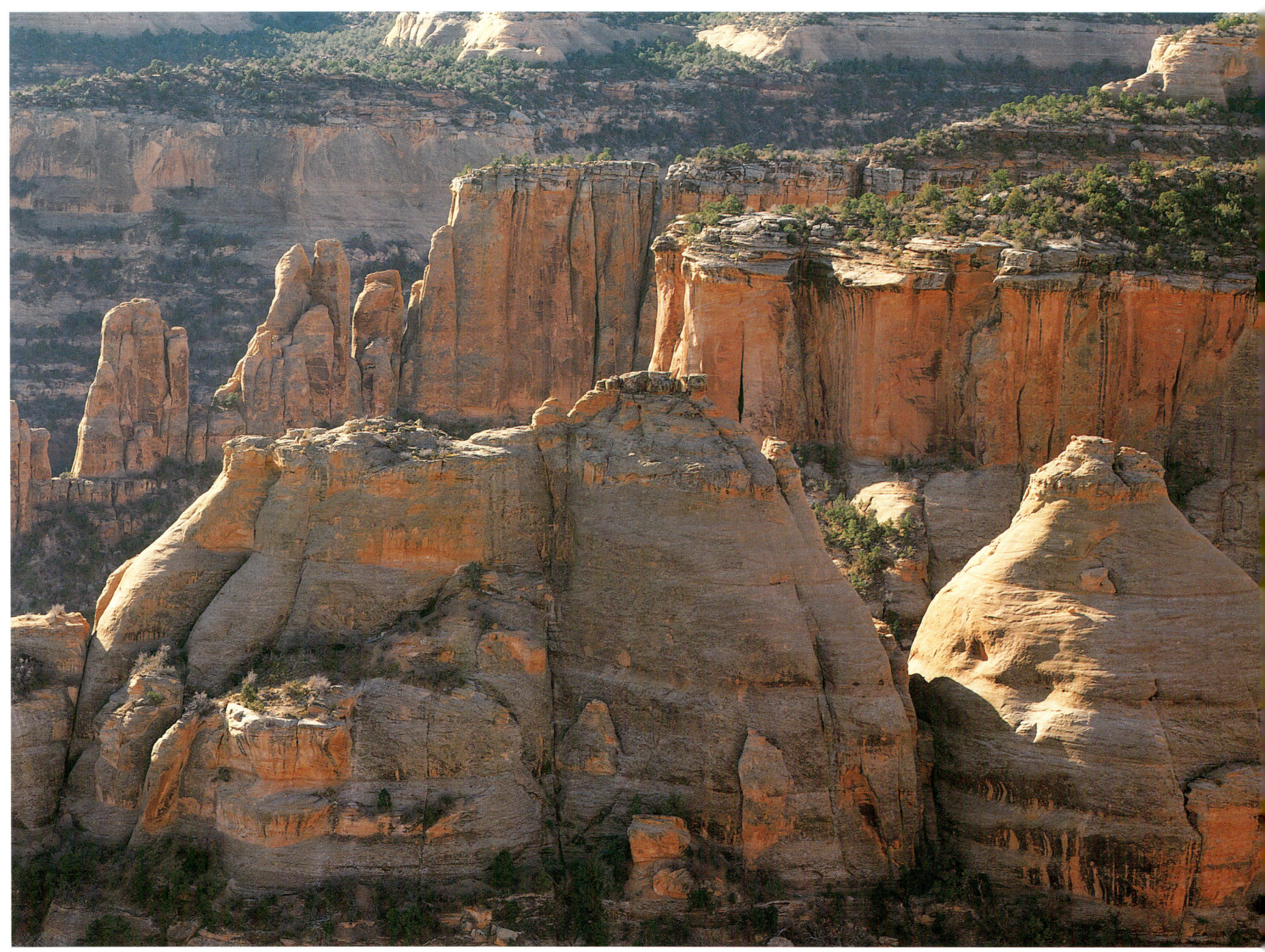

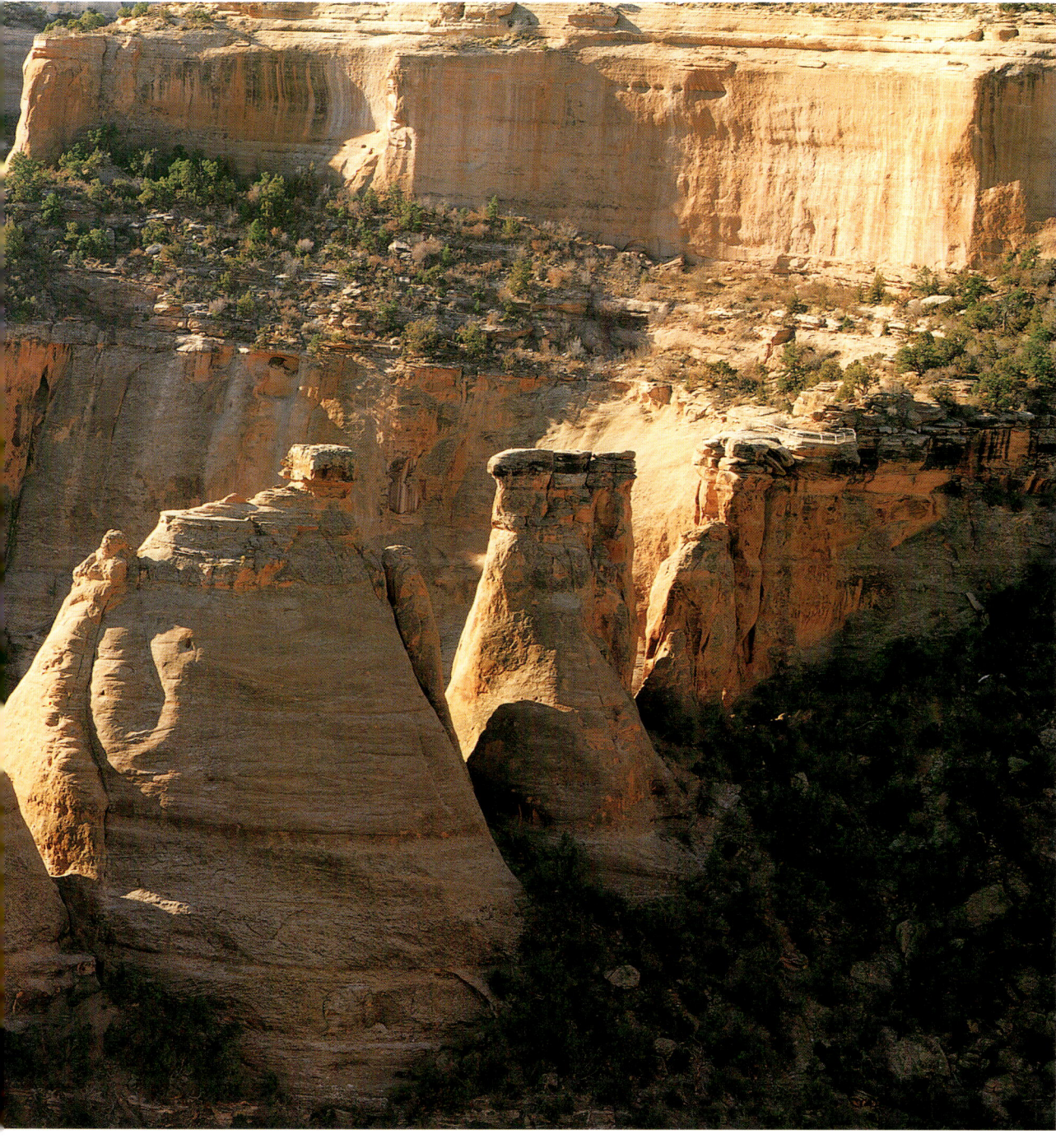

Overleaf: Yampa River Canyon, Dinosaur National Monument

Left: Colorado National Monument

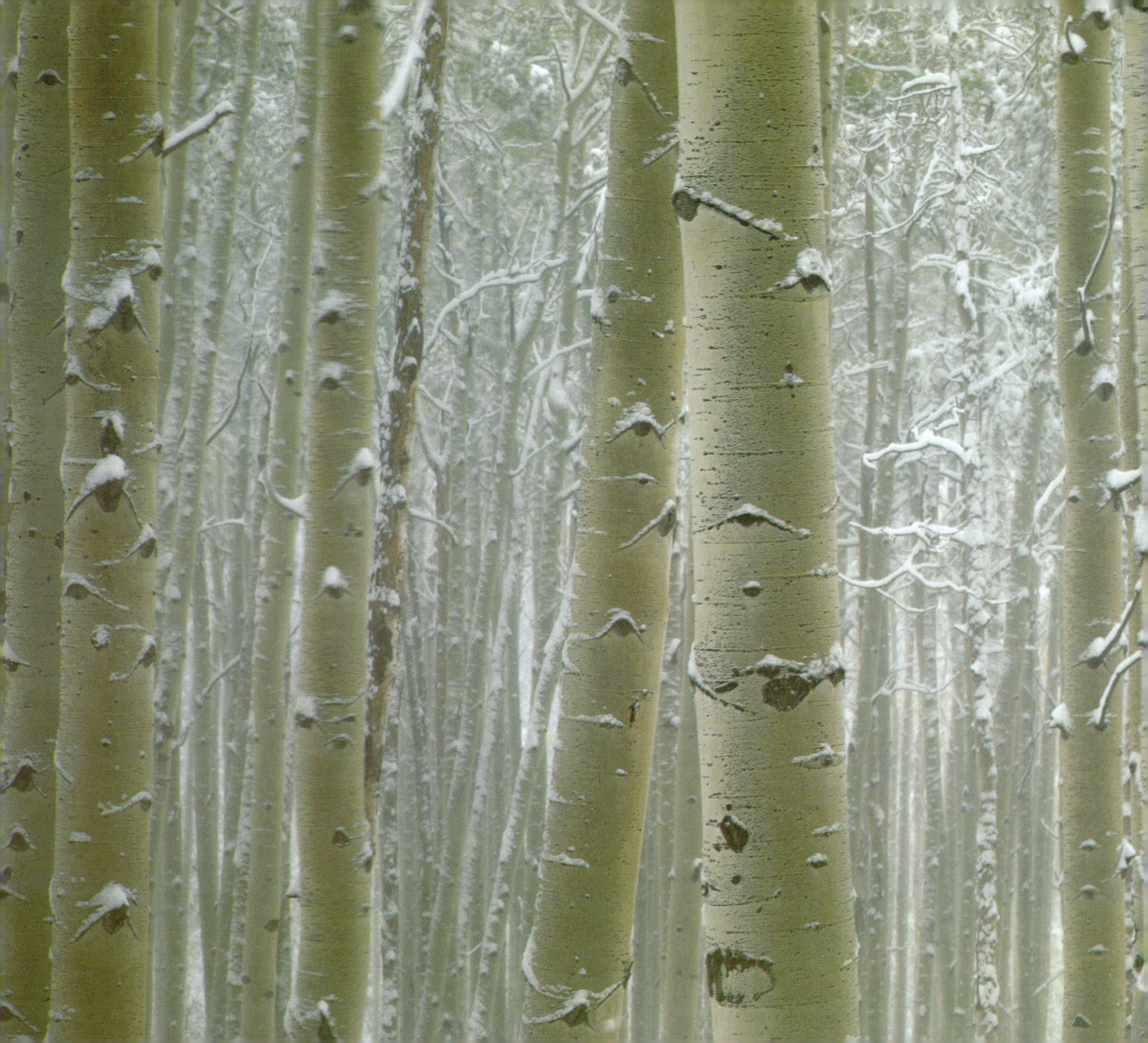

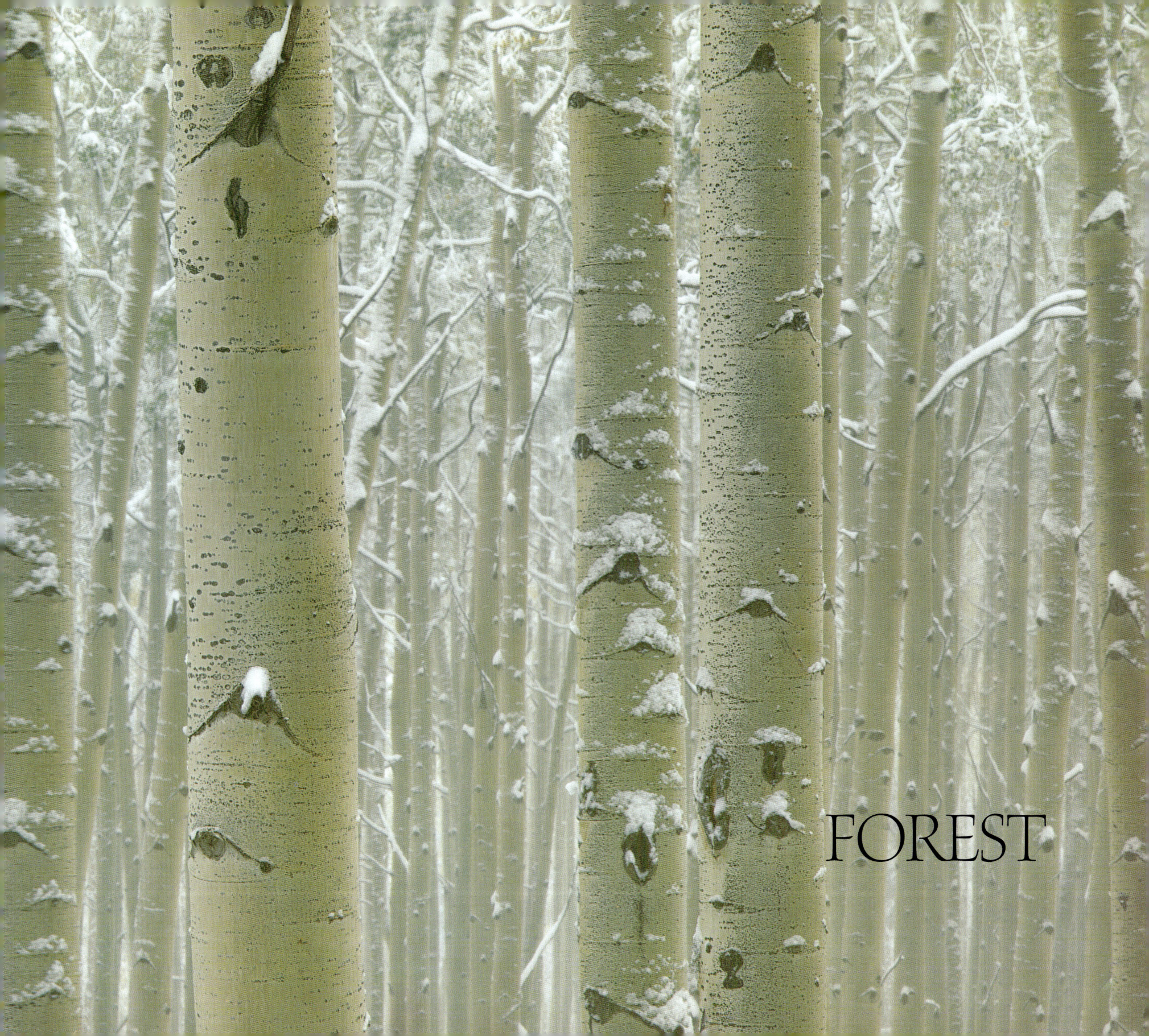

FOREST

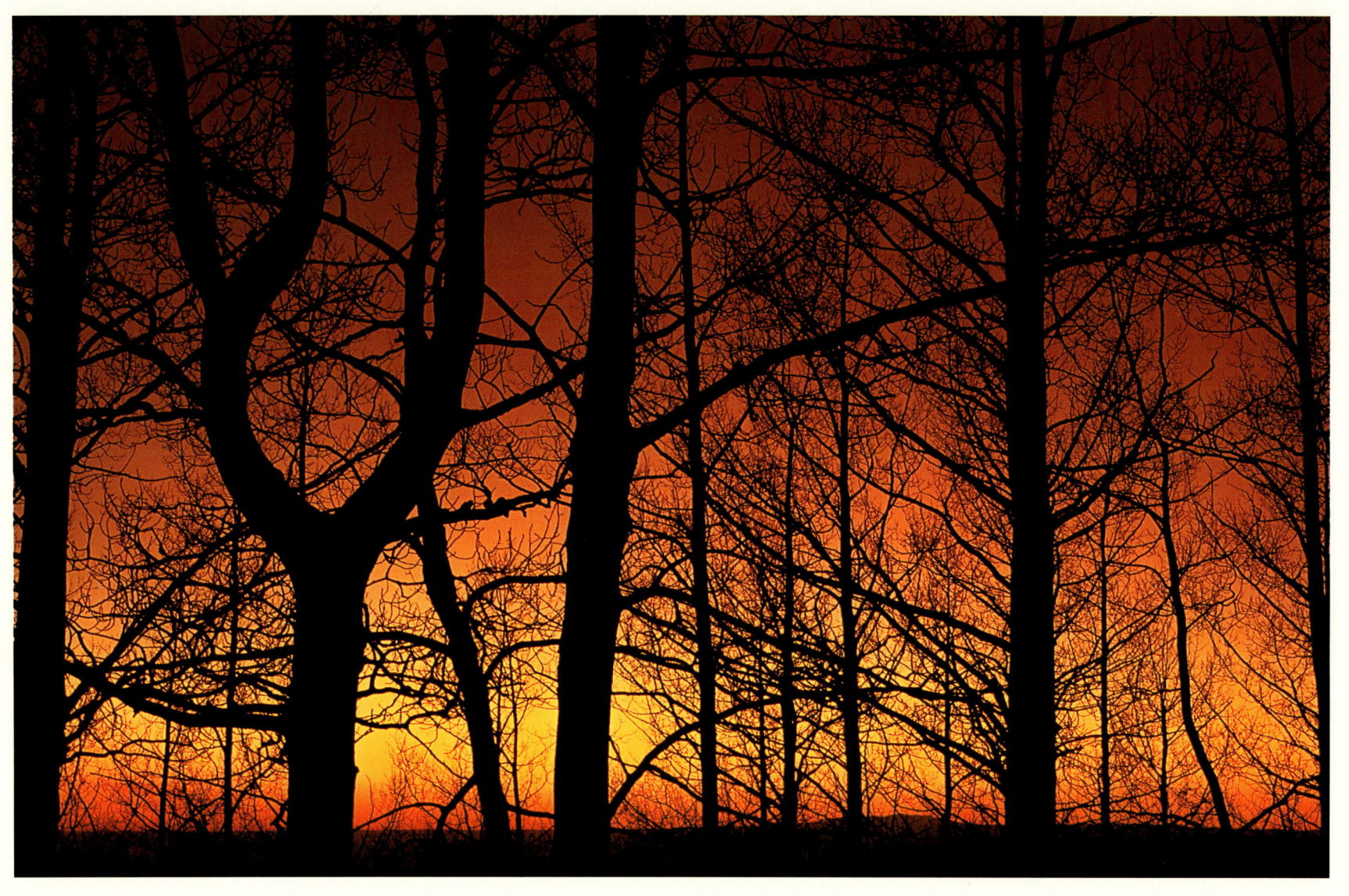

Winterkill forest. Trees fallen from last winter's heavy snows and wind, toppled over each other with crazy geometry. Even with all the dead and downed, the summer forest remains thick with living Engelmann spruce and subalpine firs, verging on black in their

Overleaf: Quaking aspen (*Populus tremuloides*), Roaring Fork River Valley

Left: Quaking aspen (*Populus tremuloides*), San Juan Mountains

ecliptic light. A messy place, these damp mountain forests. Wild rose brambles are like barbed wire. Elk listen to you, hearing your grumbles as you lumber your way through. Mountain lions keep their distance, smelling your tracks after you have gone.

Few tree species besides the spruce and fir are able to reproduce in this heavy shade, so trees come in limited variety, creating a common, stable structure around which the inundating undergrowth can spread. The majority of precipitation in Colorado falls in these subalpine forests, and the shaded cover keeps the water in place. Compared to the more arid Arizona, where 95 percent of annual precipitation is steamed and sweated back to the atmosphere, nearly all snow and rain are protected in these Colorado forests, stored to feed the rivers and aquifers in the lands below. If the subalpine ecosystem were suddenly erased, the entire state would dry like a curling sheet of mud.

As I traveled through the security of these dark lines in the high headwaters of Dallas Creek on a western mountain range, far into the timber, I saw a mule deer. This was not an unusual sighting, but encountering any living creature within the drapes and stalks of a thicket is riveting, even a chattering red squirrel. The deer stood on a steep pitch above the creek. I saw it and froze to watch. When it found my scent among the opulent, moist smells of the forest, its head lifted from grazing. Grass hung mid-chew. It was a buck, a male deer. I couldn't count its antler points between all of the trees, but I could see it had many: an old animal. Its head moved stiffly as it watched between spruce trunks. It knew all of the ins and outs of this forest, the alchemy of scents, the patterns and motions and seasons and stillness. I looked at the ground so that my eyes would not show white against the shadowy backdrop. At my feet was a mushroom broken like a yeasty biscuit, and deer tracks with the shape of praying hands, minutes-fresh in the garden dirt.

We were on the north face of the range, customarily the far wetter, far more vegetated side of the mountains. In a sanctuary forest like this, elements are judged by their lack of presence more than anything. The deer was hardly there. Dappled in heavy shadows, blocked by the stilted trunks of trees, it could barely be seen. When I walked ahead, lifting my left leg to cross a log, he bounded away. Not like an elk that will crash through branches with locomotive intent, or a coyote that will disturb the first two loose stones and then nothing, but with clean, hard bounces that would rip human tendons from the bone. Bounces that clear all obstacles, spending more time in the air than on the ground.

I followed. I climbed over mazes of downed trees slumping into the moss and mud below. I pulled myself ahead with branches and looked for motions in the half-light.

Tracks were sometimes the only things to pursue. They dug into the soil, leaving sprays of damp loam. The deer and I met again, his head flicking from one side of a tree to another because he could not see all of me at once. He shook loose from me and leapt away. I found his prints again. I followed them, stepping over the fallen wood and the great heaps of moss. Seedling trees twined up through the debris. It takes forty years for a spruce to reach a height of four feet, four hundred years to go the rest of the way. The elegantly bowed flower of the fairy slipper would survive only through this season, then die. I was surrounded by an organic calendar.

I saw the deer, moving between the trees like a trickster in a hall of mirrors. He was observing, safely keeping track of me. Ears held rigid, head still. Wet, black nose. Antlers like branches. This animal watched me and thought of me in the way animals think, making a decision without a single comment or complete sentence; with a sniff, reading a hundred books at once. You never know what is a beginning or an ending for a wild animal in a place like this. Or even if there is such a thing.

When you think of wilderness, likely you are thinking of places you can touch, the land that presses back against the weight of your foot. You think of the frontier pushed by Lewis and Clark or the water that carries the name of the creek you walk beside. You think of the pristine piece of ground accessed by some vague animal trail.

But there is another wilderness down in the forest. It is not so simple that it can be told here on paper. It comes in the secrets of club moss, in a constellation of white mushrooms. It is what a deer sees through a hundred trees. It is darkness in the middle of the day. It is the hive of mystery, each of the small, complex things brought together, heaped on each other, making walking difficult, revealing the details.

The deer eventually got away from me. It moved behind clumps of trees and darted off before I knew it was out of sight. I could not find its tracks again. Even smelling the air, I found nothing but the fertile scent of decaying wood.

Right: Dallas Divide, Uncompahgre National Forest

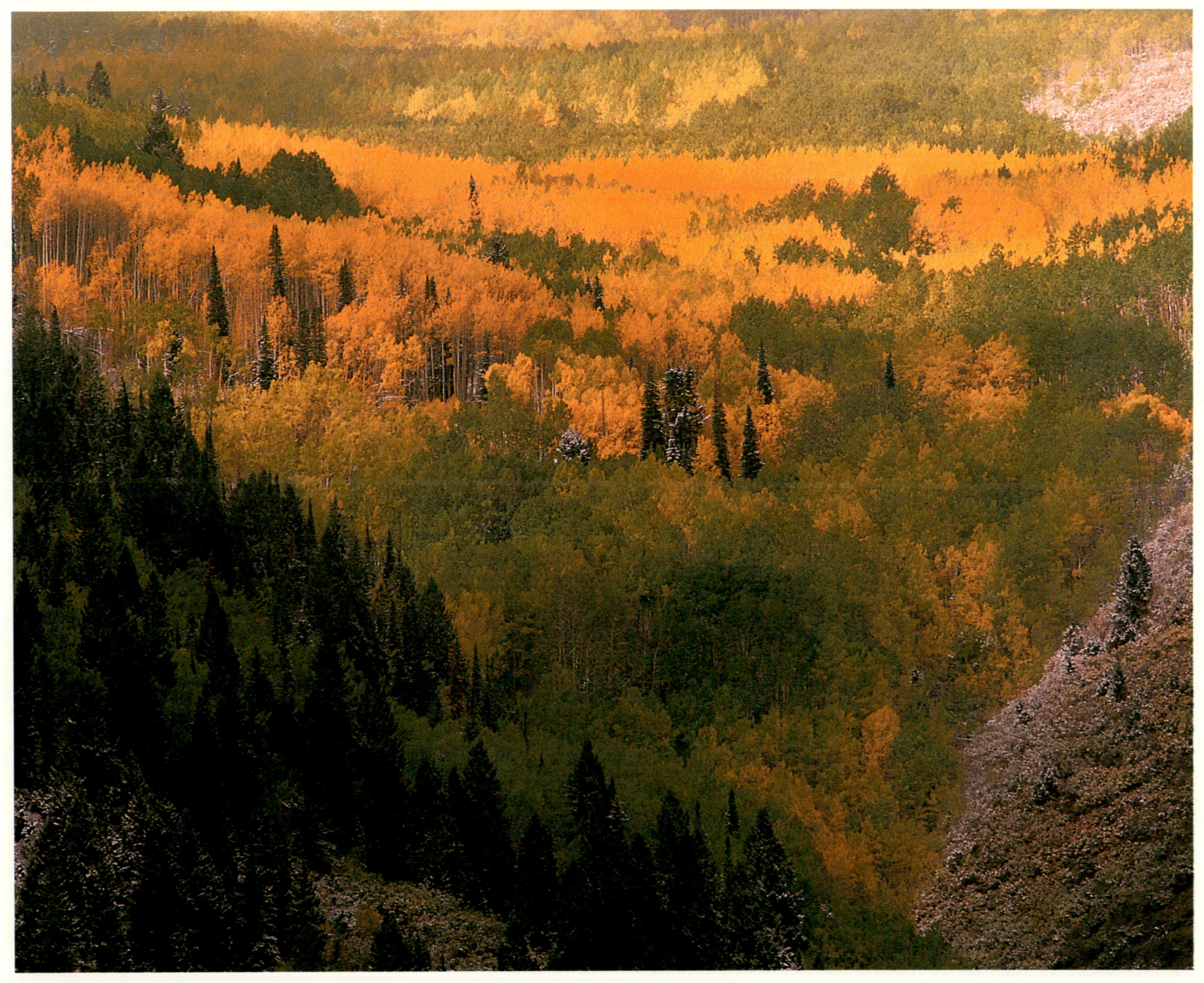

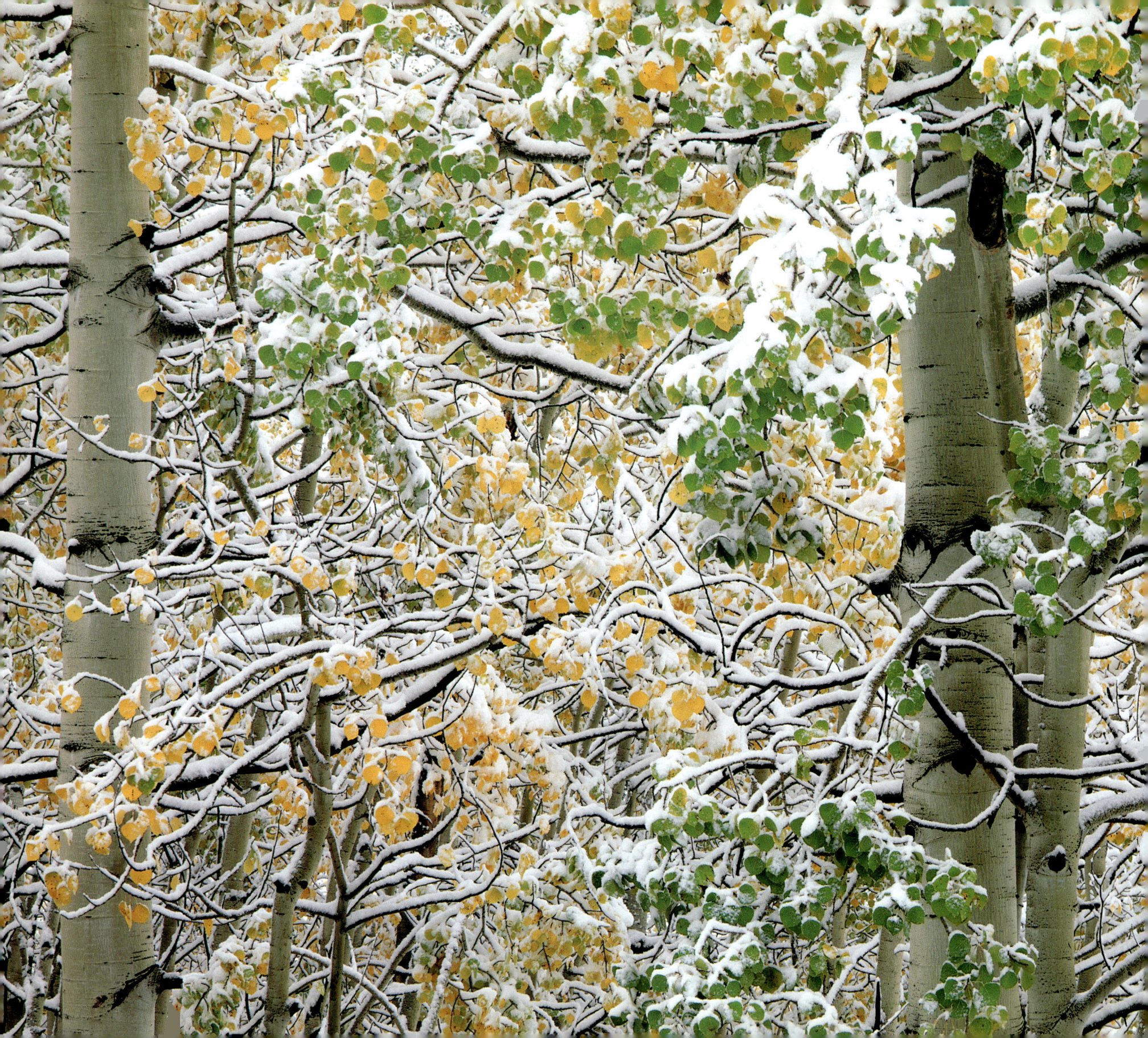

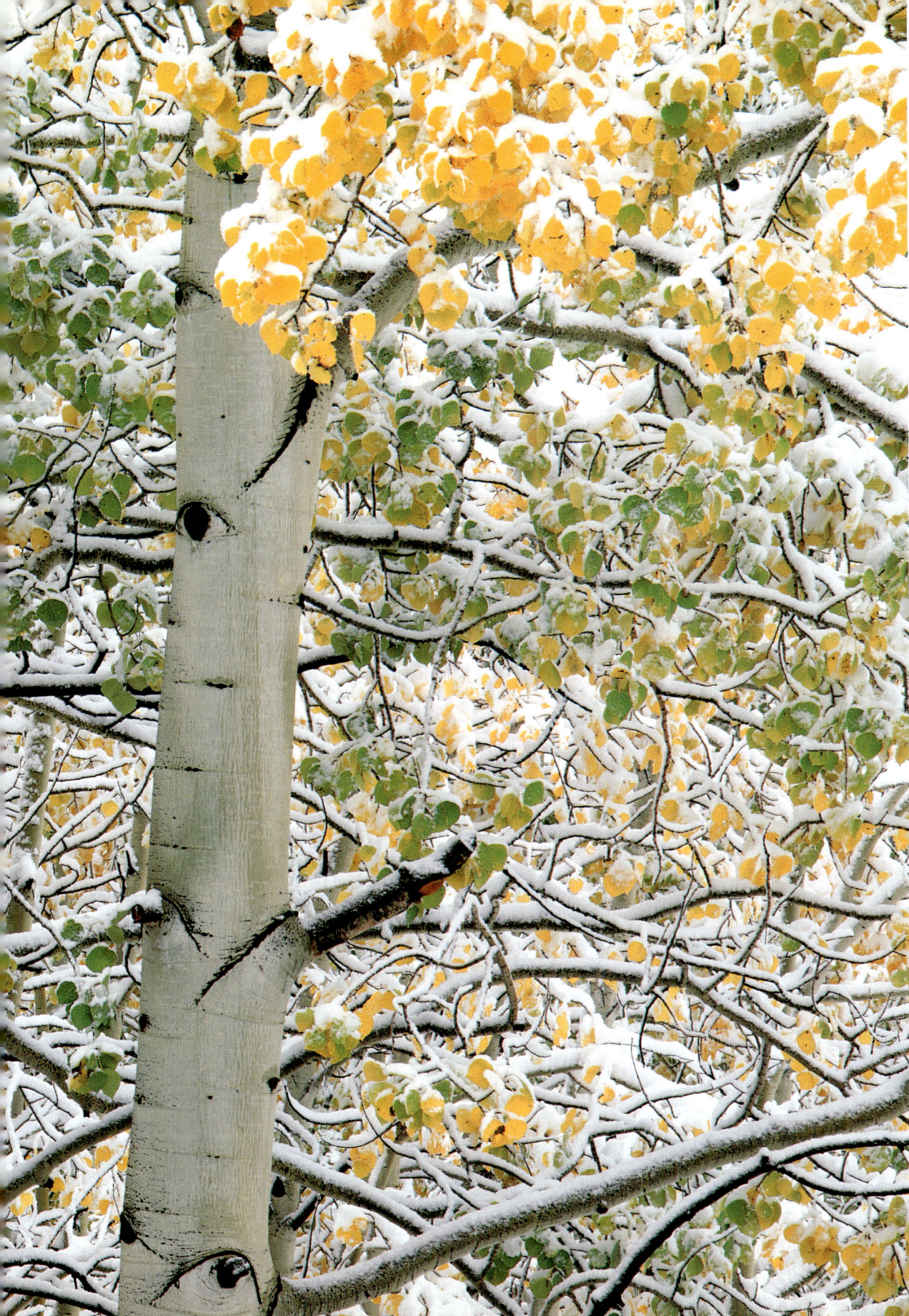

Quaking aspen (*Populus tremuloides*), Maroon Creek Valley

Below: Northern saw-whet owl (*Aegolius acadicus*), Rocky Mountain National Park

Right: American pine marten (*Martes americana*), Rocky Mountain National Park

Far right: Quaking aspen (*Populus tremuloides*), Maroon Bells-Snowmass Wilderness

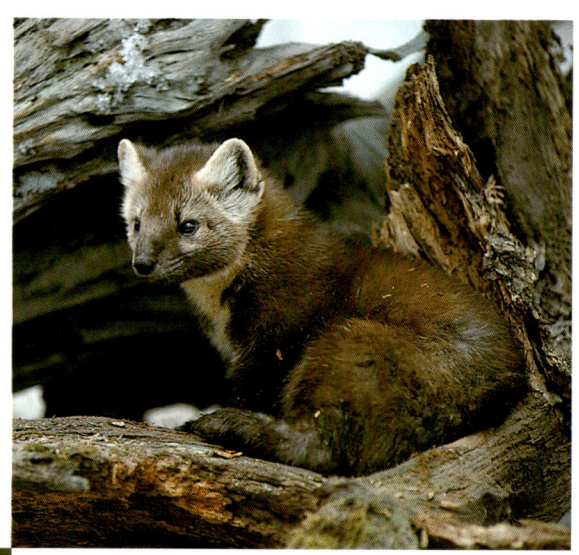

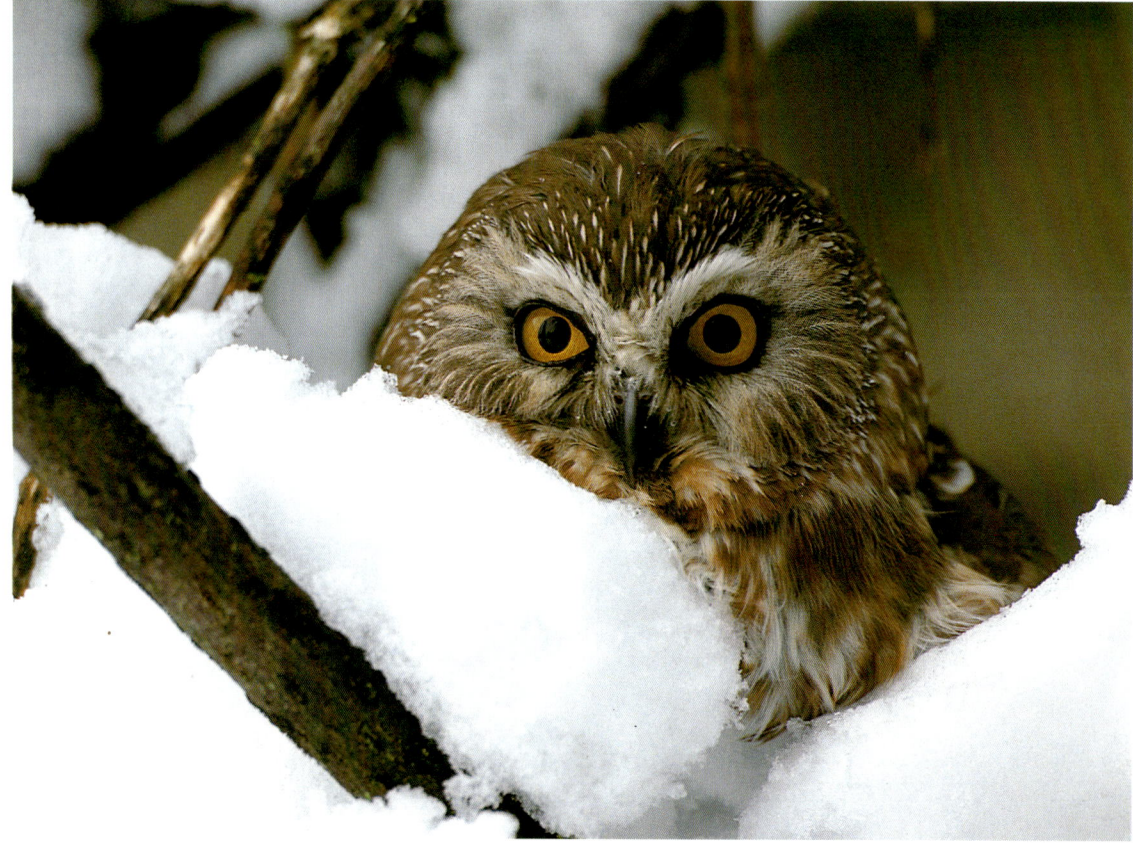

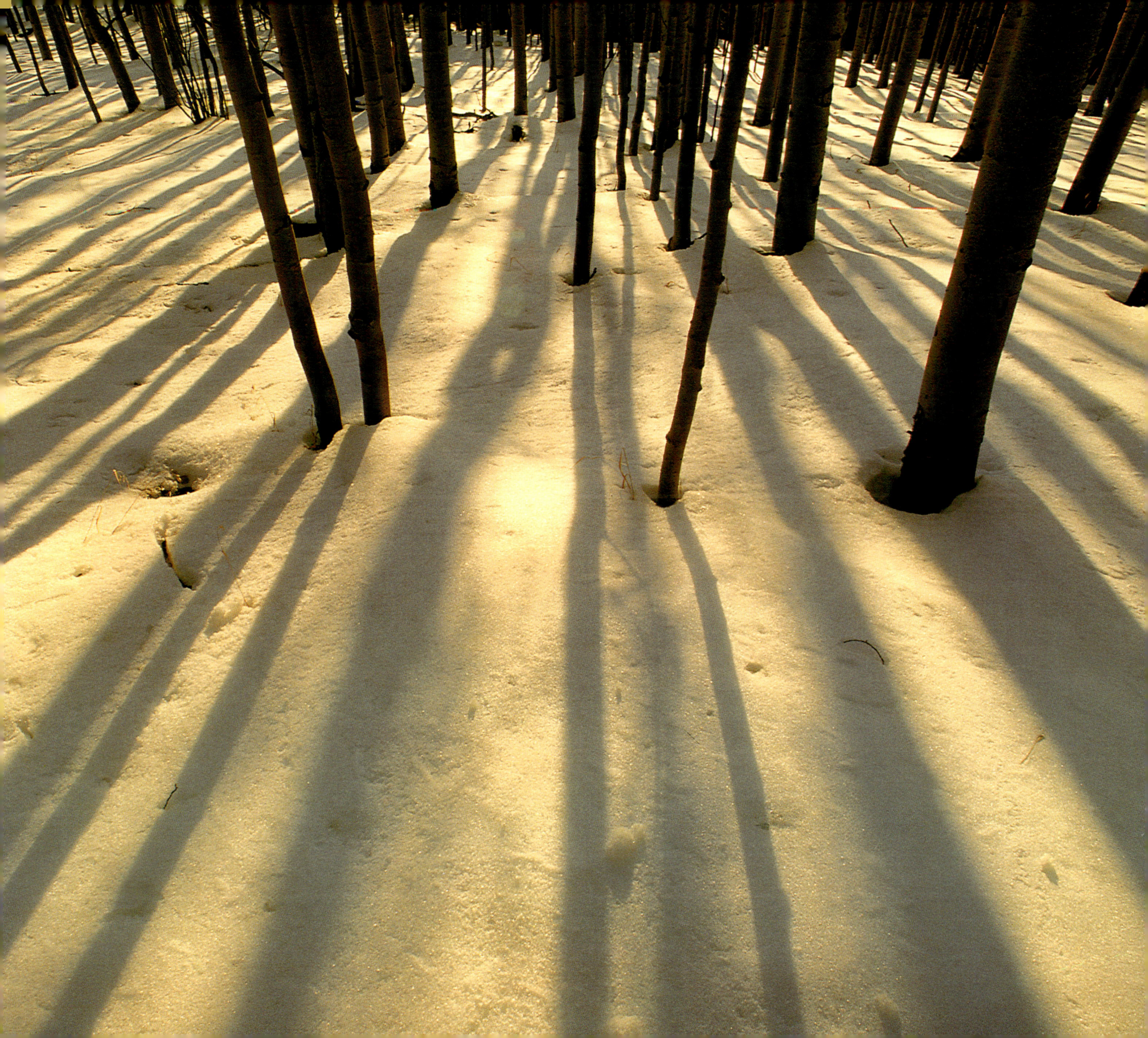

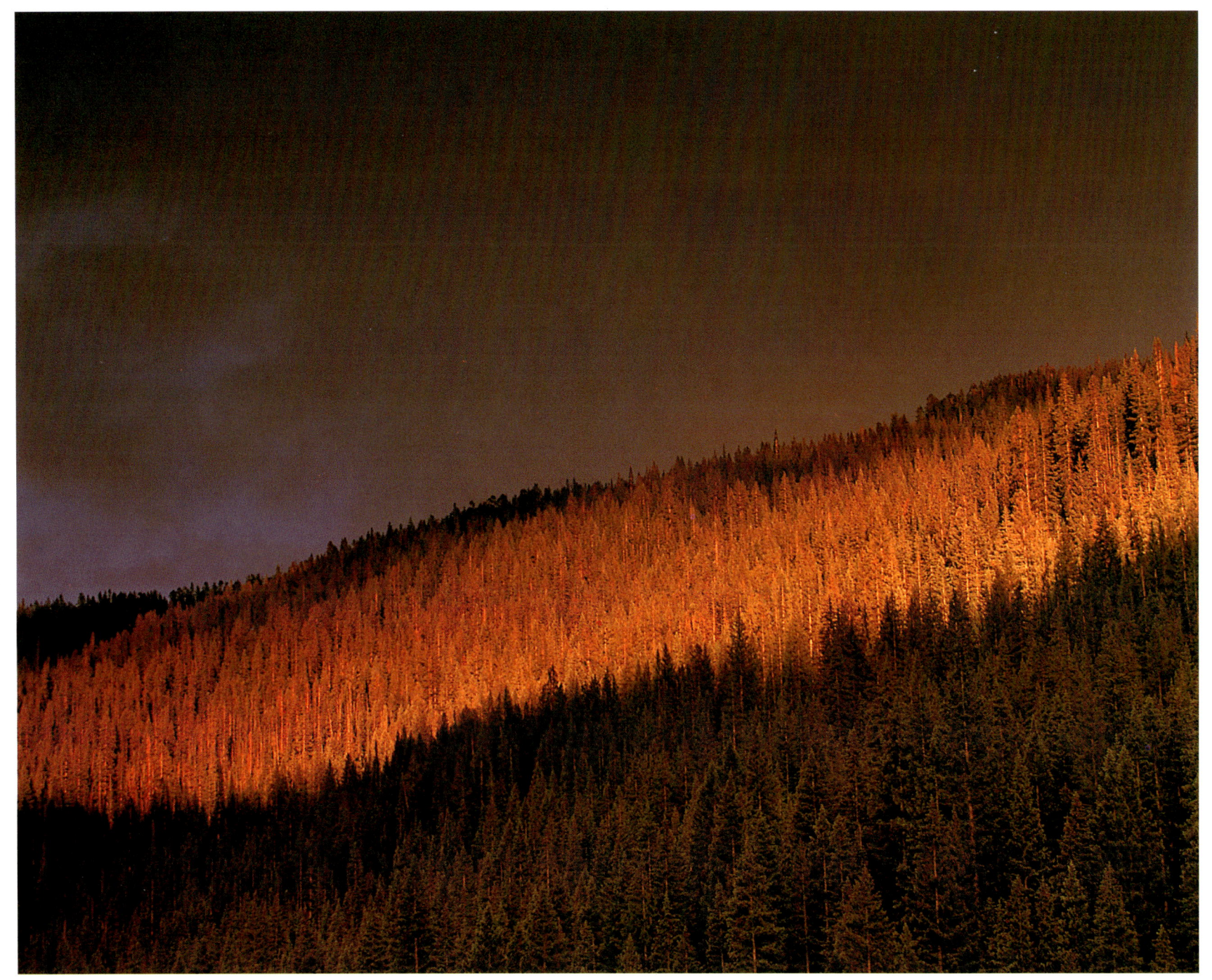

Spruce (*Picea* sp.), Rocky Mountain National Park

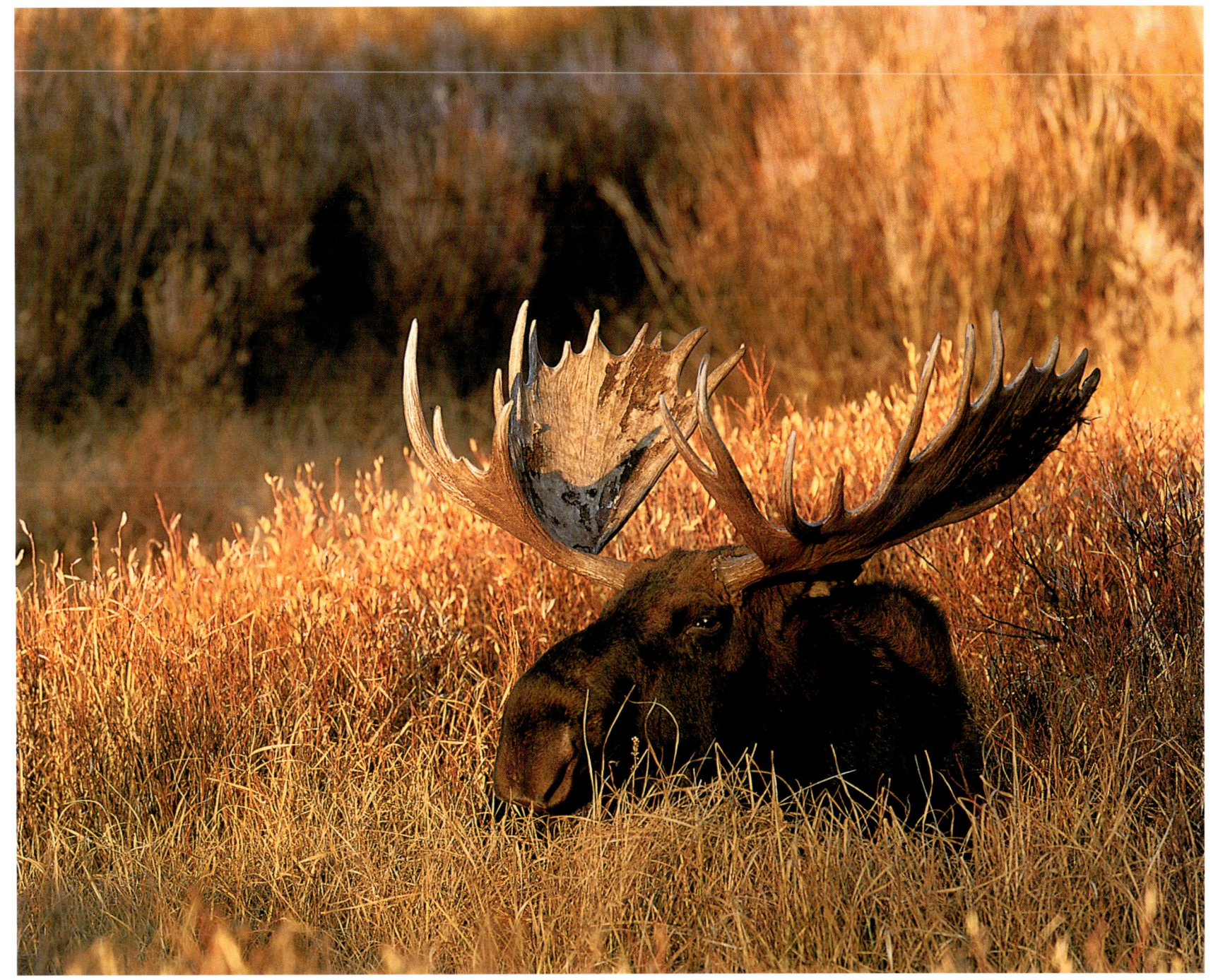
Moose (*Alces alces*), Rocky Mountain National Park

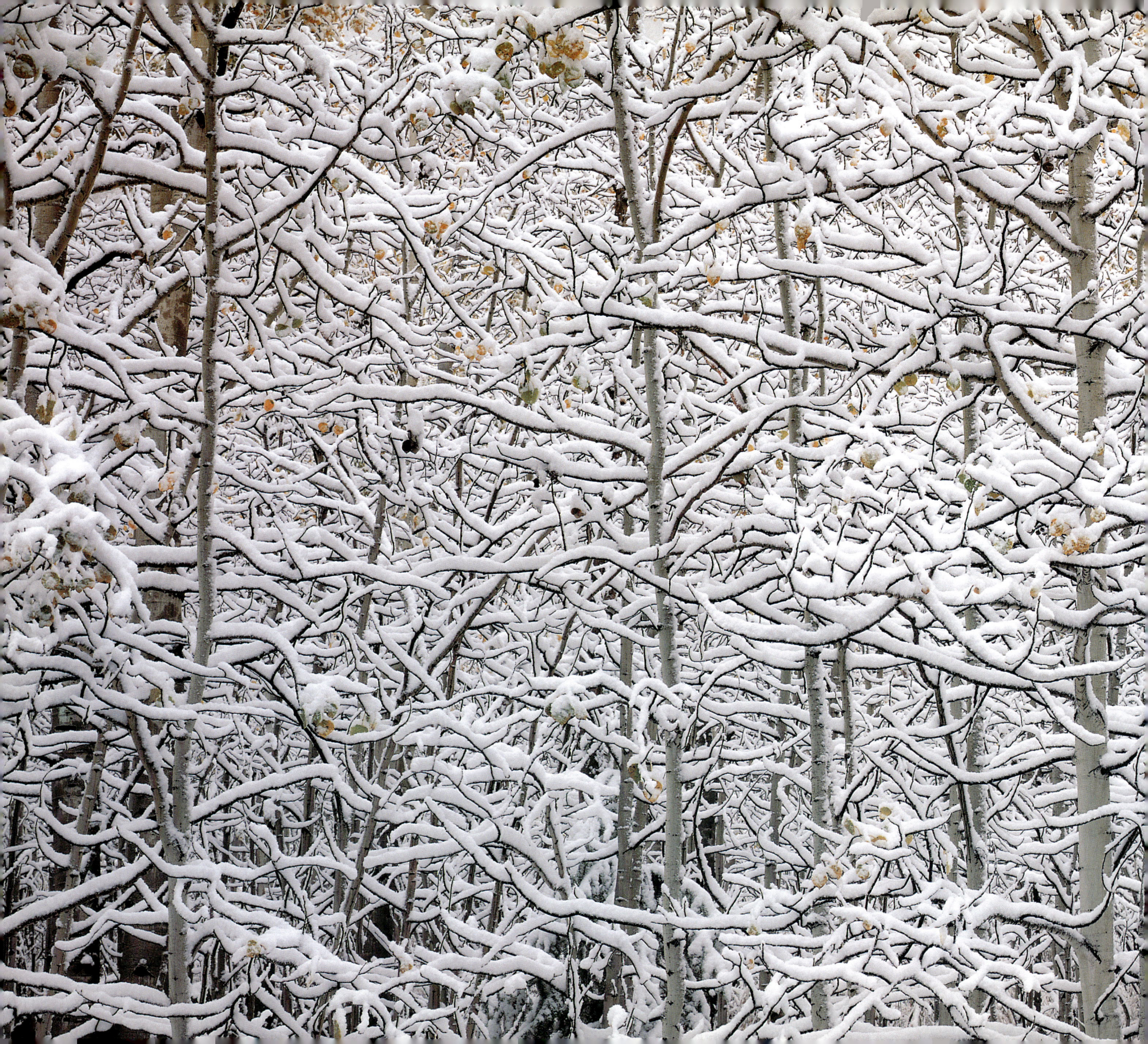

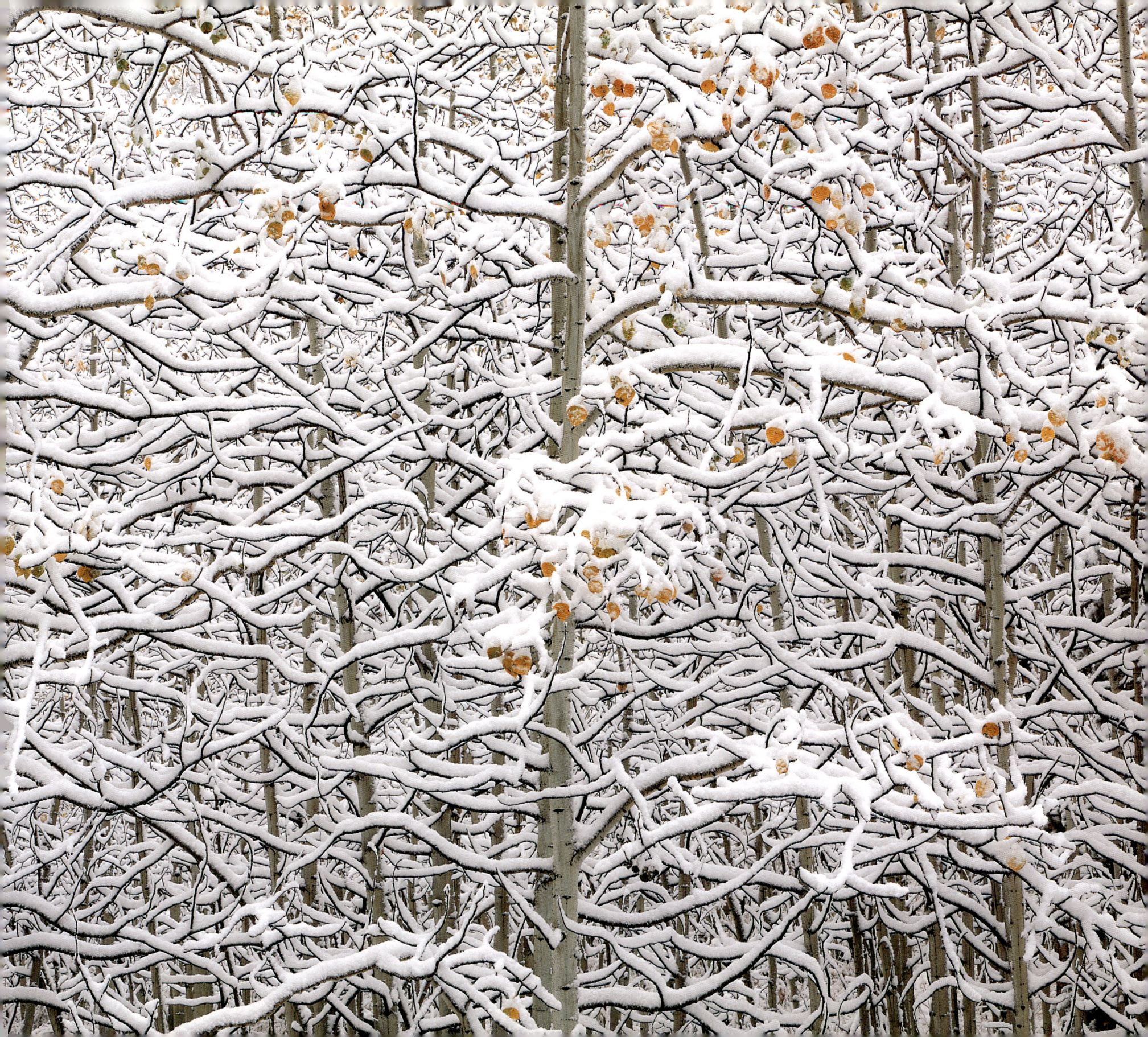

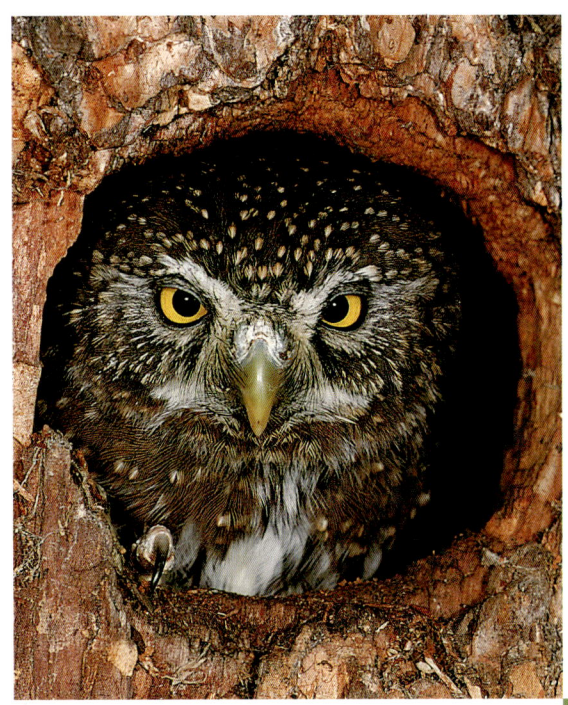

Overleaf: Quaking aspen *(Populus tremuloides)*, Maroon Creek Valley

Left: Northern pygmy-owl *(Glaucidium gnoma)*, Rocky Mountain National Park

Below: Boreal owl *(Aegolius funereus)*, Laramie Mountains

Right: Elk *(Cervus elaphus)*, Rocky Mountain National Park

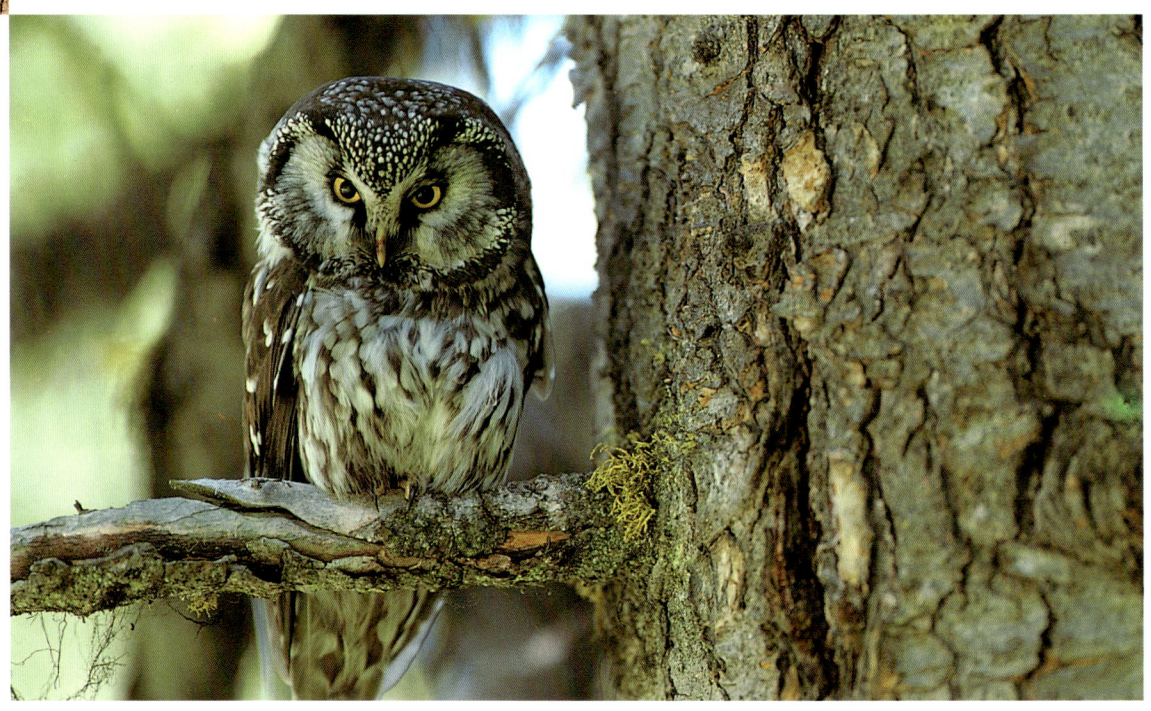

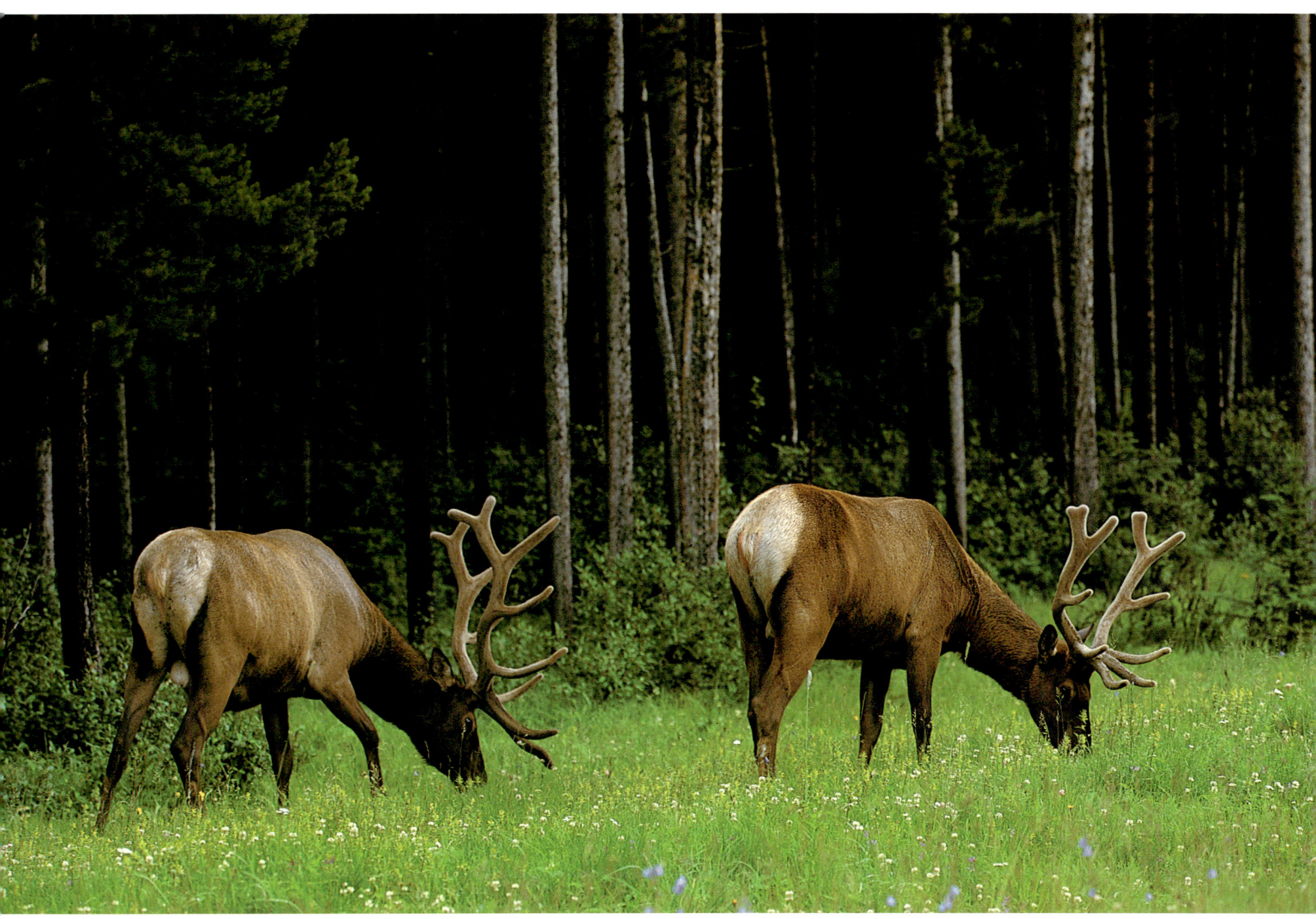

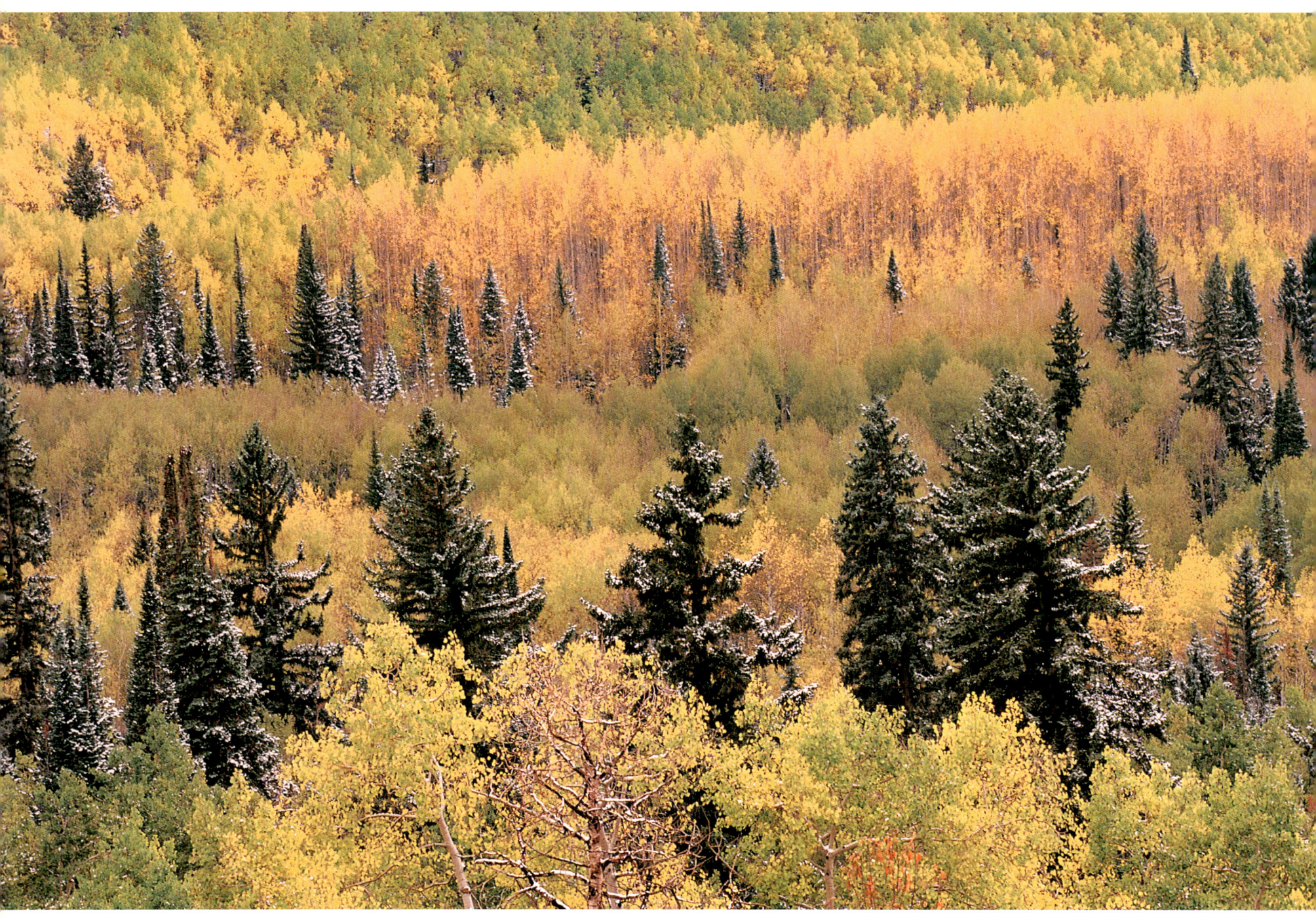

Left: Uncompahgre National Forest

Right: Quaking aspen (*Populus tremuloides*), Uncompahgre National Forest

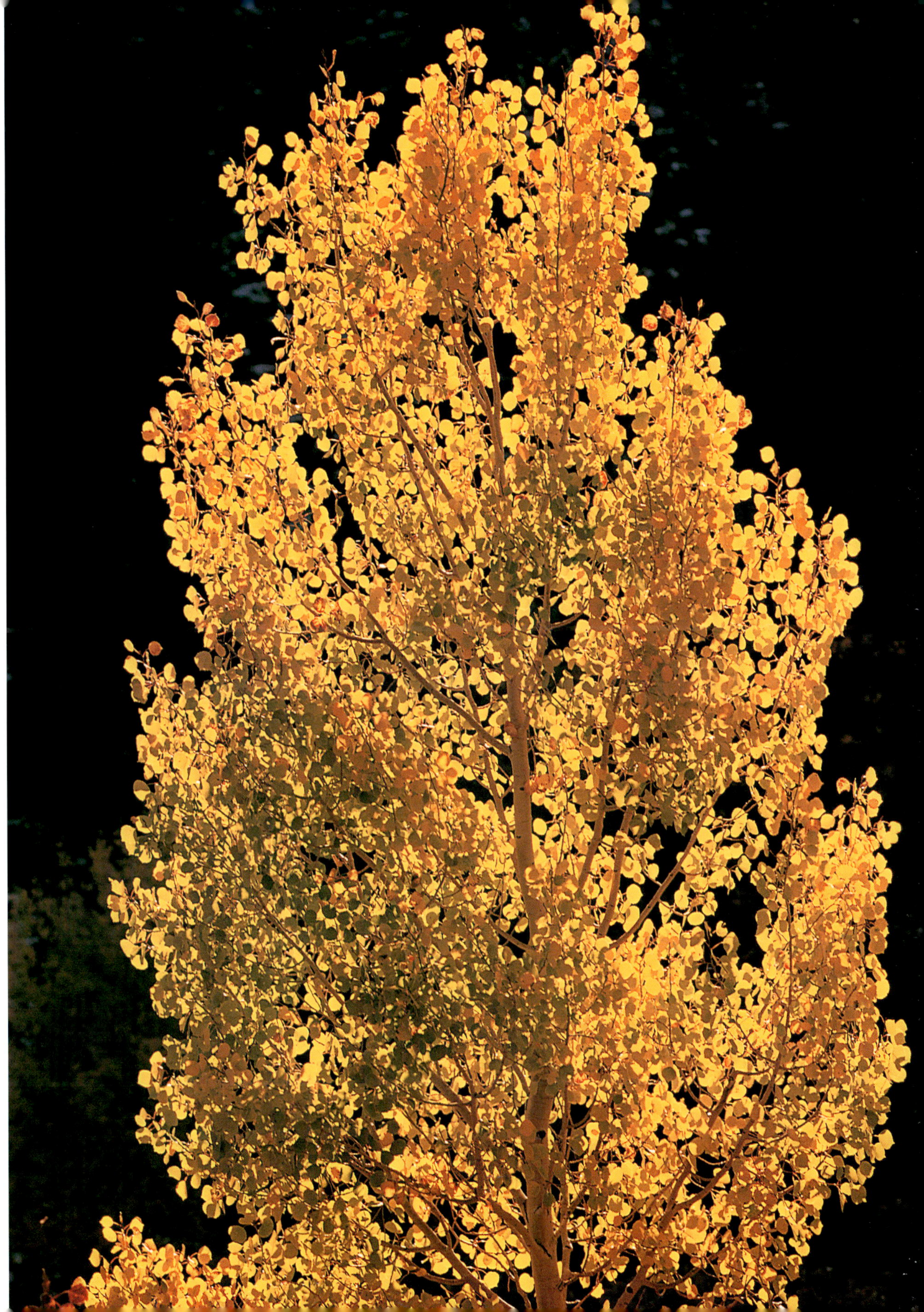

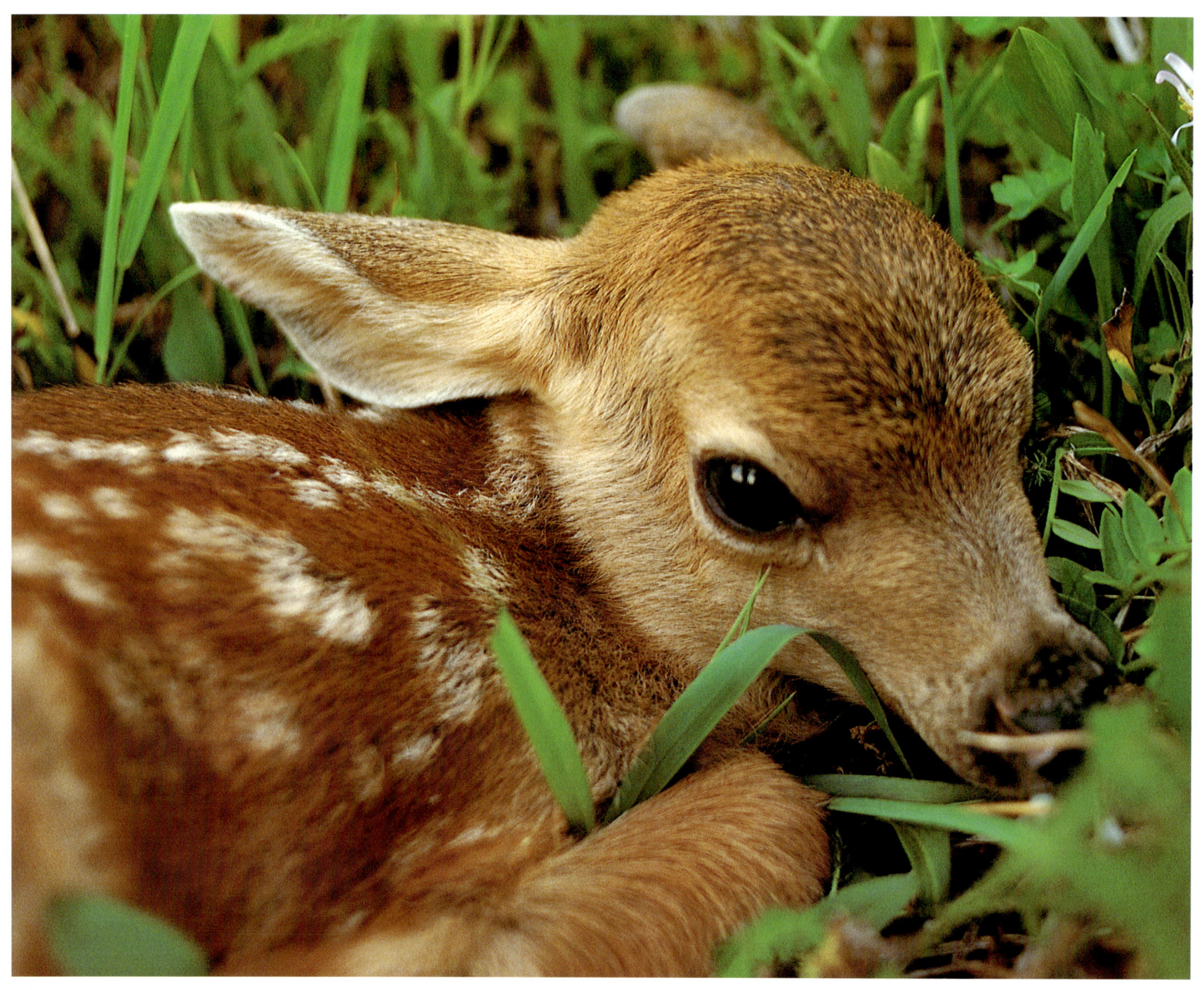

Mule deer (*Odocoileus hemionus*), Rocky Mountain National Park

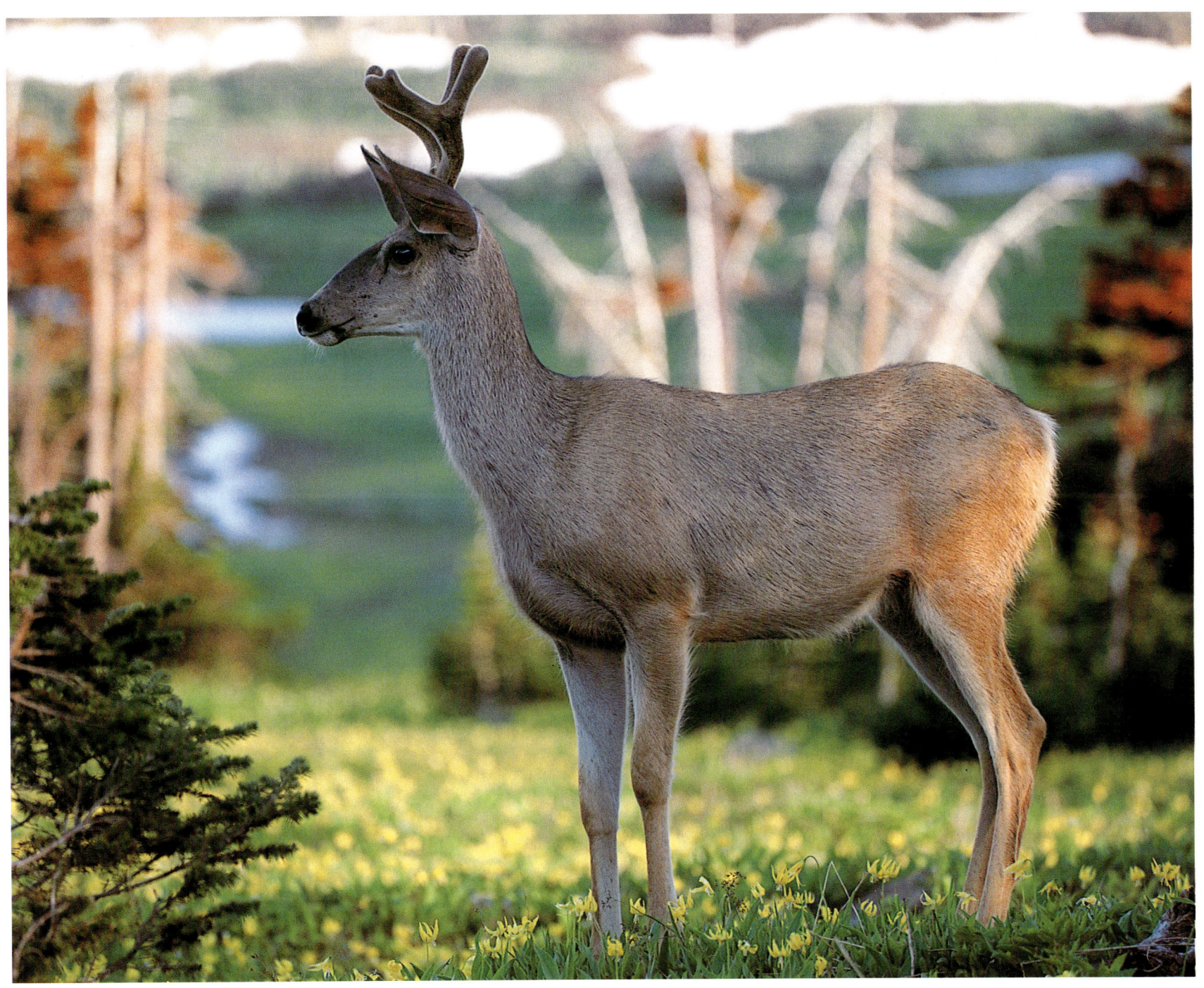

Mule deer (*Odocoileus hemionus*), Rocky Mountain National Park

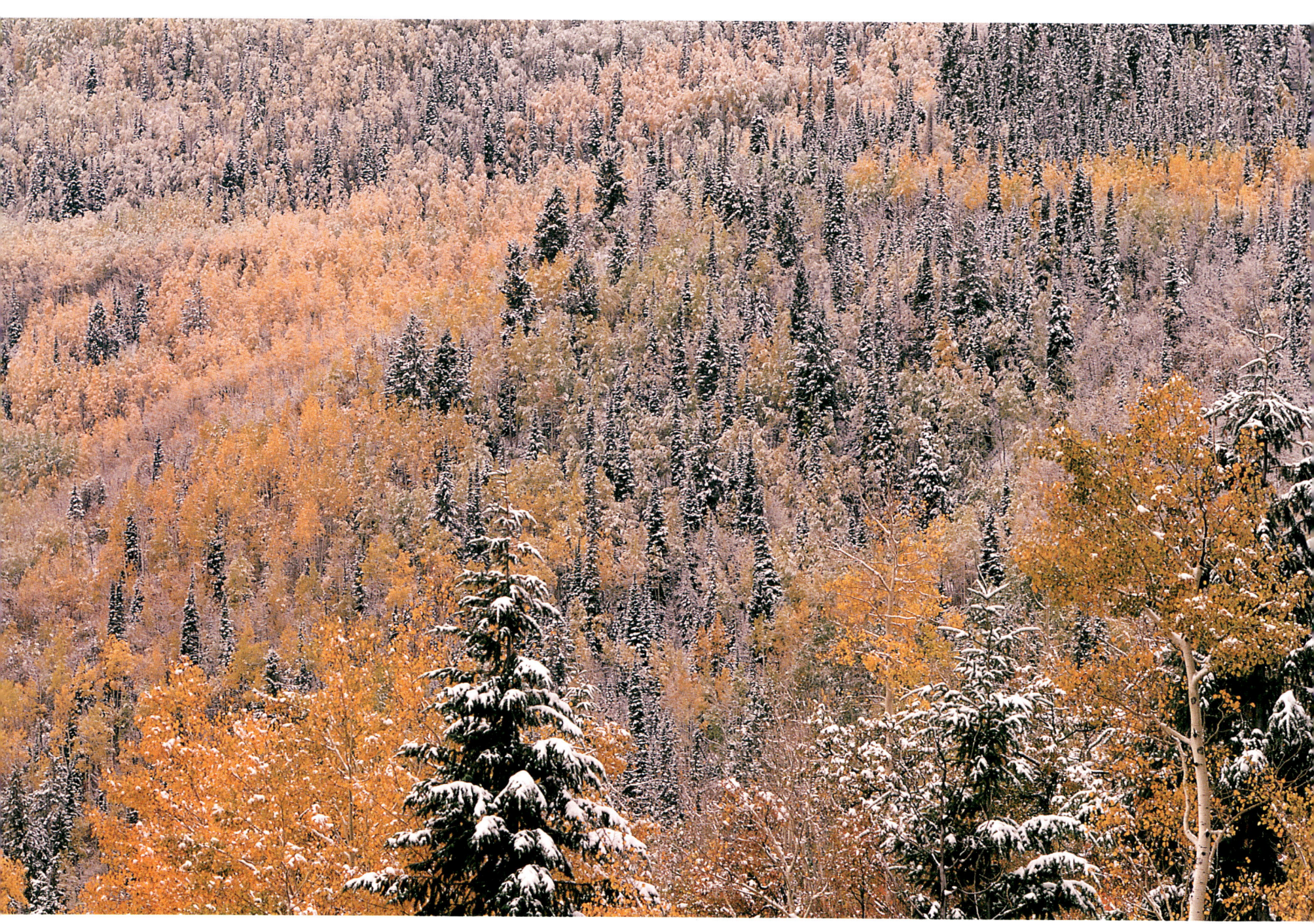

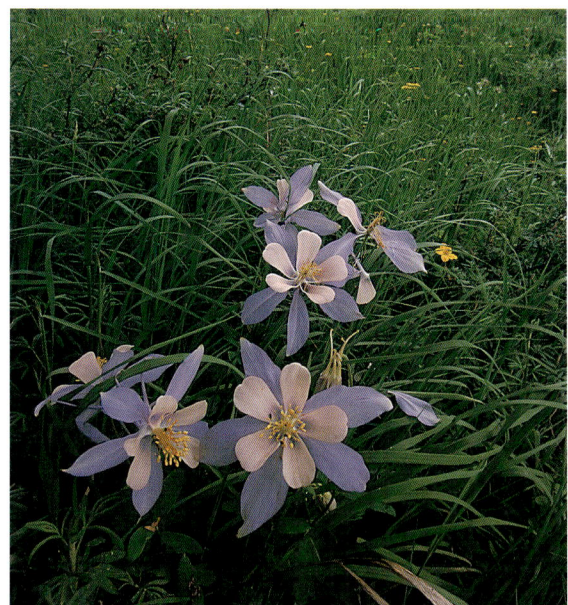

Far left: Dallas Divide, Uncompahgre National Forest

Left: Blue columbine (*Aquilegia coerulea*), San Juan Mountains

Below: Maroon Bells-Snowmass Wilderness

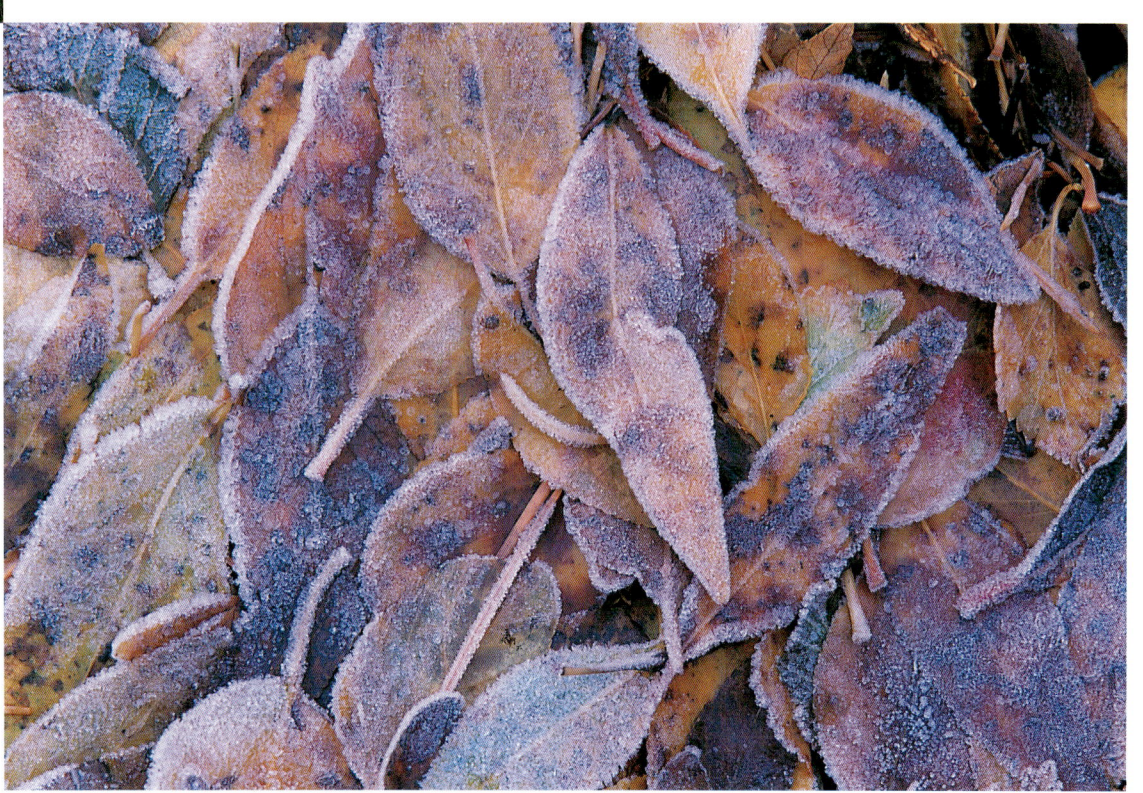

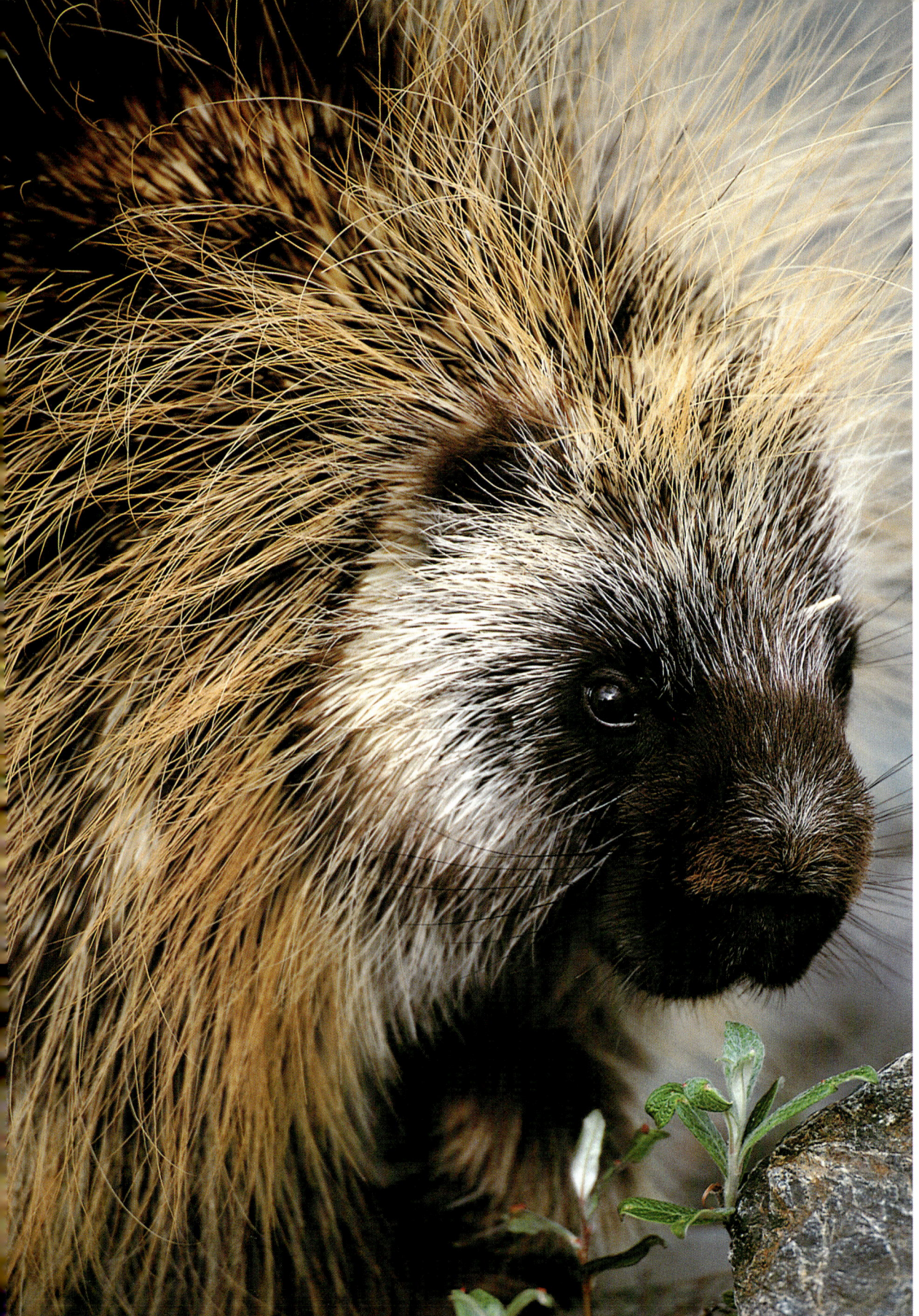

Left: Porcupine (*Erethizon dorsatum*), San Juan Mountains

Right: Quaking aspen (*Populus tremuloides*), Maroon Bells–Snowmass Wilderness

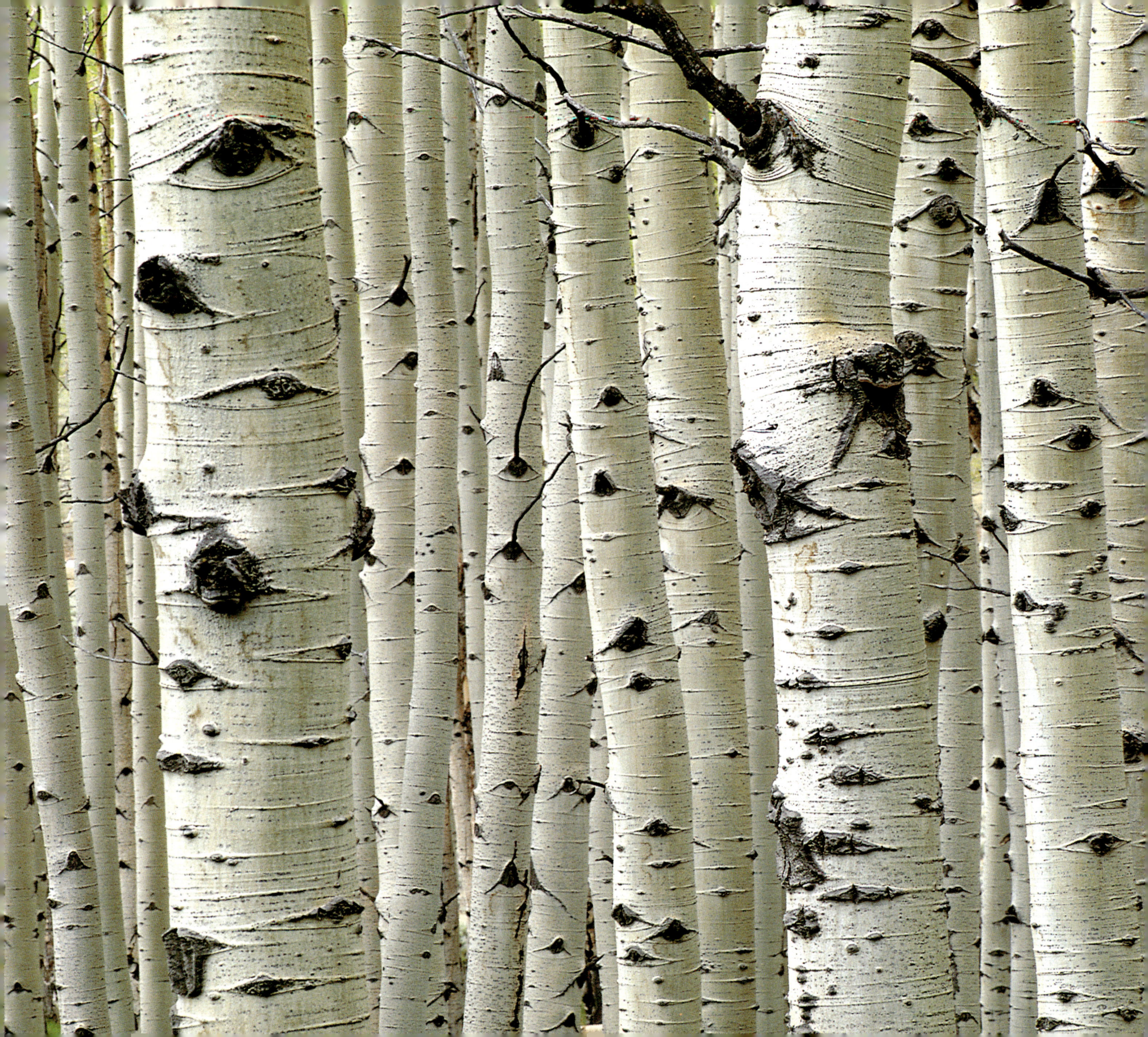

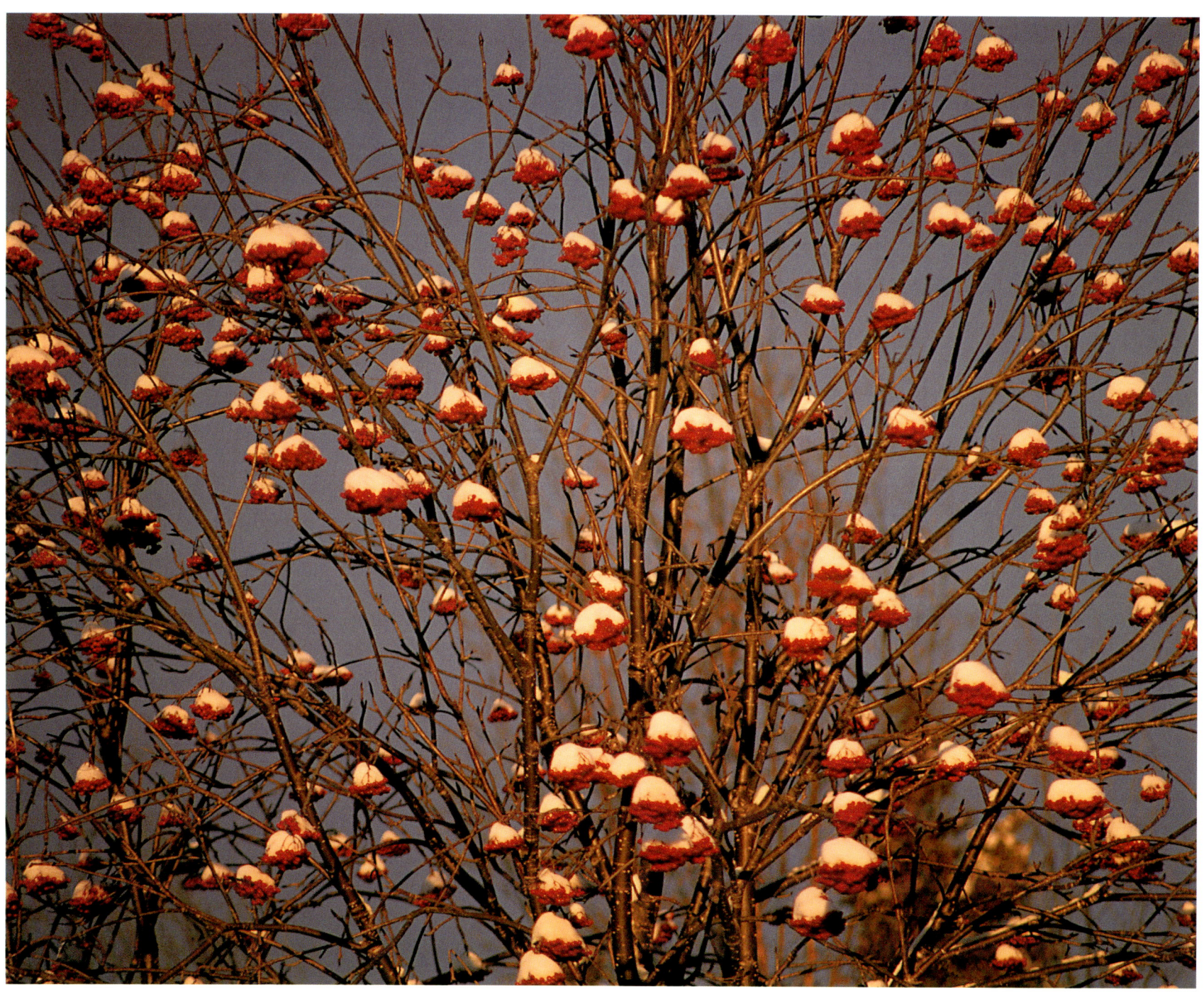

Mountain-ash (*Sorbus scopulina*), Maroon Bells-Snowmass Wilderness

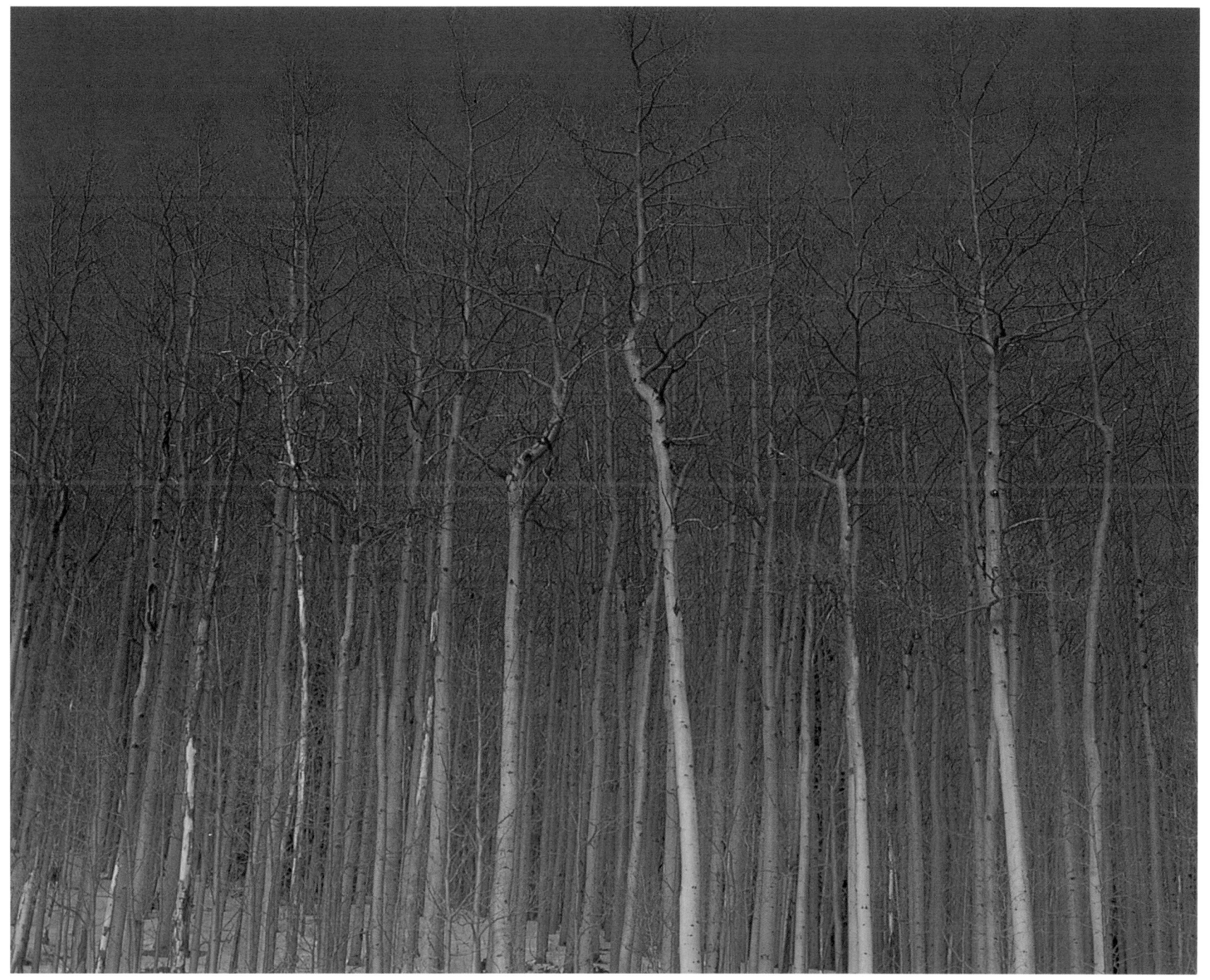

Quaking aspen (*Populus tremuloides*), Elk Mountains

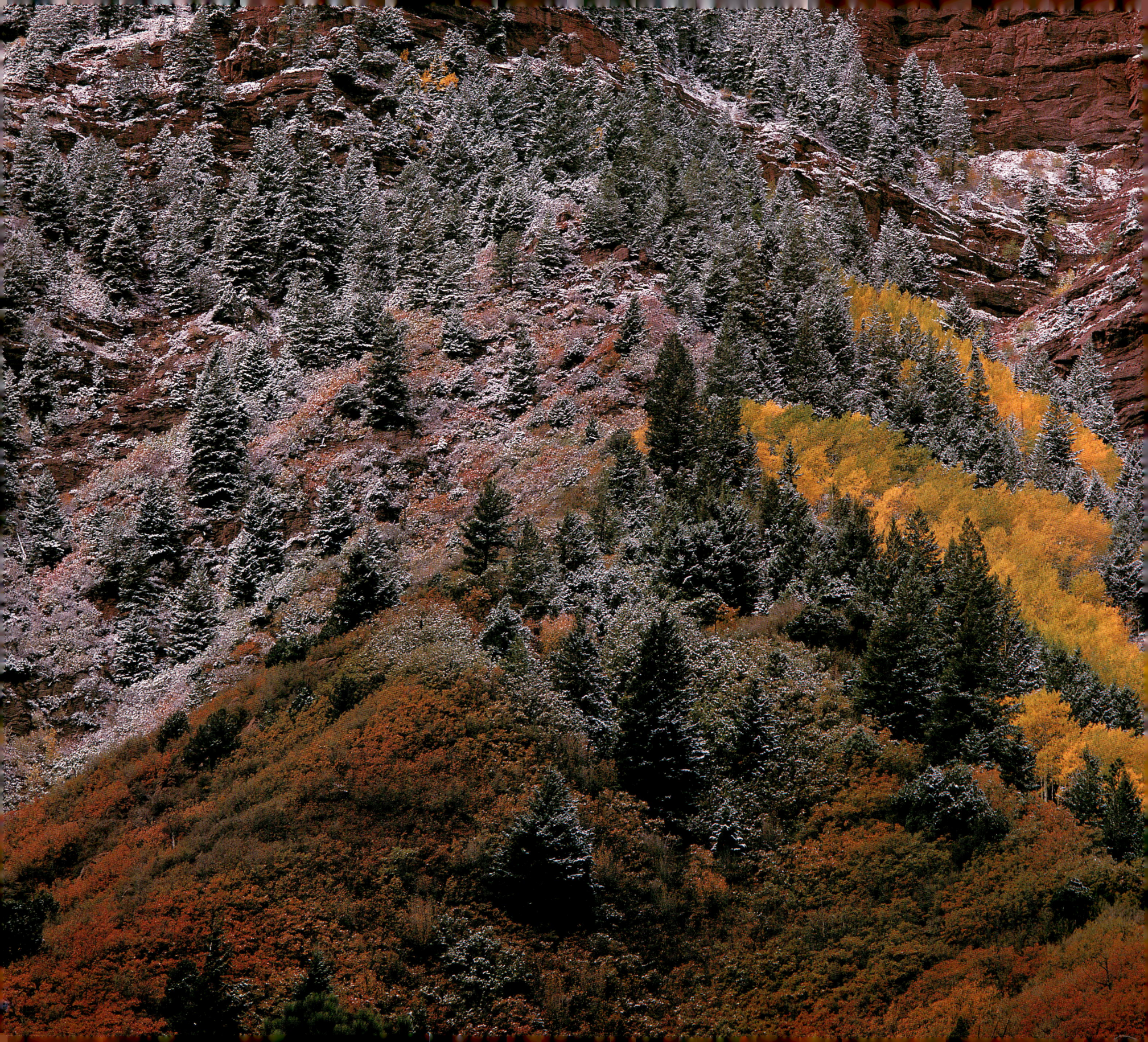

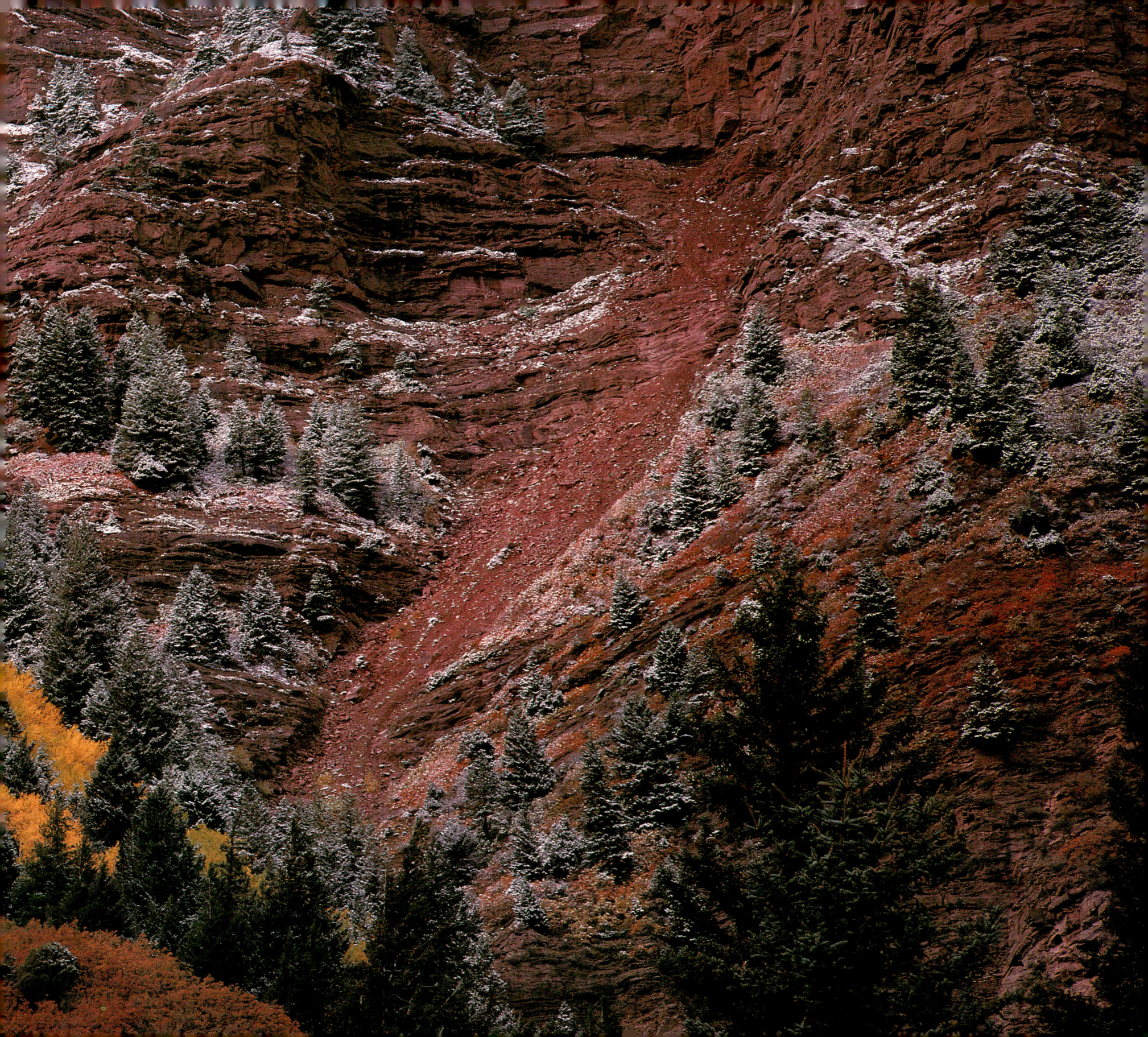

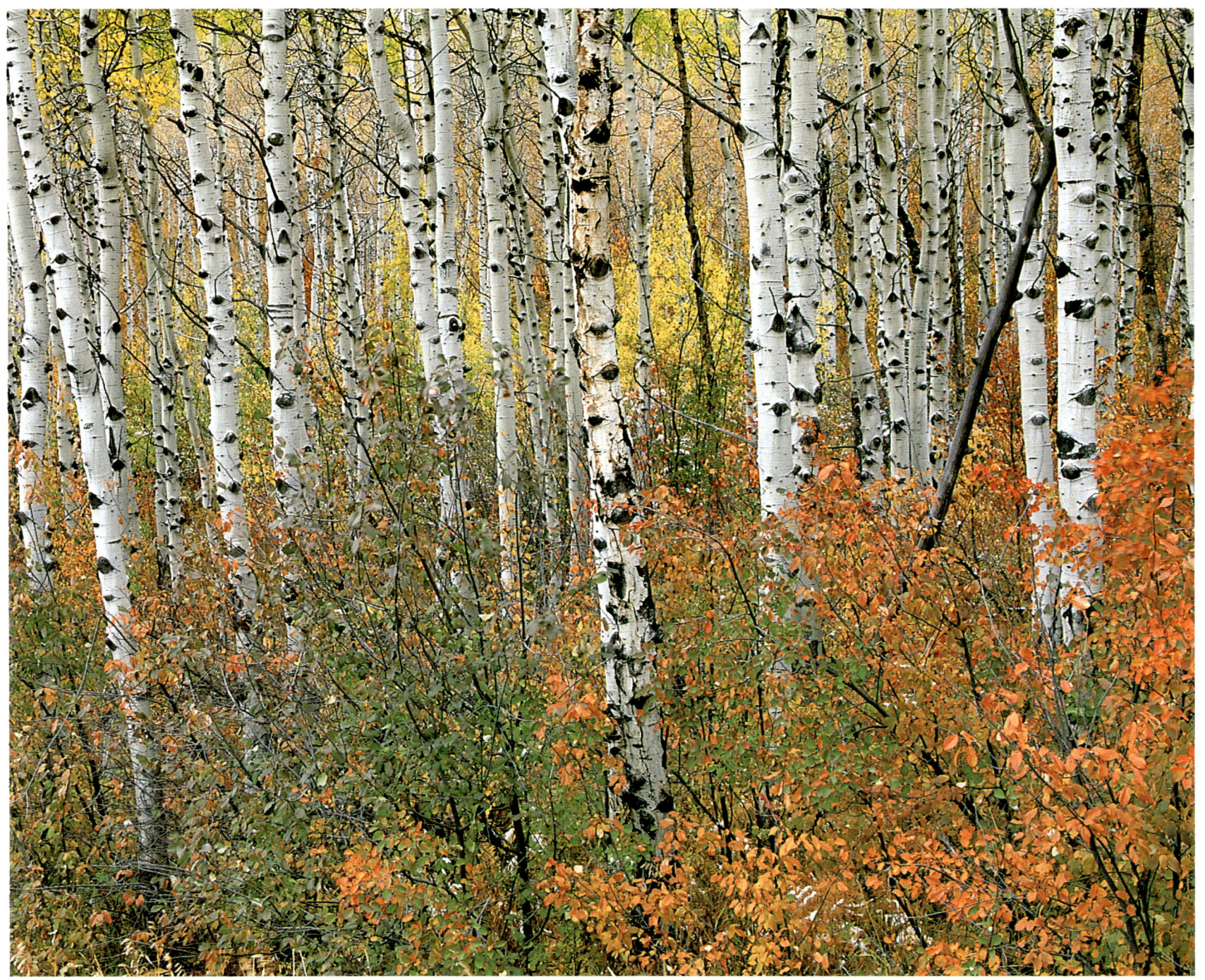

Overleaf: Sawatch Range

Above: Quaking aspen (*Populus tremuloides*), Maroon Bells-Snowmass Wilderness

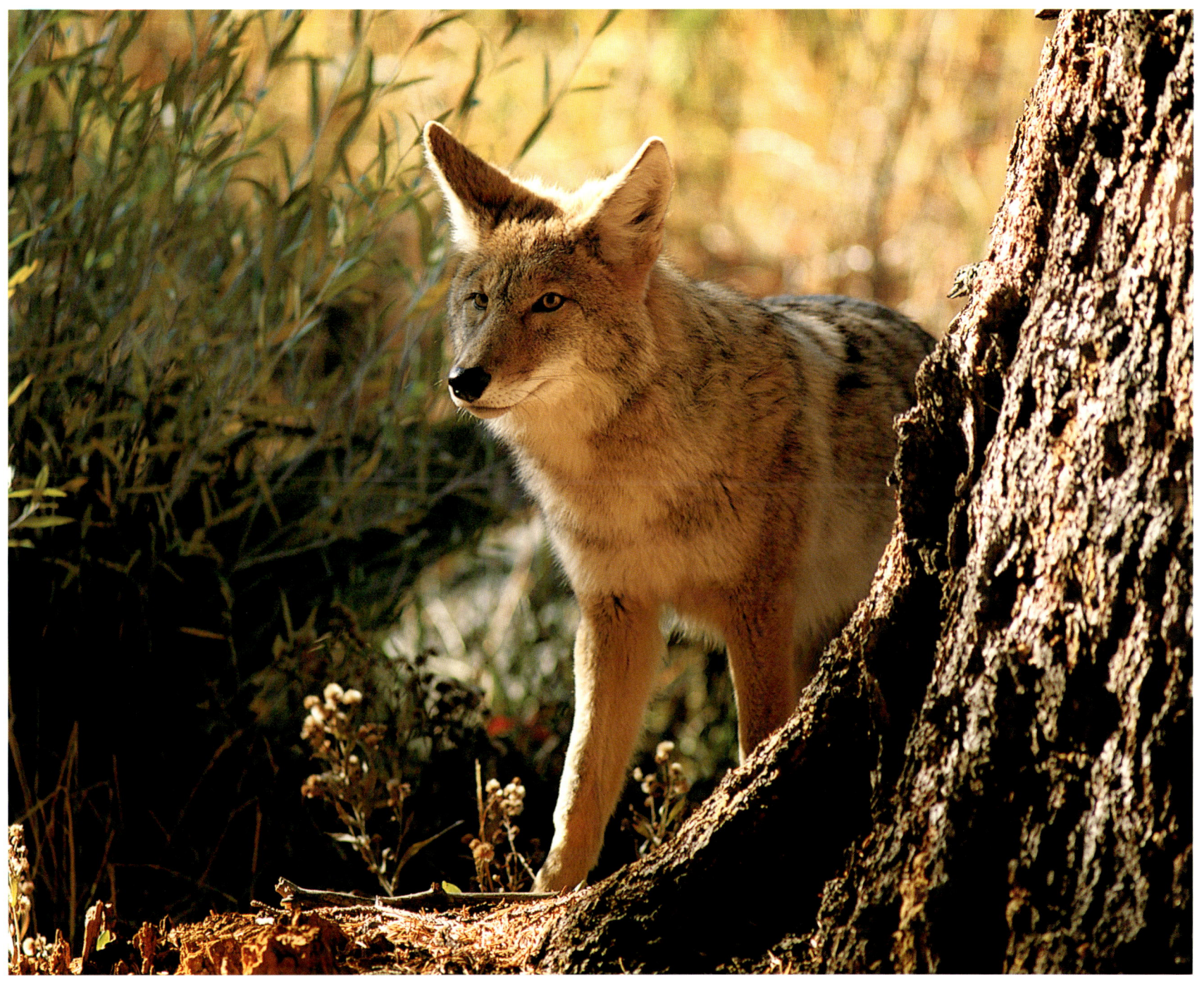
Coyote (*Canis latrans*), Mount Evans

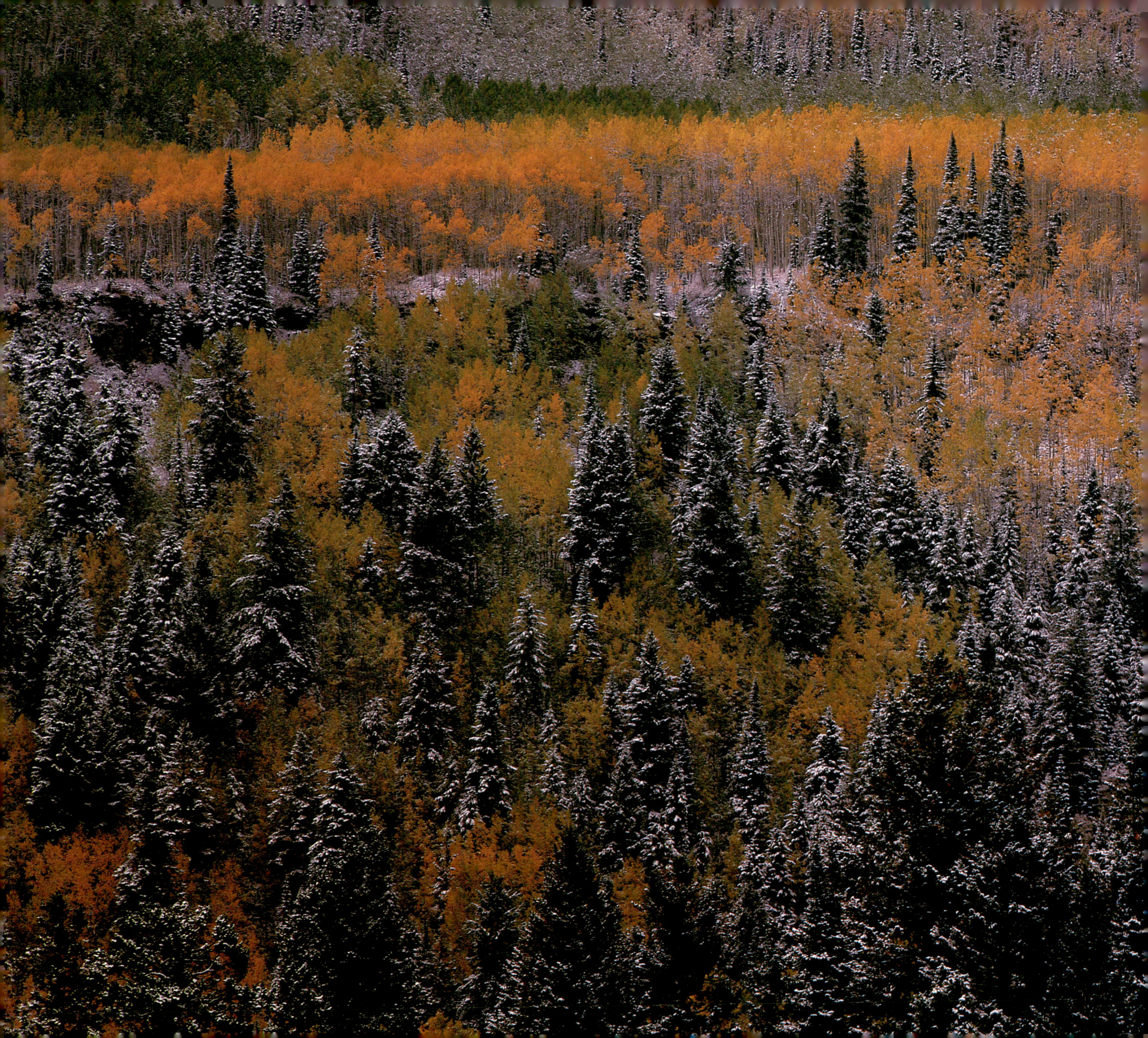

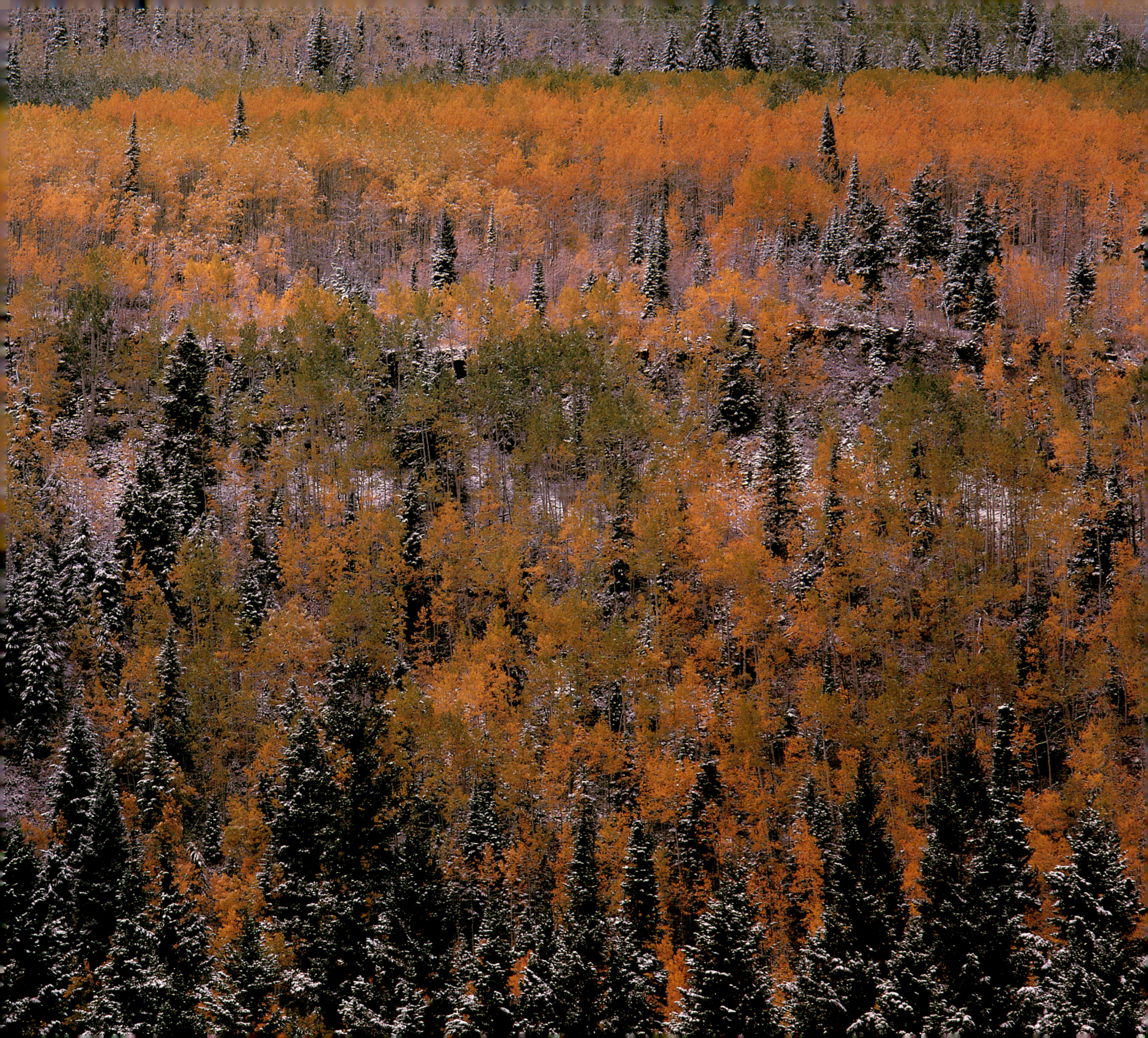

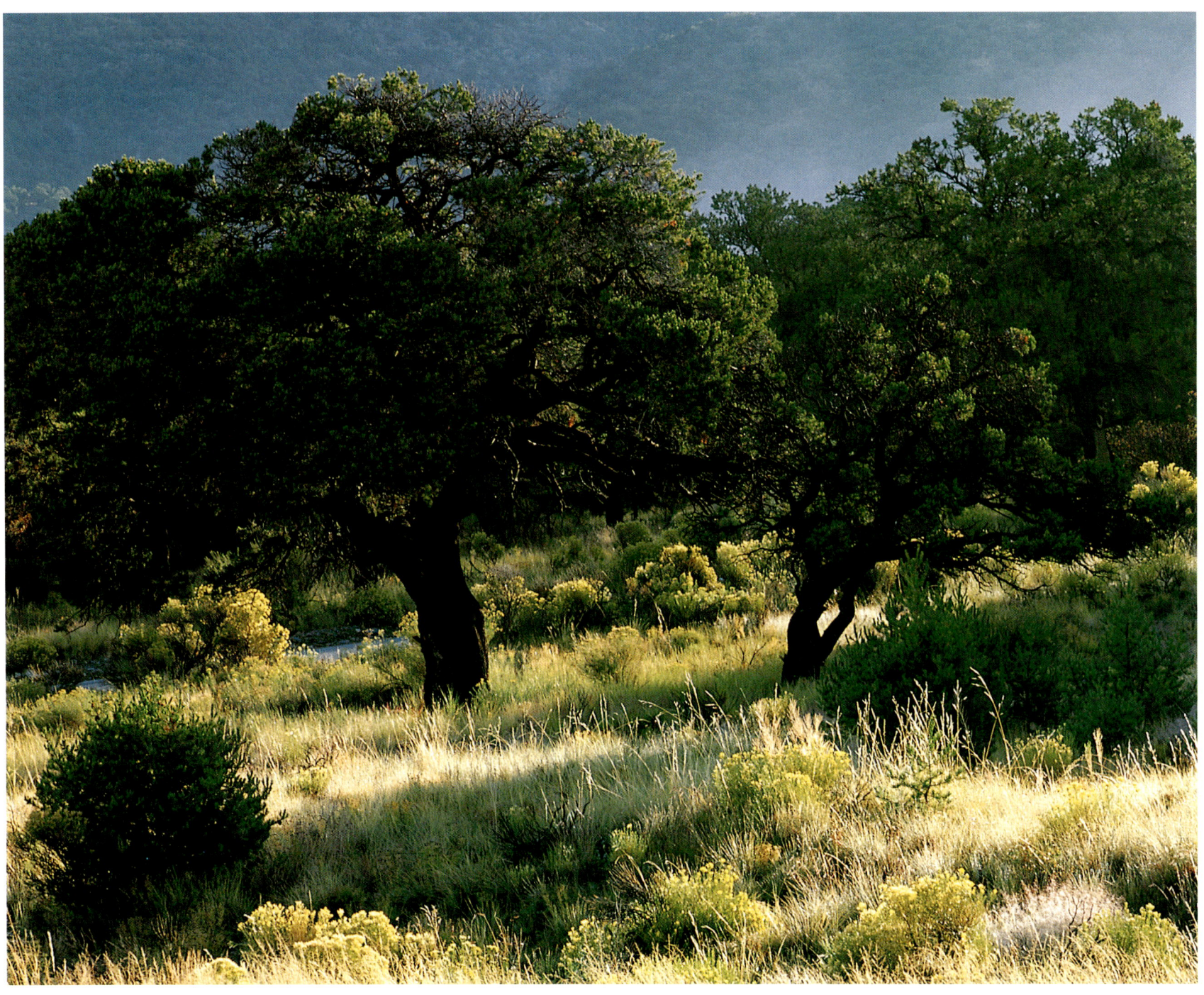

Overleaf: Sawatch Range

Above: Pinyon (*Pinus edulis*), Great Sand Dunes National Monument

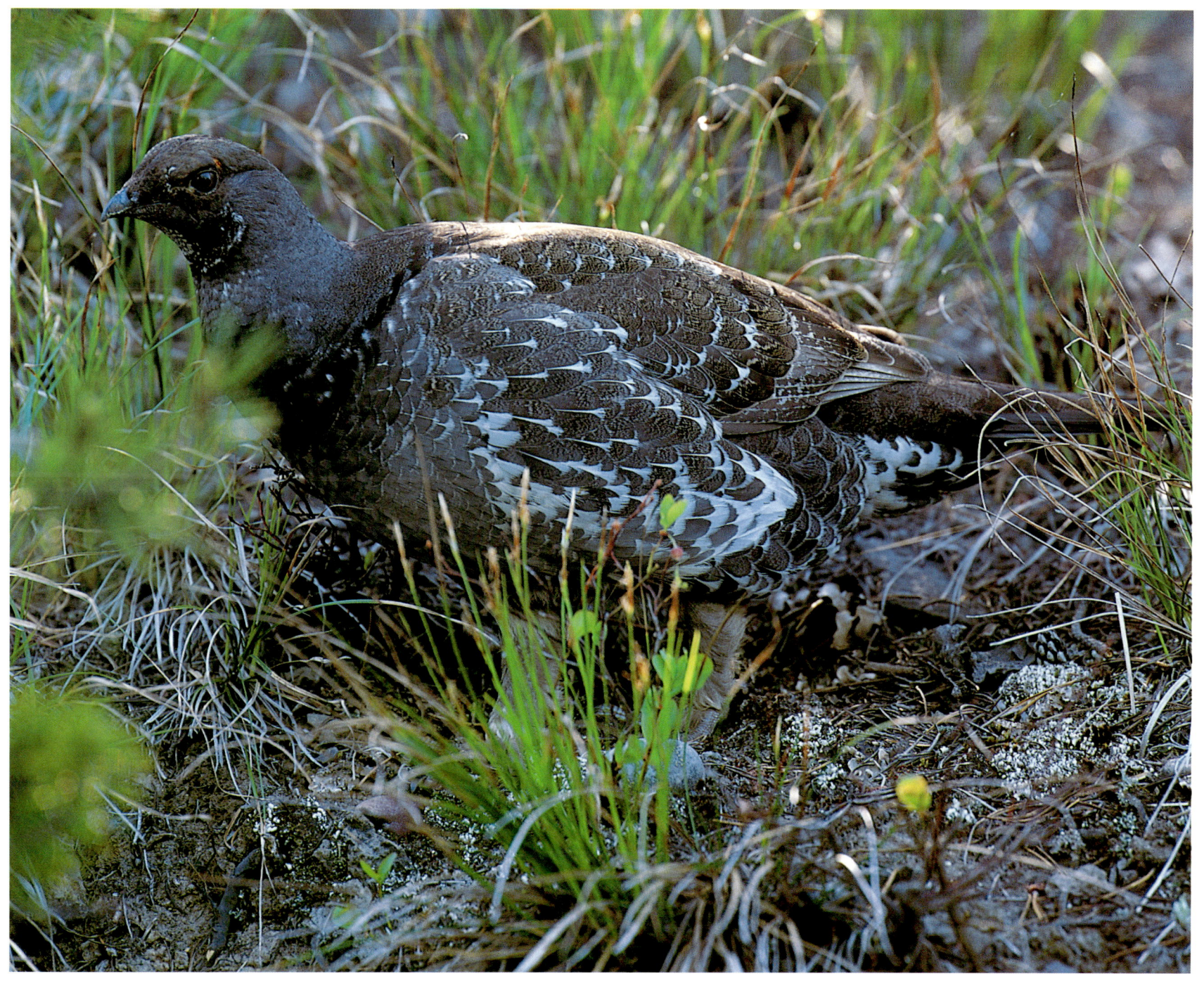

Blue grouse (*Dendragapus obscurus*), Mount Evans

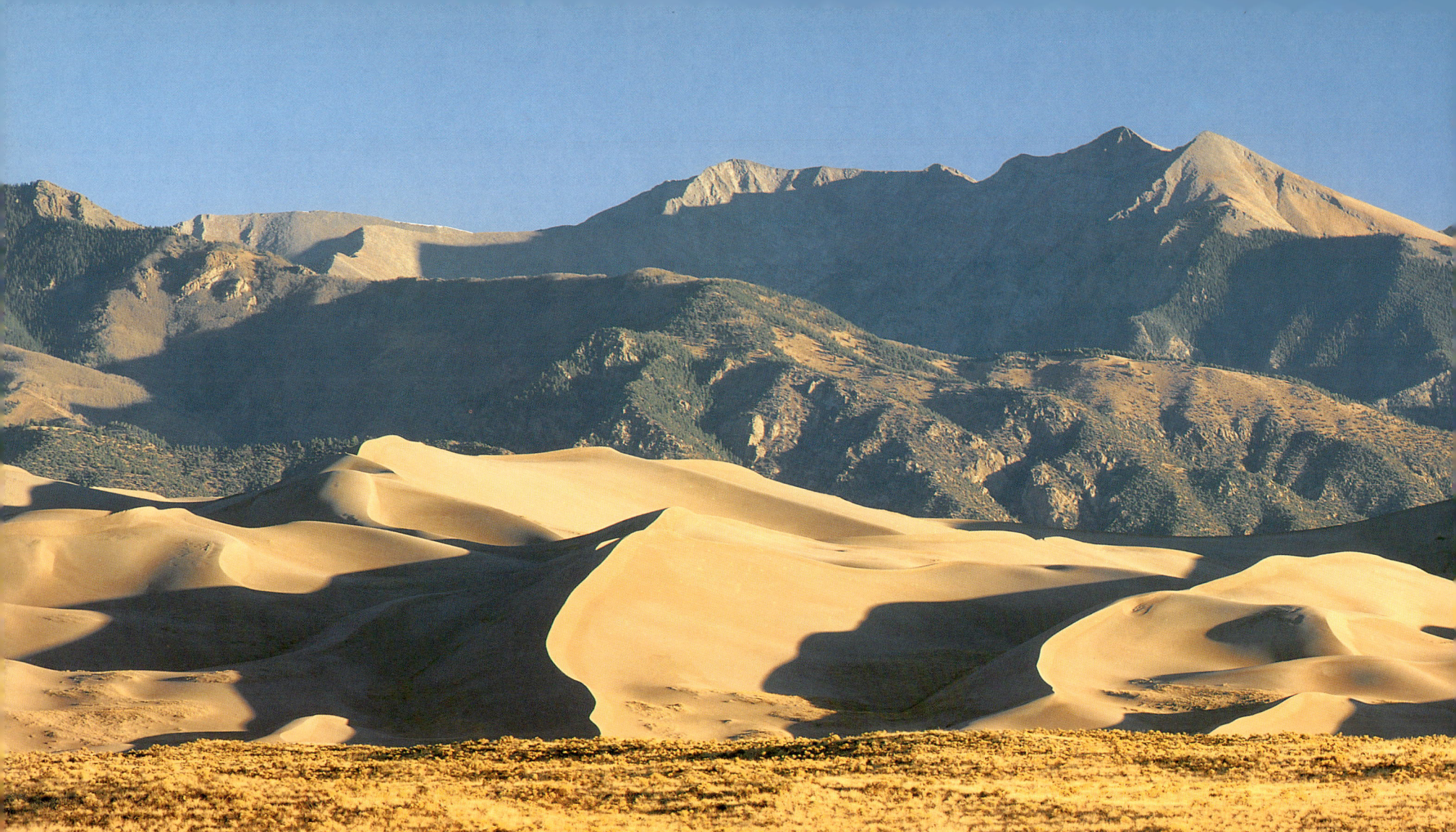

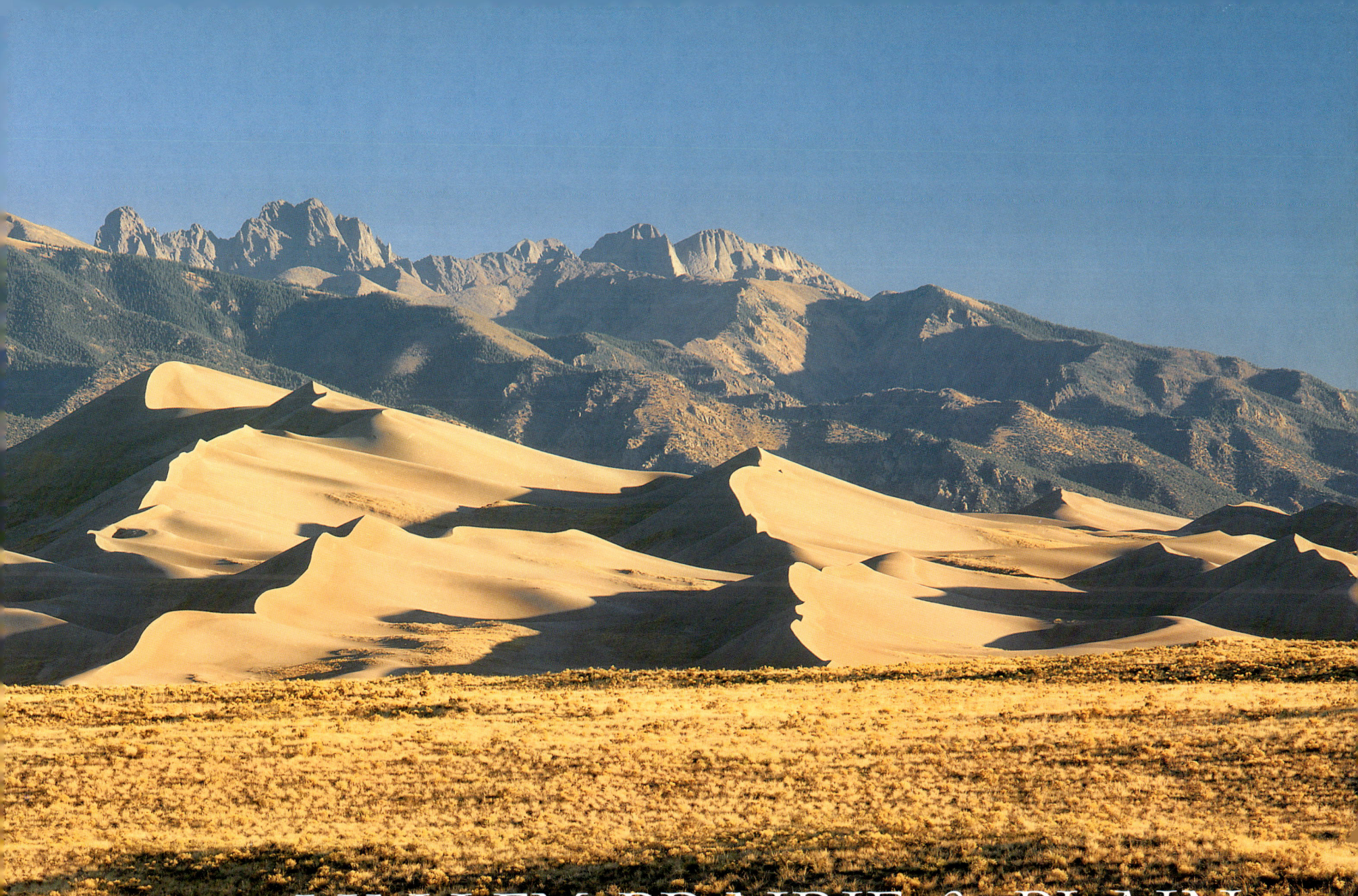

VALLEY, PRAIRIE & PLAIN

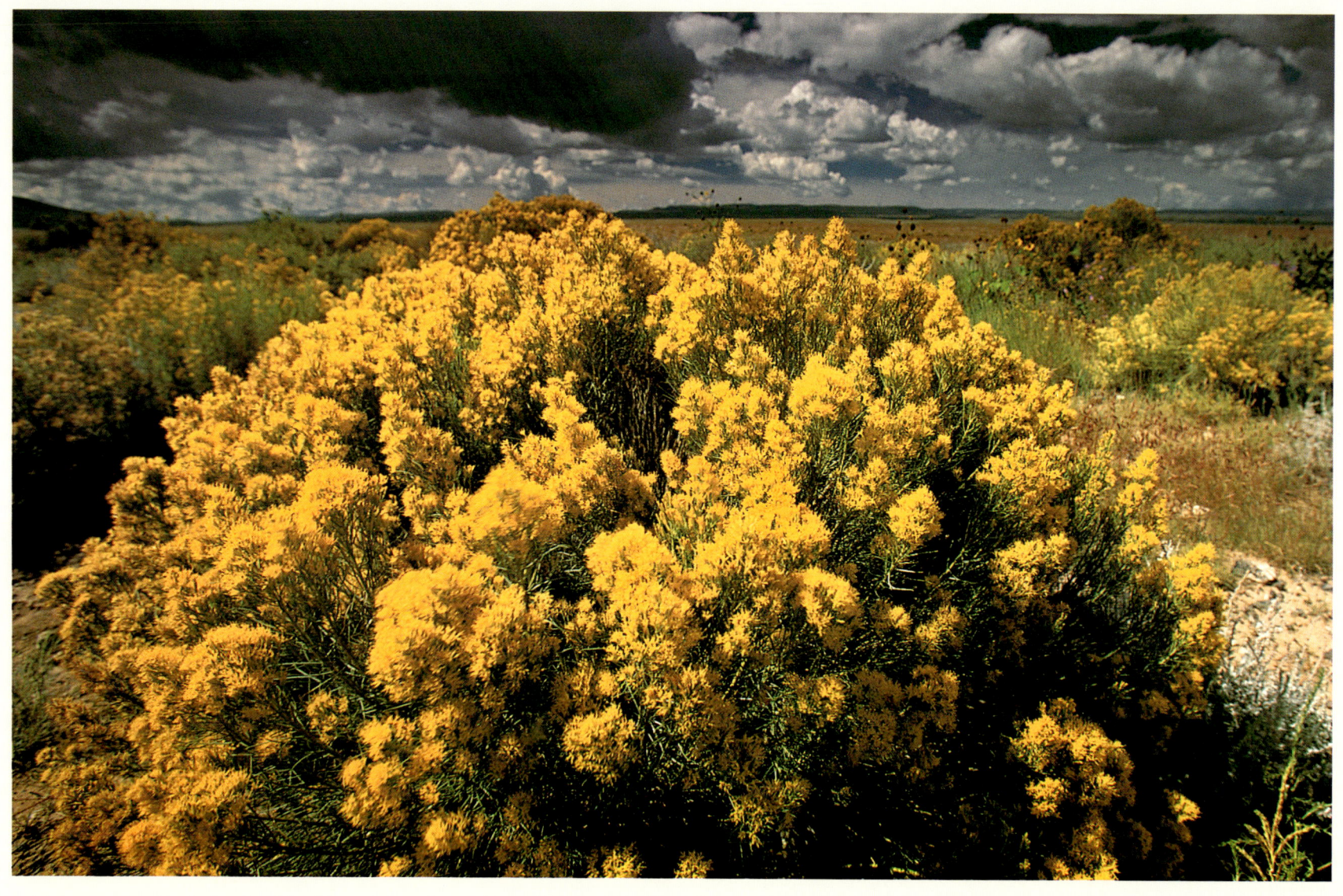

The road is straight. It exceeds the horizon, and I don't think it ends until it hits the East Coast. At least I have never gone far enough to find its completion. Not an interstate with a cement median and sparkles of broken glass, it is a modest paved road with one faded yellow

Overleaf: San Luis Valley

Left: Rabbitbrush (*Chrysothamnus nauseosus*), San Luis Valley

line and the occasional cluster of galvanized steel mailboxes leaning away from each other. The road changes direction once, to dip into a roll in the landscape, down by a grove of cottonwood trees, then back out to go straight again for eternity.

I used to bring a bicycle and ride until I lost sight of the Rocky Mountains far behind me. I would ride and become swallowed by the sky, watching late-spring thunderstorms bloom out of nowhere. I am something of a stranger here, having always lived in aggressive landscapes: deserts, mountains, high mesas, places with broken boulders and cliffs. This road shoots across the plains of Eastern Colorado. The prairie is not actually flat, not even as flat as a mesa top. Rather, it rolls and folds like an unmade bed, tucking away pieces of land that cannot be seen from the road.

The road is alien to me, and it makes me want to ride until dark, completely free as if in the middle of a meditation. On the prairie I don't concern myself with natural history. I don't crawl on my stomach stalking animals as in the forest. I stop on the side of the road, lay my bike in the tall seed heads of grass, species unknown. I listen to the watery voice of western meadowlarks.

The road travels through grids of farms, which, close to the rain shadow of the Rocky Mountains, are not nearly as lush as those of Iowa. Corn and watermelon farmers live out here. Sellers of horse tack and farm implements. There is order out here. People's credibility is judged on the straightness of plowed furrows. In the mountains you can build a ramshackle cabin, surround it with junked tools and heaps of firewood, and no one will think worse of you. In the desert you can throw a trailer of a house onto the rocks, build a shade ramada out of leftover material, and leave it at that. If a person on the plains bucks hay onto a flatbed and the load is slightly crooked, people avert their eyes.

The road travels farther to where farms dissolve into rare territories of unworked grasslands. Few of these places remain. Most have been fastidiously groomed and irrigated by farmers, so those that remain stand out in striking contrast. I would always discard my bicycle when I arrived at these remnant ecosystems. I would walk out, finding uneven ground and crowds of grasses, so many species of grasses that they quickly became uncountable. I would study the eyebrow curl of blue grama grass and the wheatlike tufts of buffalo grass.

Once in a patch of high grass a dozen or more infant snakes erupted at my feet. The ground seemed to twist and writhe, there were so many, some wrapping over my feet, some curling around the bases of the June grass. They slid and warped away from me, weaving themselves into the shelter of sagebrush and down dark, mounded prairie dog holes. Within thirty seconds the ground was still again.

Farther east along the road come the prairie sandhills, with their dunes and bayonets of yucca and species of grass commonly called sand bluestem and blowout. The rivers are made of sand. Waterless, covered with ornate wind ripples, they flow east. Many of the roads disappear around these sandhills, unable to find purchase. This one keeps going, linking to roads on the other side.

What has constantly impressed me about the plains is their clarity. I once came through early-morning ice on the South Platte River and hunkered in a fortress of cattails. I remained motionless, as small flocks of ducks skirted me, their wings curved, buffeting the air for a landing. But they did not land near me. They sank from view. As each flock changed formation to land in some other water source, I mapped their paths. I could see so much of their travel through the sky that without moving from the sheltering cattails, I knew the lay of the land below, the location of ponds and sloughs. That is a clarity I have received from no other landscape.

Clarity reveals itself in the ticking tail of a prairie falcon just landed on a telephone wire. The swift, clean dive to pluck harvest mice or grasshopper mice from the field. It is revealed in the poise of pronghorns two miles away, their bodies arranged closely together as if in defense against the vast openness.

I will never live on the plains. I am too disorganized and would be shamed by locals. I cannot meditate for more than a minute without getting up to do something else. And I do not have the mind of a squash farmer who knows it takes a lifetime to map the textures and species of grass and to know each detail of that one road that does not end.

Right: Prairie sunflower (*Helianthus petiolaris*), San Luis Valley

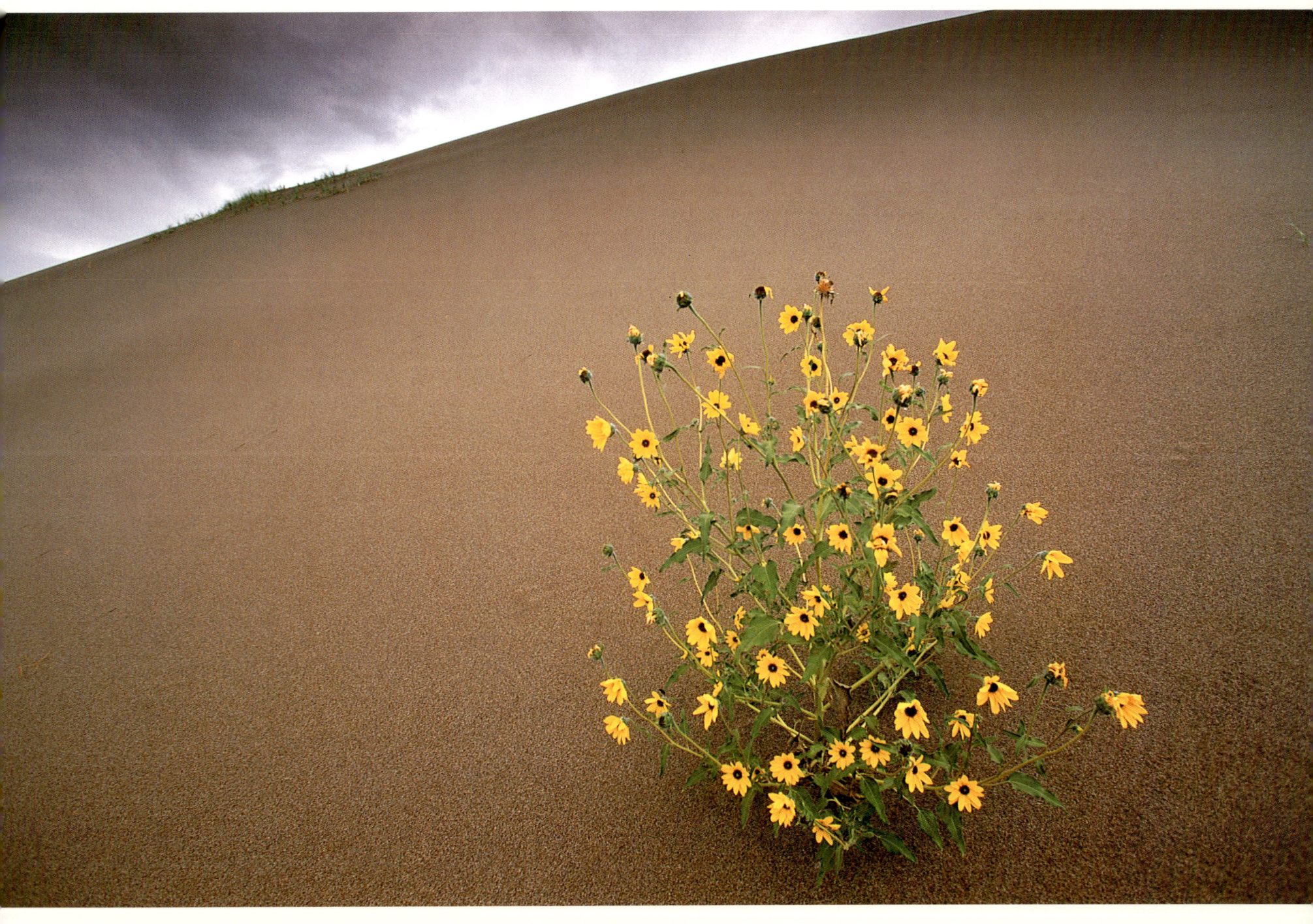

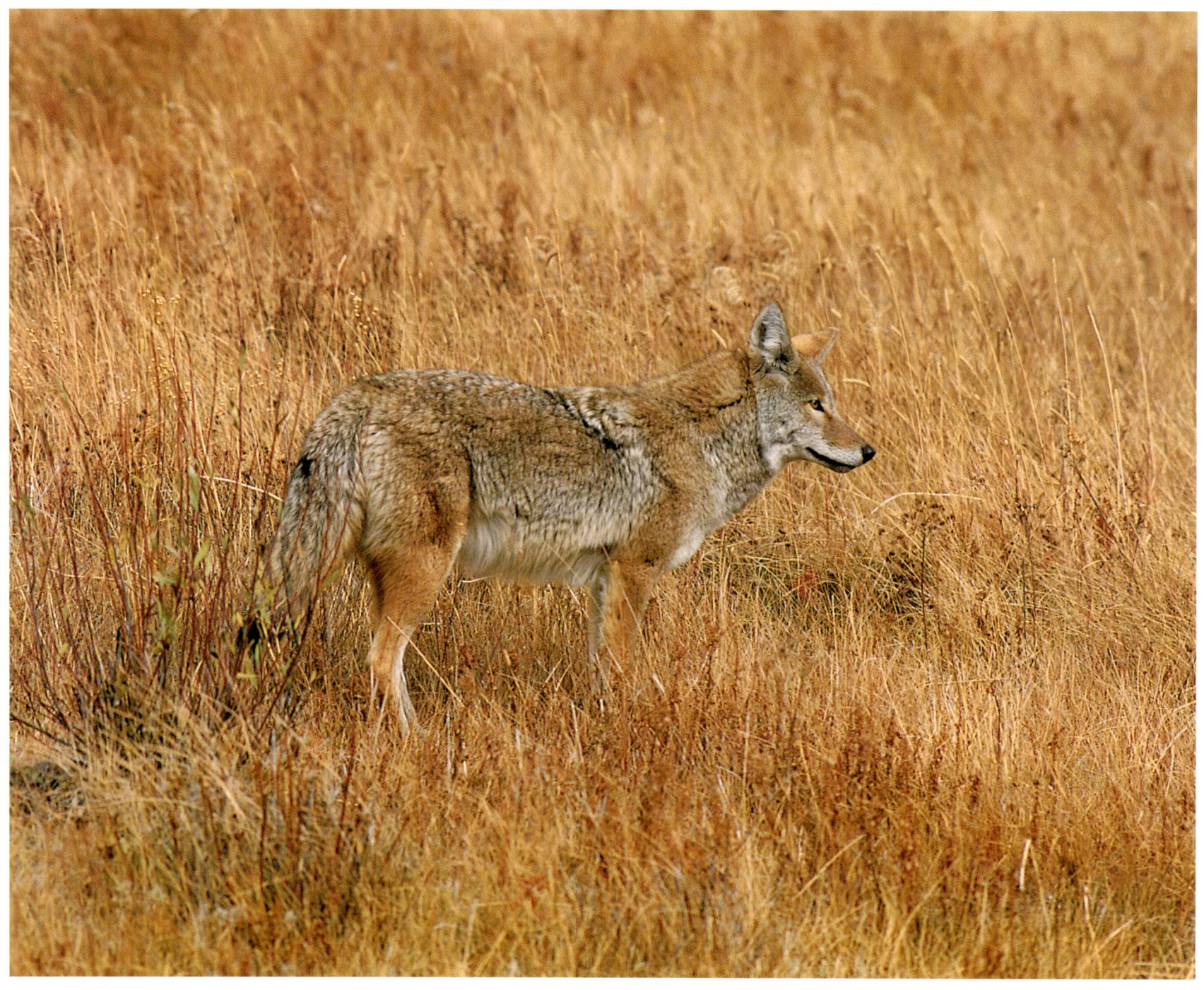

142 | COLORADO

Left: Coyote (*Canis latrans*), Pawnee National Grassland

Below: Pronghorn (*Antilocapra americana*), Pawnee National Grassland

Right: Burrowing owl (*Athene cunicularia*), Jones Flat

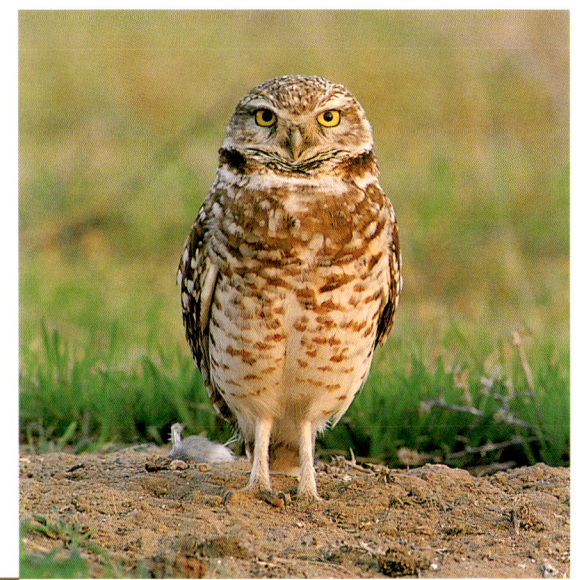

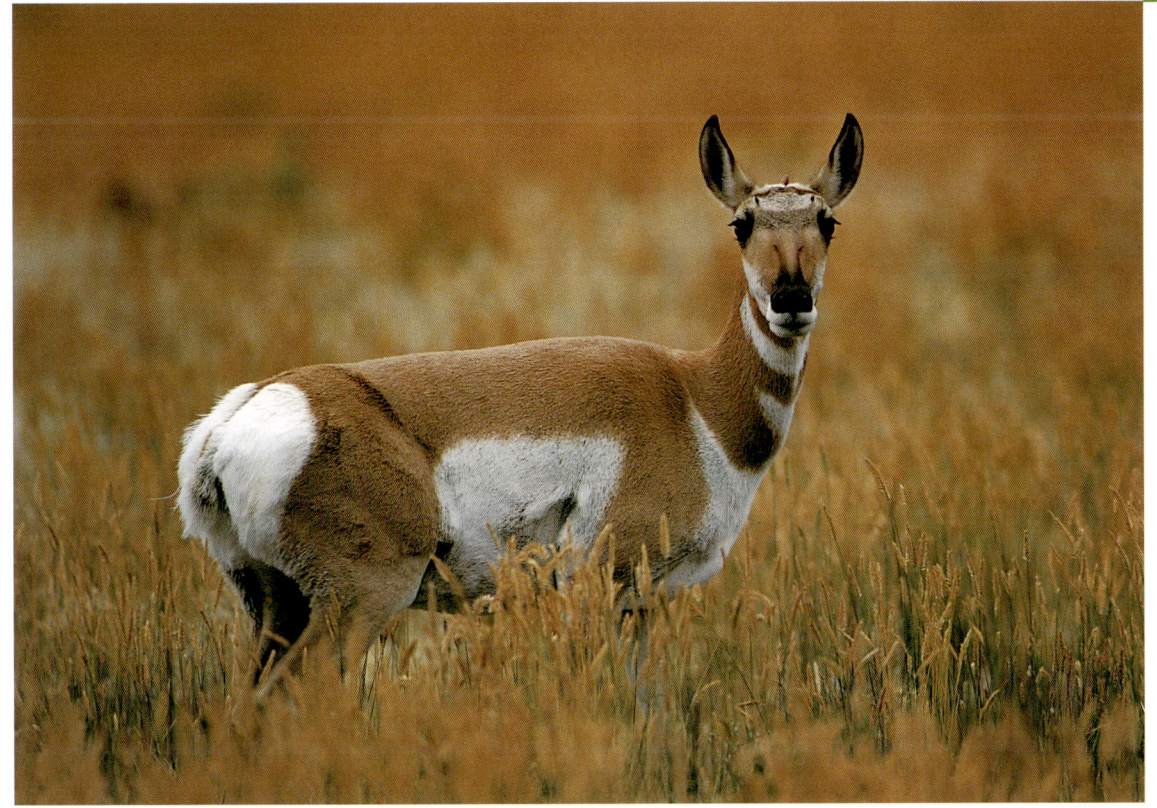

VALLEY, PRAIRIE & PLAIN

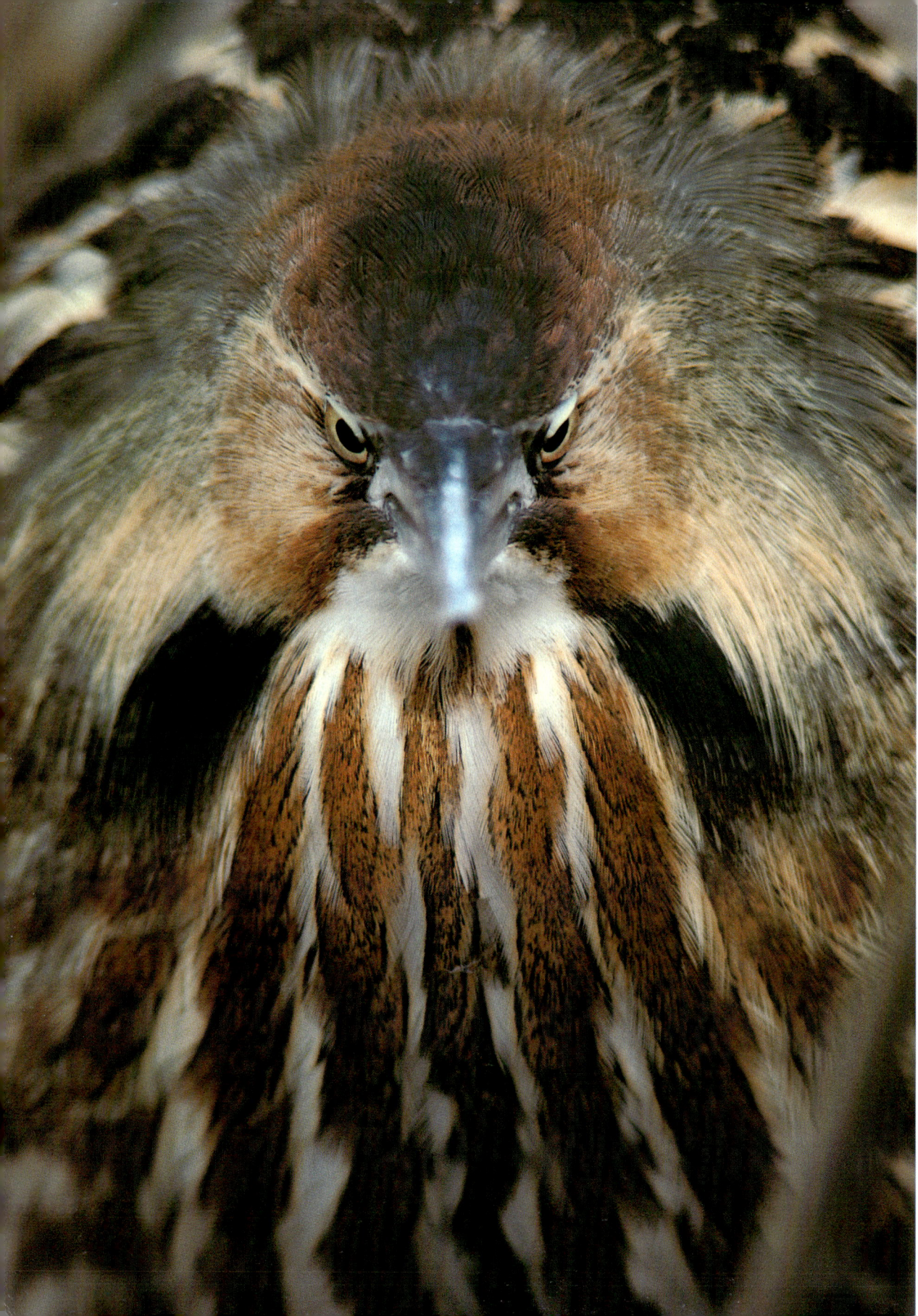

Left: American bittern (*Botaurus lentiginosus*), Seven Lakes Reservoir

Right: San Luis Valley

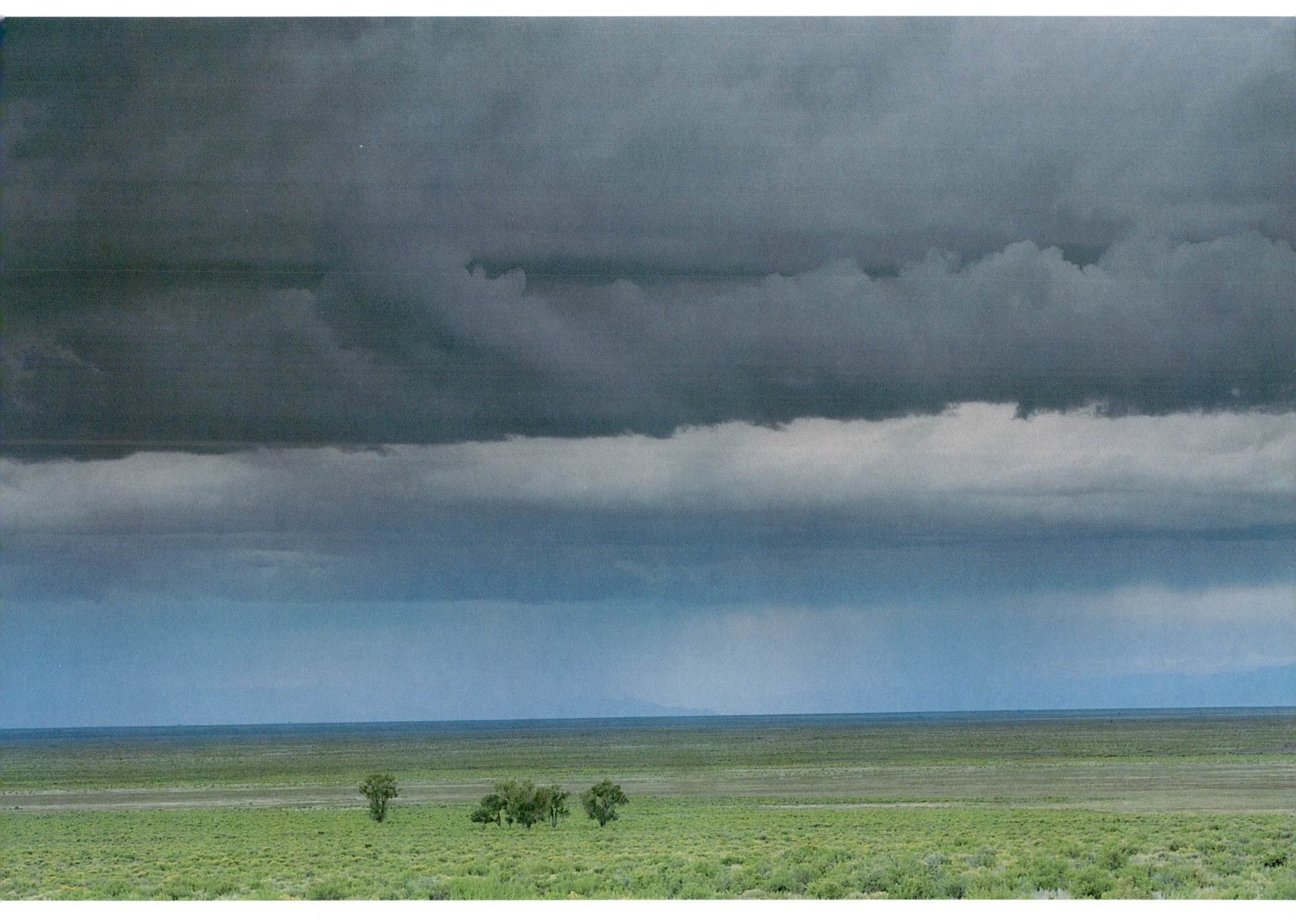

VALLEY, PRAIRIE & PLAIN

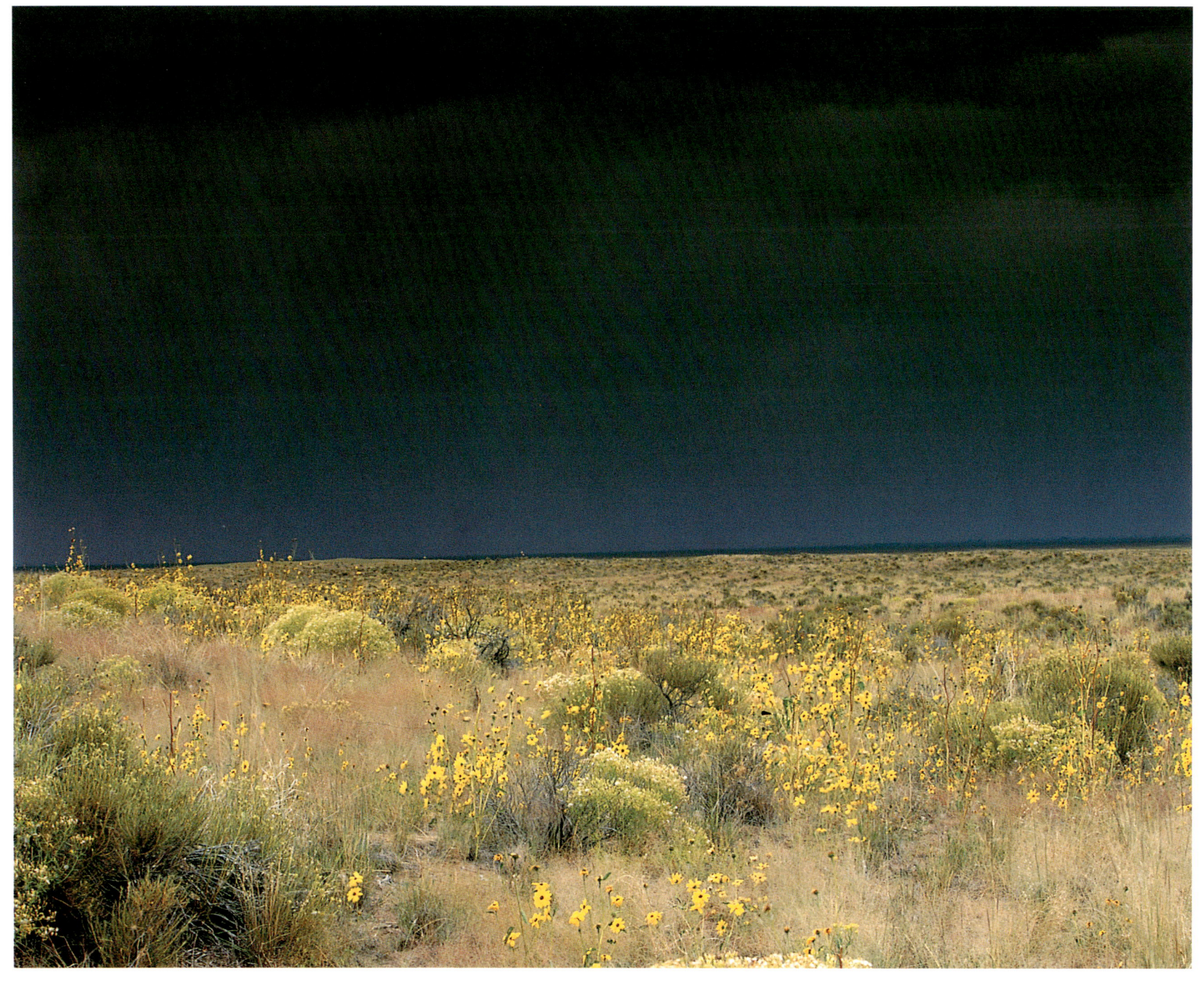

Prairie sunflower (*Helianthus petiolaris*), San Luis Valley

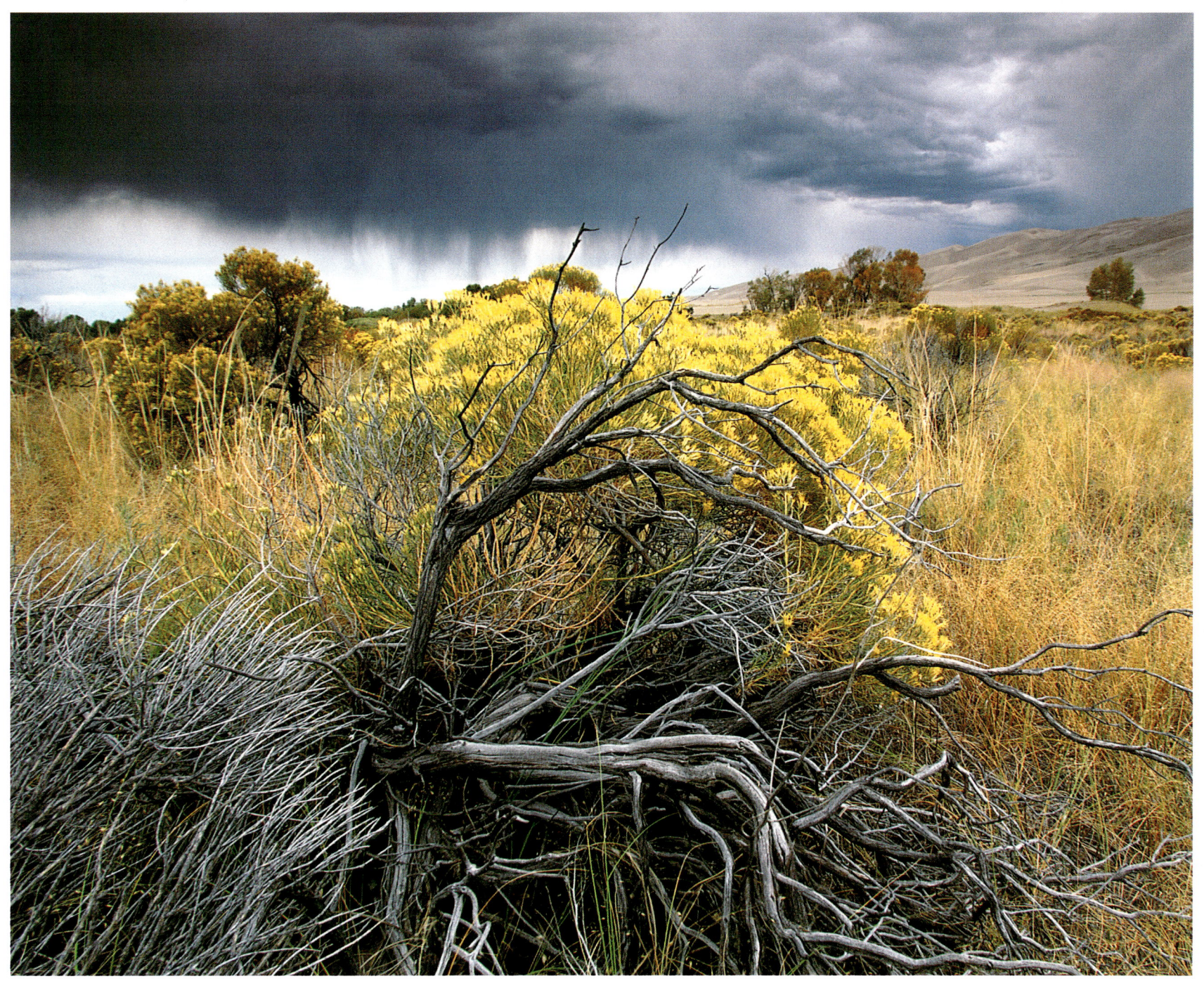

Rabbitbrush (*Chrysothamnus nauseosus*), San Luis Valley

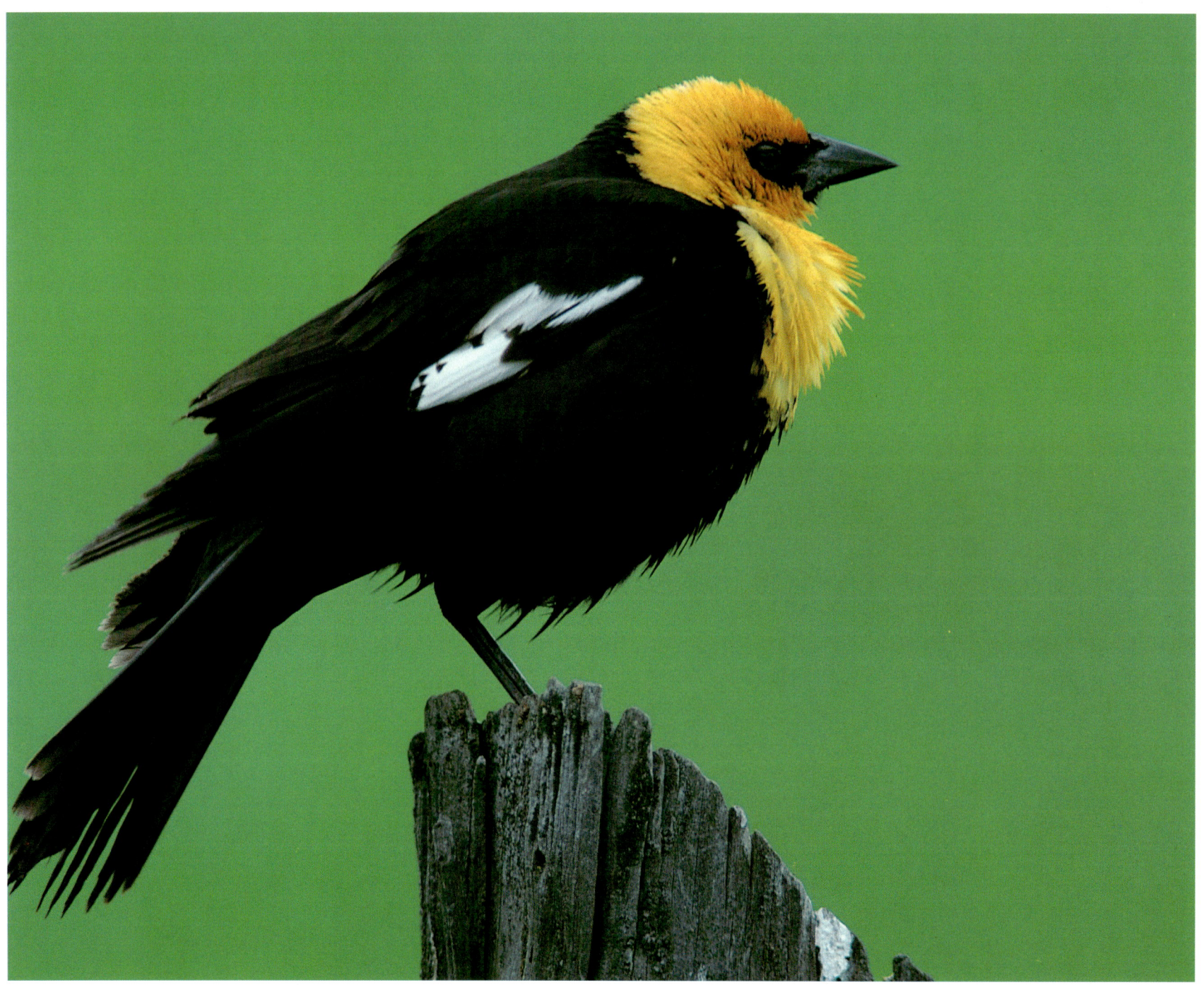

Left: Yellow-headed blackbird (*Xanthocephalus xanthocephalus*), Seven Lakes Reservoir

Below: Blanketflower (*Gaillardia* sp.), Pawnee National Grassland

Right: American kestrel (*Falco spaverius*), San Luis Valley

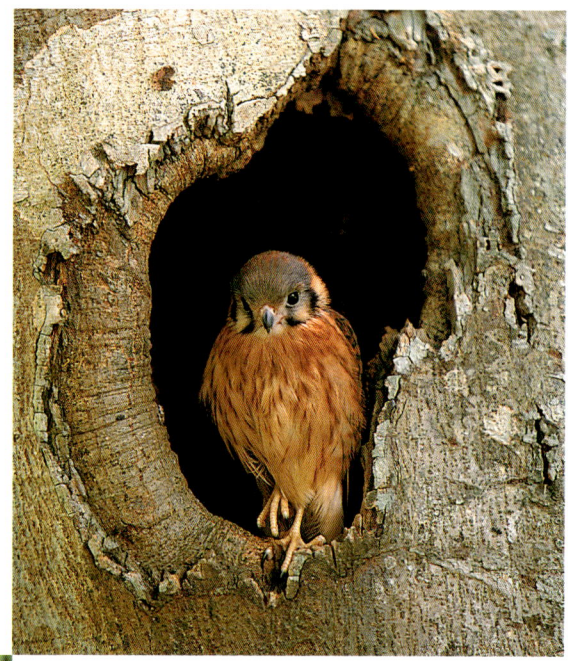

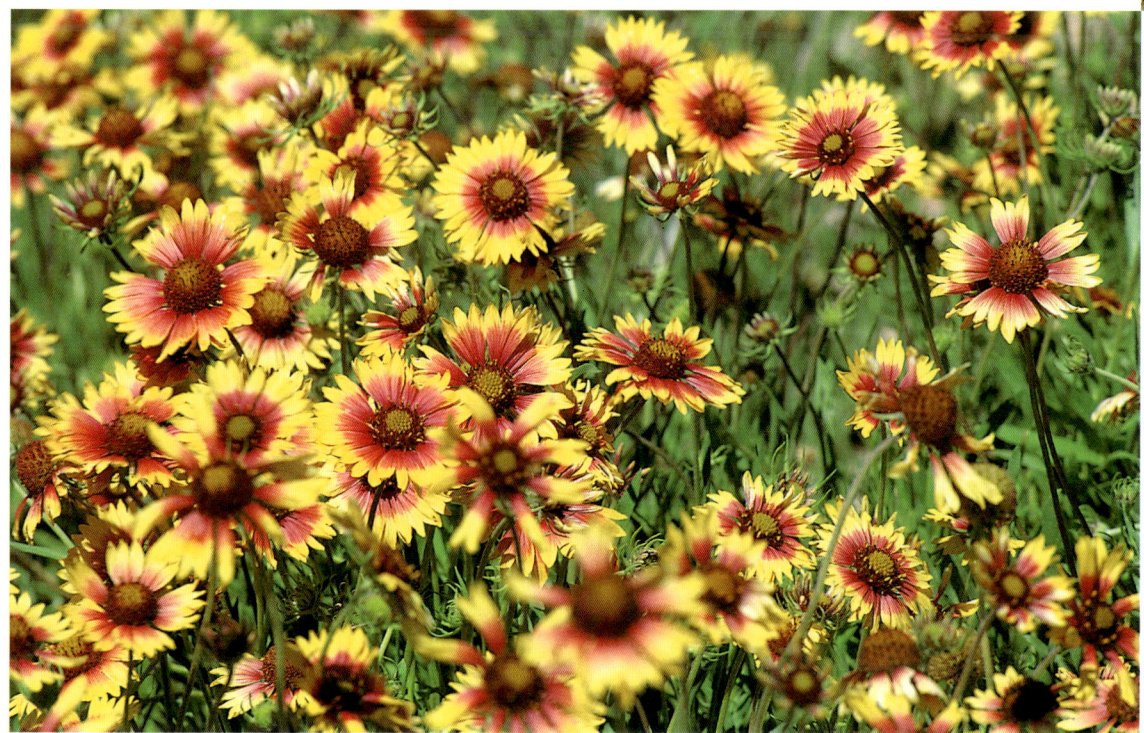

VALLEY, PRAIRIE & PLAIN

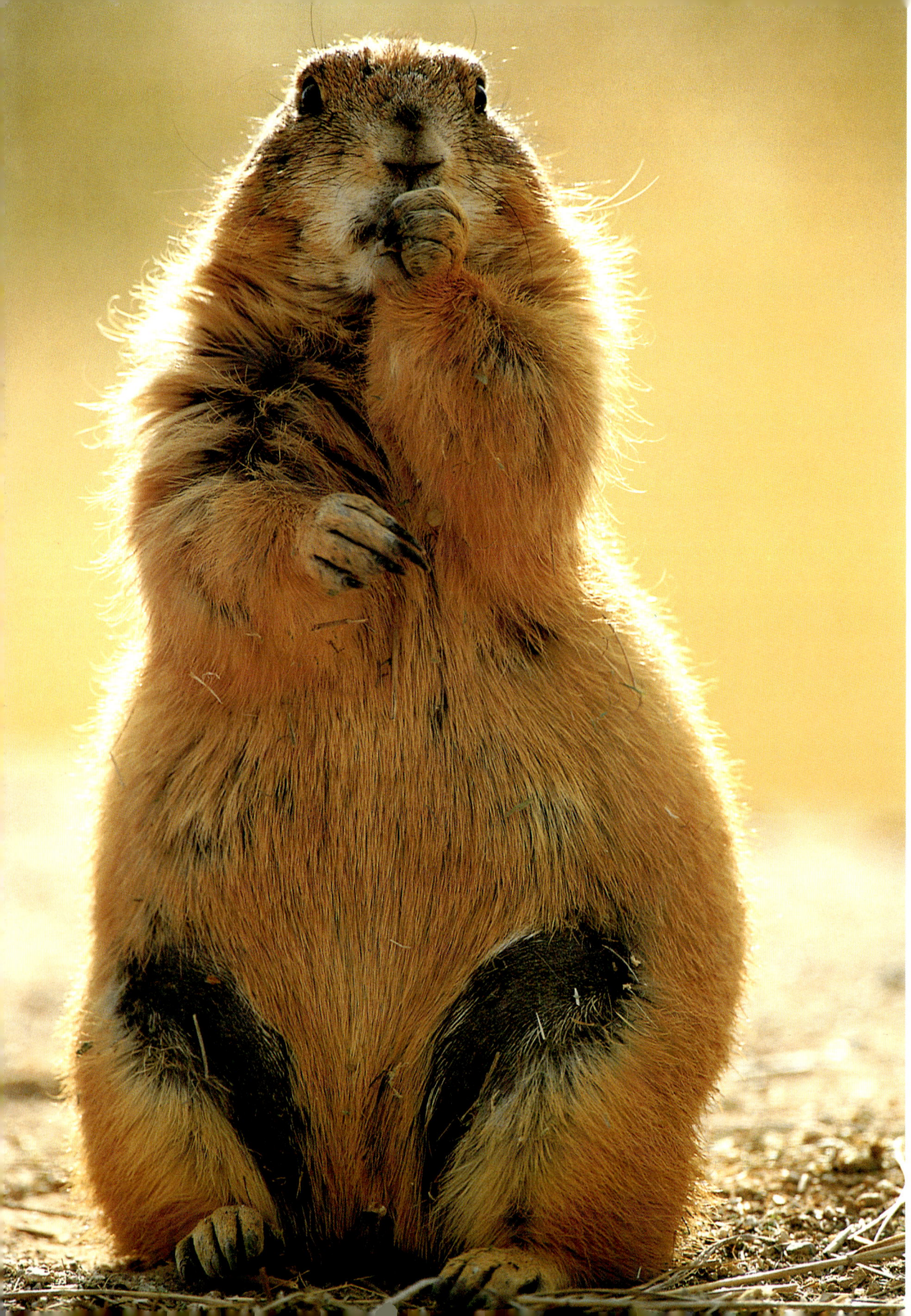

Left: Black-tailed prairie dog (*Cynomys ludovicianus*), Pawnee National Grassland

Right: Squawbush (*Rhus trilobia*) and rabbitbrush (*Chrysothamnus nauseosus*), San Luis Valley

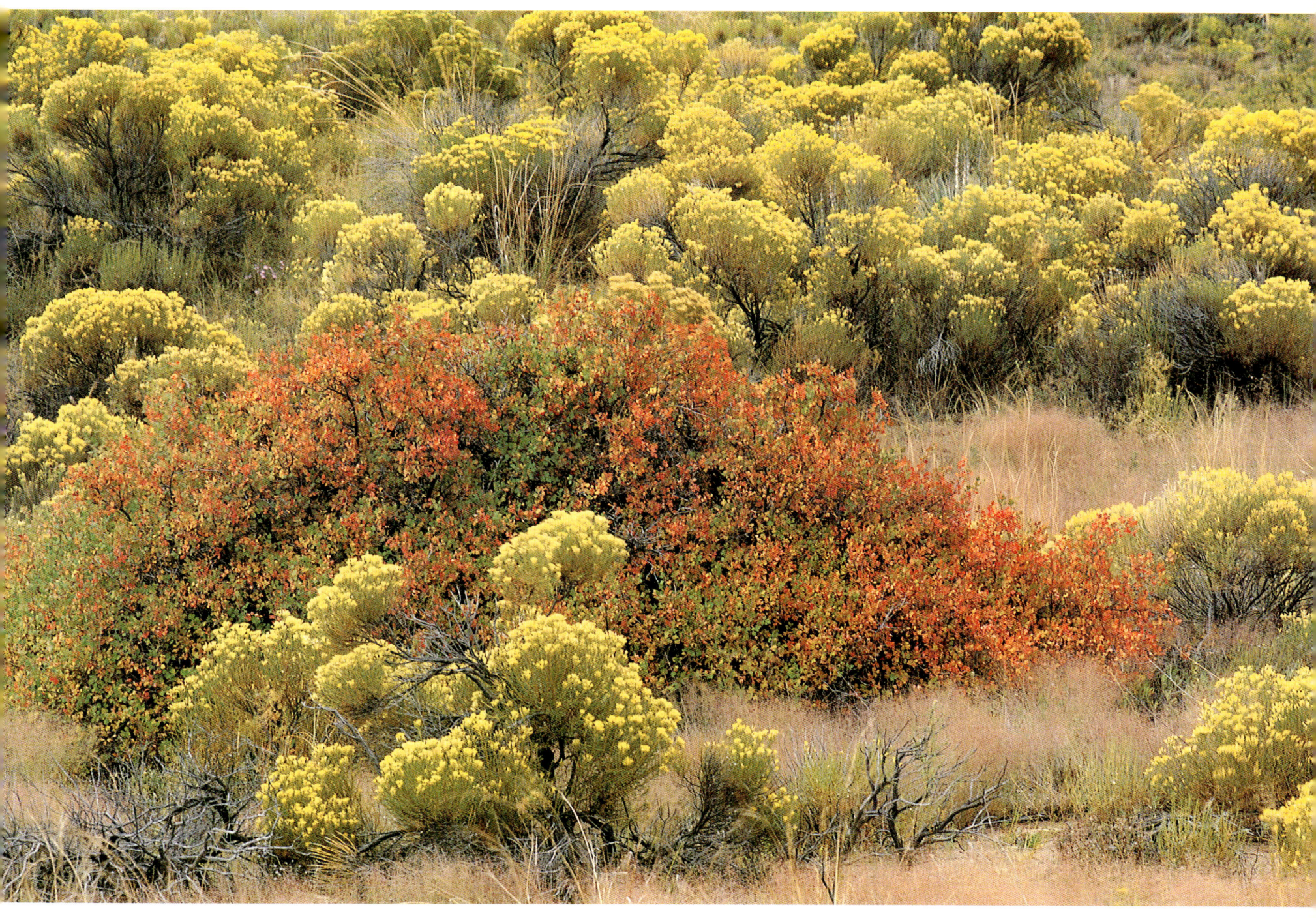

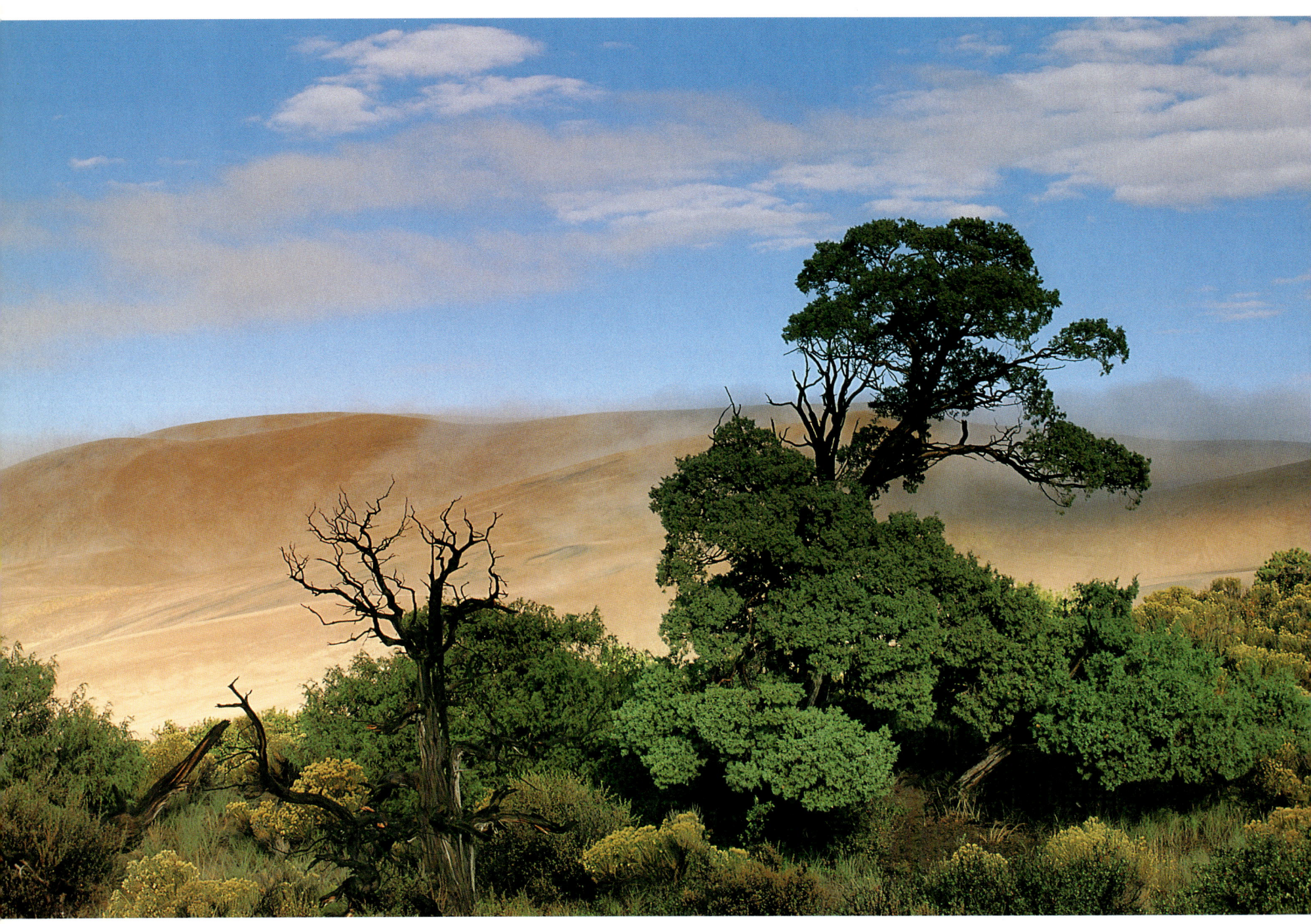

Left: Pinyon (*Pinus edulis*), Great Sand Dunes National Monument

Right: Long-billed curlew (*Numenius americanus*), Pawnee National Grassland

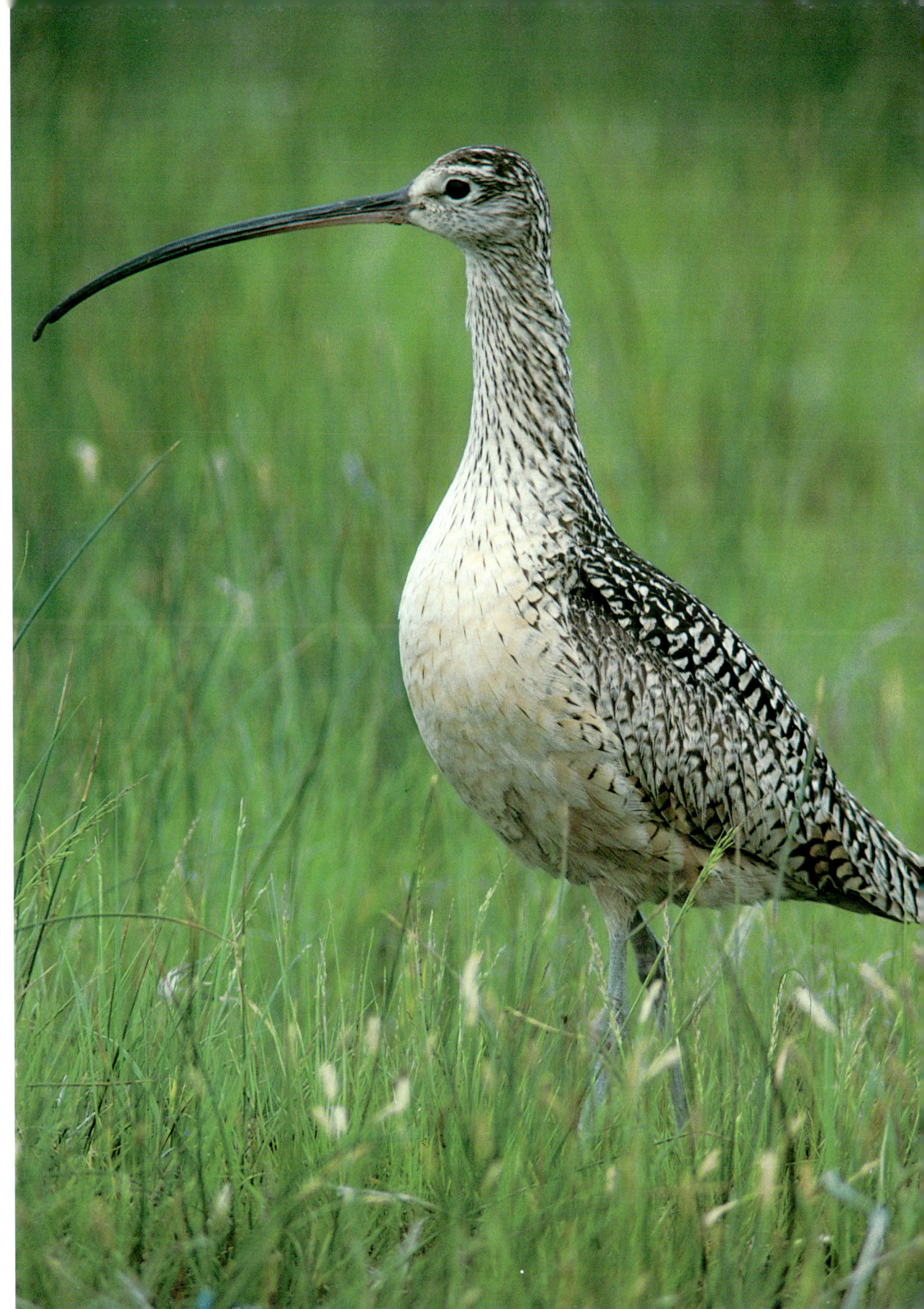

Below: Composite, Pawnee National Grassland

Right: Cattail (*Typha* sp.), San Luis Valley

Far right: Cattail (*Typha* sp.) marsh, San Luis Valley

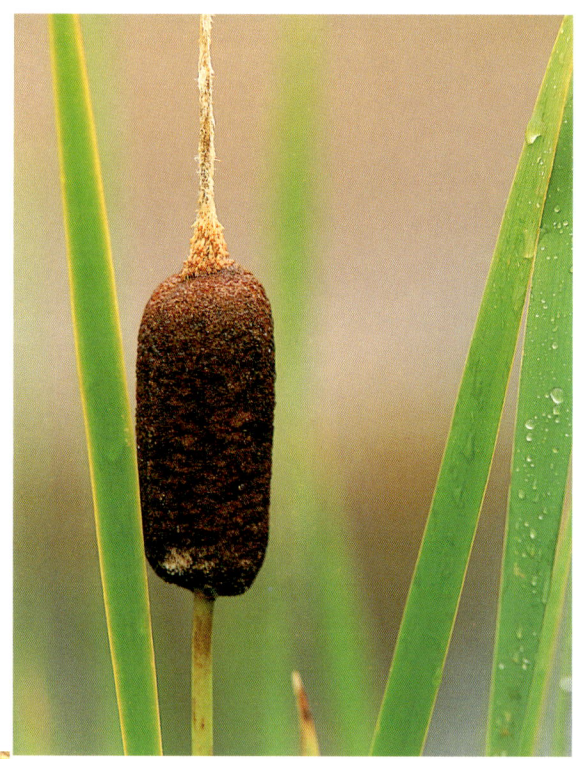

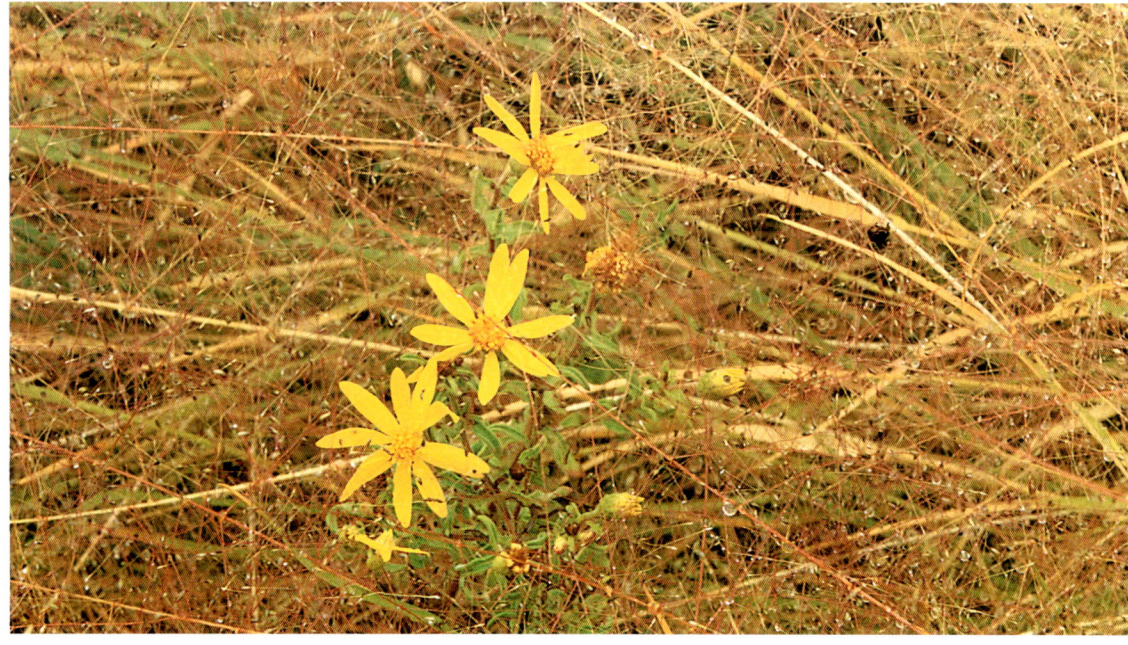

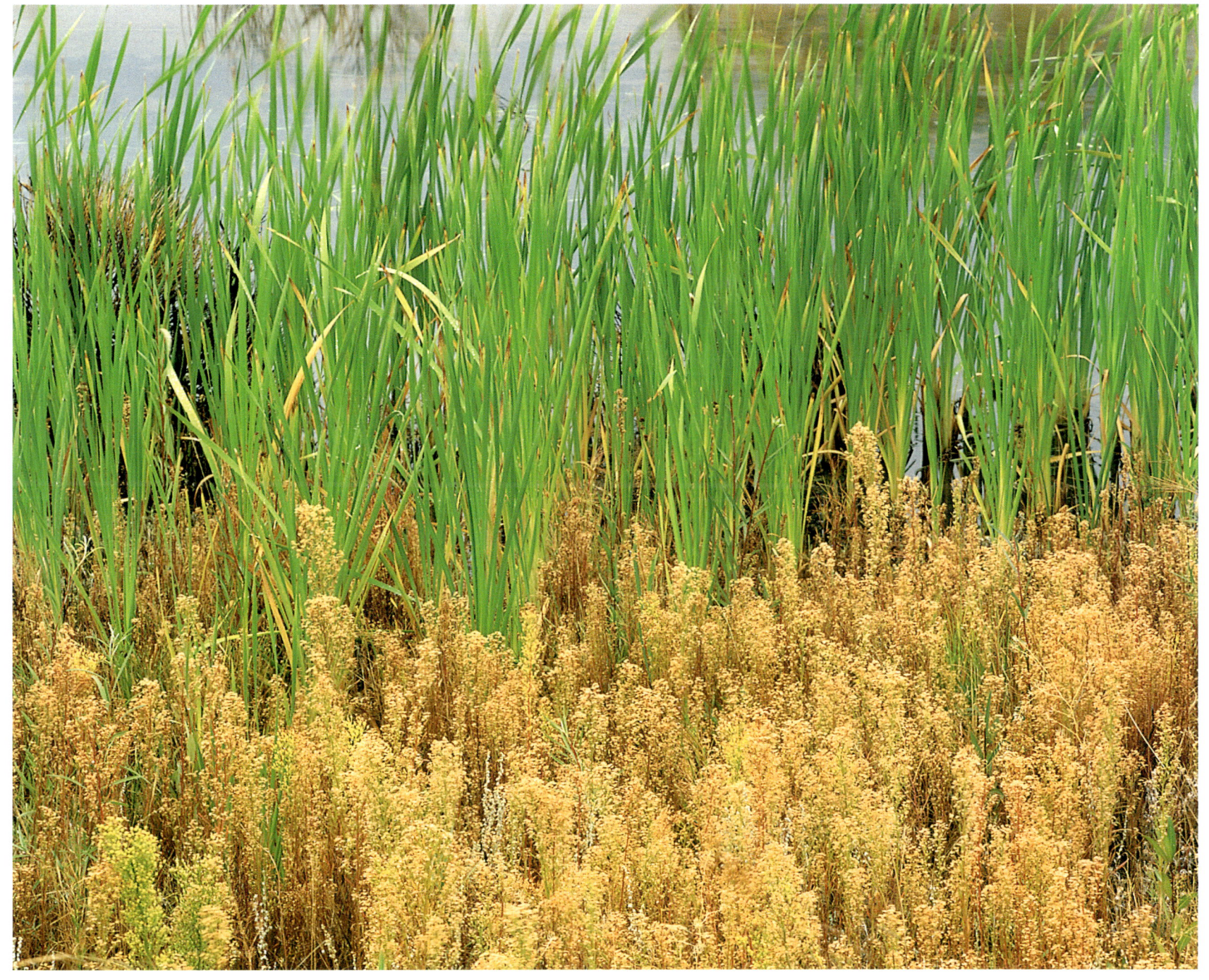

VALLEY, PRAIRIE & PLAIN

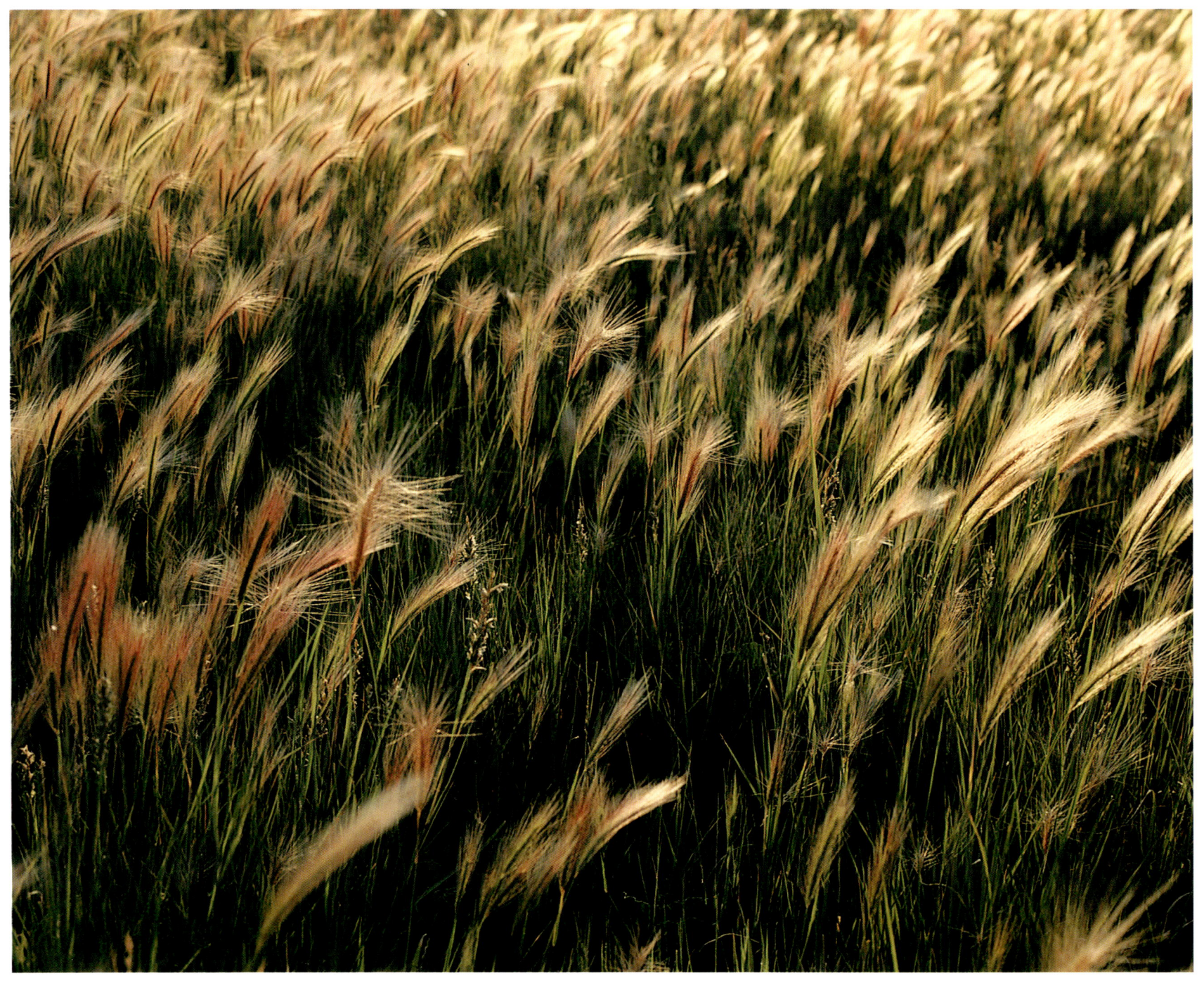

Foxtail barley (*Hordeum jubatum*), Pawnee National Grassland

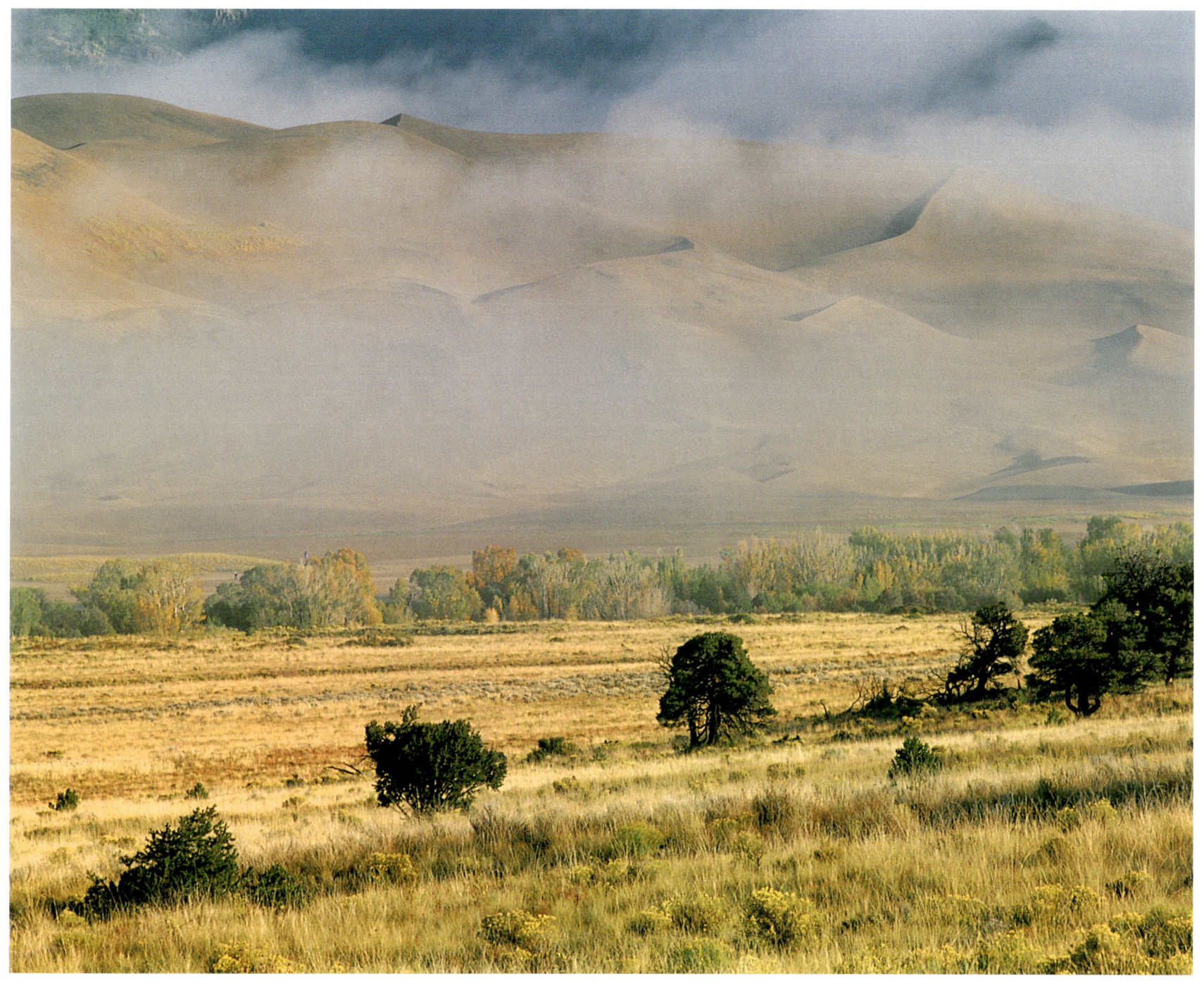

San Luis Valley

157

VALLEY, PRAIRIE & PLAIN

RESOURCE LIST

American Farmland Trust
P.O. Box 328
Palisade, CO 81526
Tel: 970-464-4963
Fax: 970-464-4973
Email: jjones@farmland.org
www.farmland.org

Audubon Society of Greater Denver
9308 South Platte Canyon Road
Littleton, CO 80128
Tel: 303-973-9530
Fax: 303-973-1038
Email: asgdoff@aol.com
www.audubon.org/chapter/cl/asgd

Clean Water Action
899 Logan Street – Suite 101
Denver, CO 80203
Tel: 303-839-9866
Fax: 303-839-9870
Email: Denvercwa@cleanwater.org
www.cleanwateraction.org

Colorado Coalition of Land Trusts
710 10th Street – Suite 117
Golden, CO 80401
Tel: 303-271-1577
Fax: 303-271-1582
Email: janeh@cclt.org
www.cclt.org

Colorado Environmental Coalition
1536 Wynkoop Street – Suite 5
Denver, CO 80202
Tel: 303-534-7066
Fax: 303-534-7063
Email: jolynne@ceceenviro.org
www.ourcolorado.org

The Colorado Mountain Club
710 10th Street – Suite 200
Golden, CO 80401
Tel: 303-279-3080
Fax: 303-279-9690
Email: beckwt@cmc.org
www.cmc.org

Colorado Open Lands
274 Union Boulevard – Suite 320
Lakewood, CO 80228
Tel: 303-988-2373
Fax: 303-988-2383
www.coloradoopenlands.org

Colorado Public Interest Research Group
1530 Blake Street – Suite 220
Denver, CO 80202
Tel: 303-573-7474
Fax: 303-573-3780
Email: copirg@pirg.org
www.copirg.org

Colorado Trout Unlimited
1966 13th Street – Suite LL60
Boulder, CO 80302
Tel: 303-440-2937
Fax: 303-440-2733
Email: rphilpott@tu.org
www.cotrout.org

Colorado White Water Association
P.O. Box 4315
Englewood, CO 80155
Tel: 303-430-4853
www.coloradowhitewater.org

Colorado Wild
P.O. Box 1525
Boulder, CO 80306
Email: jeff@coloradowild.org
www.coloradowild.org

The Colorado Wildlife Federation
445 Union Boulevard – Suite 320
Lakewood, CO 80220
Tel: 303-987-0400
Fax: 303-987-0200
Email: cwfed@aol.com
www.coloradowildlife.org

High Country Citizens' Alliance
P.O. Box 1066
Crested Butte, CO 81224
Tel: 970-349-7104
Fax: 970-349-0164
Email: hcca@csn.net
www.sni.net/hcca

Land and Water Fund of the Rockies
2260 Baseline Road – Suite 200
Boulder, CO 80302
Tel: 303-444-1188 x 216
Email: leslie@lawfund.org
www.lawfund.org

League of Conservation Voters
Education Fund – Rocky Mountain Program
2060 Broadway – Suite 230
Boulder, CO 80302
Tel: 303-541-0373
Fax: 303-449-4328
Email: Sheena_Logothetti
www.lcv.org

Light Hawk – Rocky Mountain Regional Office
303 Unit F AABC
Aspen, CO 81611
Tel: 970-925-6987
Fax: 970-925-2701
www.lighthawk.org

National Audubon Society – Colorado State Office
3109 28th Street
Boulder, CO 80301
Tel: 303-415-0130
Fax: 303-415-0125
Email: skirkpatrick@audubon.org
www.audubon.org/chapter/cl

The Nature Conservancy
1881 Ninth Street – Suite 200
Boulder, CO 80302
Tel: 303-444-02950
Fax: 303-444-2986
www.tnccolorado.org

San Juan Citizens Alliance
P.O. Box 2461
Durango, CO 81301
Tel: 970-259-3583
www.sanjuancitizens.org

Sierra Club – Rocky Mountain Chapter
1410 Grant Street – Suite B205
Denver, CO 80203
Tel: 303-861-8819
Fax: 303-861-2436
Email: scrmc@rmi.net
www.rmc.sierraclub.org

Southern Rockies Ecosystem Project
P.O. Box 1182
Nederland, CO 80466
Tel: 303-258-0433
Fax: 303-258-7665
Email: srep@indra.com
www.csf.colorado.edu/srep

Trust for Public Land
1410 Grant Street
Denver, CO 80203
Tel: 303-837-1414
Fax: 303-837-1131
Email: copo@tpl.org
www.tpl.org

Western Colorado Congress
P.O. Box 472
Montrose, CO 81402
Tel: 970-249-1978
Fax: 970-249-1983
Email: info@wccongress.org
www.wccongress.org

The Wilderness Society – Four Corners Office
7475 Dakin Street – Suite 410
Denver, CO 80221
Tel: 303-650-5818
Fax: 303-650-5942
Email: Denver@twf.org
www.wilderness.org

All photographs copyright ©2000 by Art Wolfe, except pages 24, 38-39, 48-49, 52, 56, 57, 62, 69, 71, 72-73, 74, 76-77, 79, 80, 82, 83, 84-85, 88, 89, 90-91, 94-95, 98-99, 100-101, 120, 130, 131, 136-137, 143 (top), back cover flap, and back cover (center) copyright ©2000 by Gavriel Jecan
Art Wolfe logo copyright ©2000 by Art Wolfe
Text copyright ©2000 by Craig Childs
All rights reserved. No portion of this book may be reproduced or utilized in any form, or by any electronic, mechanical, or other means without the prior written permission of the publisher.

Published by Sasquatch Books
Distributed in Canada by Raincoast Books, Ltd.
Printed in Hong Kong
04 03 02 01 00   5 4 3 2 1

Cover and interior design: Karen Schober
Map illustration: Jane Shasky

Cover photograph: Alpine buttercup (*Rununculus adoneus*), alpine forget-me-not (*Eritrichium elongatum*), and lichen, Rocky Mountain National Park. **Photograph page 1:** Mountain bluebird (*Sialia currucoides*), Dinosaur National Monument. **Photograph pages 2-3:** Garden of the Gods. **Photographs page 5:** Snow-covered rocks, Taylor River; quaking aspen (*Populus tremuloides*), Maroon Bells-Snowmass Wilderness; blanketflower (*Gaillardia* sp.), Pawnee National Grassland. **Photograph pages 6-7:** Quaking aspen (*Populus tremuloides*), Maroon Bells-Snowmass Wilderness.

Library of Congress Cataloging-in-Publication Data

Wolfe, Art.
    Colorado / Art Wolfe ; text by Craig Childs.
      p. cm.
    Includes bibliographical references.
    ISBN 1-57061-252-8 (h : alk. paper) — ISBN 1-57061-253-6 (p : alk. paper)
        1. Colorado—Pictorial works. 2. Colorado—Description and travel. 3. Landscape—Colorado—Pictorial works.
        4. Natural history— Colorado—Pictorial works. I. Childs, Craig Leland. II. Title.

F777 .W65 2000
779'.3'09788—dc21

00-036996

Sasquatch Books
615 Second Avenue
Seattle, Washington 98104
(206) 467-4300
www.SasquatchBooks.com
books@SasquatchBooks.com